ESSAYS ON MUSIC
IN THE WESTERN WORLD

Source Readings in Music History

ESSAYS ON MUSIC IN THE WESTERN WORLD

OLIVER STRUNK

Princeton University

FOREWORD BY LEWIS LOCKWOOD

W · W · NORTON & COMPANY · INC · *New York*

Copyright © 1974 by W. W. Norton & Company, Inc.
FIRST EDITION
All Rights Reserved
Published simultaneously in Canada
by George J. McLeod Limited, Toronto

Library of Congress Cataloging in Publication Data

Strunk, William Oliver, 1901–
    Essays on music in the Western World.

    "The majority of the essays in this volume were written
between the late 1920s . . . 1950."
    Includes bibliographical references.
    CONTENTS: Erich Hertzmann (December 14, 1902–
March 3, 1963)—The historical aspect of musicology.
—Sources and problems for graduate study in
musicology.
[etc.]
    1. Music—Addresses, essays, lectures. I. Title.
ML60.S862E8   780'.8   74–5414
ISBN 0-393-02178-5

This book was designed by Andrea Clark
The type is Garamond and Aeterna.
The book was manufactured by Haddon Craftsmen

Printed in the United States of America
1   2   3   4   5   6   7   8   9   0

*To my colleagues past and present,
and to all my students.*

CONTENTS

FOREWORD

By Lewis Lockwood

IN June, 1895, in his inaugural lecture on the study of history given at the University of Cambridge, Lord Acton wrote:

> For our purpose, the main thing to learn is not the art of accumulating material, but the sublimer art of investigating it. . . . It is by solidity of criticism more than by the plenitude of erudition, that the study of history strengthens, and straightens, and extends the mind.

It can come as no surprise that few historians have risen fully or consistently to Acton's standard, since what it presupposes is vast knowledge of the substance of a field that is completely informed by critical judgment and lit by imagination. Scholars on this plane are rare in any branch of studies; even rarer are those whose gifts of expression match their intellectual visions and whose influence through writing and through teaching is equally potent. In the field of musicology I can think of no one who has come closer to exemplifying these ideals than Oliver Strunk.

To the reader with considerable background these essays will suffice by themselves to convey the special qualities that Strunk has brought to the study of the history of Western music. Several are classics of long standing in their respective fields, well known in the inner byways of the profession. But since they are now collected for the first time and can therefore be seen as contributions to the growth of musicology, especially in the United States, during the earlier decades of Strunk's professional career, they should emerge in new perspective even for those who have known them individually before.

For those who have not, a few words of explanation may be of
value. The majority of the essays in this volume were written
between the late 1920s, when Strunk returned to the United States
from his studies in Berlin, and 1950, when his active research
turned altogether to the field of Byzantine chant, in which he had
already become a leading figure. The only essays reprinted here
that were written after 1950 show some influence of either his
Byzantine studies or of events in Italy since 1966, when after
almost thirty years of teaching at Princeton University he retired
to the venerable town of Grottaferrata near Rome. Four later
essays are included here. They are, in order of writing, "A Cypriot
in Venice," published in 1962 in a volume honoring Knud
Jeppesen on the occasion of his seventieth birthday: the memorial
essay for Erich Hertzmann, an old friend and colleague who was
for many years professor of music at Columbia University; the
survey of Verdiana in the Library of Congress, which was prepared
for the Primo Congresso Internazionale di Studi Verdiani held in
Venice in 1966; and the essay on a late medieval polyphonic fragment found in the Badia greca of Grottaferrata, published in 1970.

Most of these essays, then, are products of the 1930s and 1940s,
a period that began with Strunk's membership in, and eventual
leadership of, the staff of the Music Division of the Library of
Congress and continued, from 1937 on, with his appointment to
the faculty of Princeton University, the first music historian so
appointed in Princeton's history. During these years he was partly
engaged in problems that had aroused his interest while studying
in Berlin under Johannes Wolf and partly in Haydn studies, a field
that had grown out of his work at the Library of Congress. From
his period at Berlin and from later research stem the essays that deal
with fifteenth-century music, especially the path-breaking article on
the "L'homme armé" complex. From his investigation of the rich
source materials on Haydn owned by the Library of Congress came
the article on the Haydn baryton divertimenti and the other Haydn
articles. At the same time there were other phases of his activity
that underlie these essays. One was his important role in the estab-
lishment of musicology as a recognized branch of studies in the
United States, signaled by the founding of the American Musicological Society in 1934. He not only made a valuable survey of
American resources for the field of musicology that was published

in 1932 (it is not included here) but also delivered the two important papers on the discipline itself that are reprinted in this volume. During these same years much of his time was also occupied by two major tasks of editing and of compilation. One of these was his work on the revised translation of Alfred Einstein's *The Italian Madrigal,* published in 1949; the other was the preparation of his own monumental *Source Readings in Music History.* And beyond all these activities of research and writing and collaboration in forming the professional character of the field in the United States, was Strunk's extraordinary role as teacher. Not only is a whole generation of younger scholars permanently indebted to him as teacher, but there is a natural and intimate relationship between the particular qualities of his teaching and the modes of thought and expression that the discerning reader will discover in these essays.

Five years ago a sympathetic and penetrating portrait of Oliver Strunk as scholar and teacher was contributed by Harold Powers as preface to the volume of essays that was published by Princeton University Press under the title *Studies in Music History: Essays for Oliver Strunk.* In the course of that preface the methods employed in several articles contained in the present volume were expertly evaluated, among them the paper on sixteenth-century motet types, the Haydn articles, the article on Palestrina and Duke Guglielmo Gonzaga, the postscript to Manfred Bukofzer's study of the Old Hall Manuscript, and the review of Father Feininger's edition of the *Missa Alma redemptoris mater* by Leonel Power. I therefore feel no need to dwell on the methodological importance of any of these essays, and if I turn to one in particular it is to say a few words about it from a different point of view.

It is not too much to say of Strunk's essay "Some Motet-Types of the 16th Century" that in a few scant pages of lucid prose it shapes a concept that could lead to the emergence of a whole field of research. I put that in the conditional since even now, thirty-five years after the publication of the essay, its implications have yet to be taken up with care and insight by specialists in the subject. The proposed classification of the motet literature of the sixteenth century, with emphasis on Palestrina but with numerous references to his predecessors and contemporaries, could only have been conceived by a scholar whose approach to the sixteenth century was rooted in knowledge of its medieval background, especially the

complex hierarchies of liturgical function and musical form in
Western chant. This way of looking at the motet literature inevitably stressed, yet without insisting upon it, the partial preservation
of earlier modes of thought and practice within a particular branch
of post-medieval music. The paper thus implicitly conveyed a sense
of the historical continuity between two eras while yet maintaining
a sense of their distance from one another. The result is not simply
a means of classification that is heuristically valuable; the essay adds
to this a quality of historical richness that gives insight into the
musical thought of the period and gains in force from the percep-
tion that the musicians of the period themselves had a consciousness of the past that can yet be recaptured by historians. It goes
without saying that parallel implications are to be found in many
of these essays.

    This same persuasive sense of the way of things in history was
always of the essence in Strunk's teaching, and I cannot close this
foreword without a few remarks based on my own experience of
that teaching, which I knew both as a graduate student and later
as a younger colleague and junior partner in the giving of several
undergraduate courses during Strunk's last eight years of teaching
at Princeton. The craftsmanship of his undergraduate lectures was
remarkable, yet one could wonder at times whether students of
limited background could fully perceive their quality. The summit
of his teaching was at the graduate level, typically within the framework of a three-hour weekly seminar. Speaking as a rule without
notes, quietly, and at a pace so measured that at times long pauses
would intervene between discrete segments of thought, with no
trace of rhetorical exaggeration and with no more than a few
telegraphic phrases on the blackboard, he would gradually shape
the physiognomy of a problem, leading it at length to whatever
seemed a proper stopping place. Sometimes the problem would
have a sharply defined conclusion, sometimes it would simply
break off. In either case its very clarity of formulation left it newly
open to further study and individual discovery. The breadth was
extraordinary. My own casual recollections are of sessions of one
kind or another on such subjects as the order of the plainsong
Alleluias in the Sundays after Pentecost in the Roman rite; the
problem of the choice of tenor patterns in the clausulae of the
Notre Dame school; the concept of the *Ars nova* and its customary

misunderstandings; the chronology of the Masses of Dufay; the structure of a scene from a Handel opera; the sources of the quartets of Haydn; the relationship of the young Wagner to Beethoven. A classic moment in any graduate student's short career was the Strunkian exegesis of the central problems in the study of ancient Greek music.

Yet the depth was equally remarkable, whether in matters of musical style or of historical development. The requirements of synthesis were mastered with no sacrifice of subtlety, and the evidence was weighed not at some other time, but before one's eyes. Most telling of all was the impression, shared by all his students, of how much more knowledge, and hard work to achieve that knowledge, lay beyond the specific content of his lectures and seminars, just as they lie beyond these often abbreviated essays. As Harold Powers observed, Strunk's vast preparatory work in fields as diverse as Notre Dame polyphony and Wagner remains without representation in his published essays, although he taught extensively in both.

This special combination of judgment and restraint in the service of scholarship gave his students an unforgettable model, whatever their own interests and the particular paths of their own development. Strunk has always had his own highly personal preferences and style in intellectual matters, but one hadn't to share it; although he set forth his views unequivocally, he imposed nothing on students. What was perceived by all was that while the whole concept of scholarship depends on courtesy and good will toward one's peers, no field is closed because others are working in it and no topic can be thought of as being exhausted. Whatever is within the conceptual framework of the field is open to the exercise of informed judgment and to the revision of received ideas by virtue of new factual knowledge leading to new interpretations. It is not that such ideals are in any way restricted to Strunk's teaching, for they are manifestly shared by other scholars and certainly by other superior scholars. It is rather that, as teacher, he exemplified them with rare insight and humanity.

Finally, a word on style. The same qualities of expression that went into his teaching—balance, precision, brevity—will be found throughout these essays. The attentive reader will see them not simply as contributions to the advance of knowledge as their fields

stood at the time of writing, but as models of different kinds of
scholarly elucidation. The way of beginning, the marshaling of
evidence, the playing off of reflections upon a particular nest of
problems against the larger background, the coupling of fact and
inference, the omission not only of needless words but of extraneous matters altogether—these features are of lasting importance.
They should have as much to say to future readers as to those of
the present not only as important essays in music history, but for
what they may contribute to what Acton called the strength and
straightness and extension of the mind.

Princeton, New Jersey
July, 1973

PREFACE

WITHOUT my believing that it would ever be realized, the wish to see my scattered writings gathered together and made more conveniently accessible is one that I have long entertained. That it is now a reality is due to the zealous devotion of two former students and present colleagues, Professors Lewis Lockwood and Kenneth Levy of Princeton University, who have planned the whole and in large measure relieved me of the task of collecting, editing, and proofreading, unselfishly setting their own work aside. And that these writings are to form part of the Norton music list, a fact in which I take particular pride, is due to a third former student, David Hamilton, Norton's music editor, and to his confidence and lively interest. To him is due also the decision to divide the whole into two volumes—the present one, with the essays on Western music edited by Lewis Lockwood, and a companion volume, already in preparation, with the essays on Byzantine music edited by Kenneth Levy.

The essays in the present volume are printed not in the order in which they were written, but in a logical order that should make for more satisfactory consecutive reading. This has meant that the three essays on Haydn, written long ago in Washington, come near the end, while a relatively recent item, the little tribute to my old friend Erich Hertzmann, to whom I am immeasurably indebted for wise counsel, heartening encouragement, and congenial companionship over the years, stands at it should at the very beginning. The essays are almost wholly independent—indeed, the sole reference in any one of them to any other occurs in the paper on relative

sonority, in which I have questioned a view advanced in the paper
that precedes it. Thus for this volume it has seemed possible to
dispense with an index. For the companion volume I have preferred a different plan, printing the essays in the order in which
they were written, not only to demonstrate the way in which our
knowledge of the field has developed during the past thirty years,
but also because most of the essays there printed presume a
familiarity with what has gone before. An index will be an absolute
necessity.

The essays on Marchetto da Padova and on the resources in
Washington for the study of Verdi's works and their history were
addressed to Italian readers and first printed in Italian translation.
Here I have substituted my original English text. The remaining
essays have been left just as they stood, barring only the correction
of obvious misprints, the engraving or reingraving of some of the
music examples, and the addition of a few new plates. To have
attempted to bring certain of the earlier items up to date would
have been to falsify and could only have resulted in confusion. In
1932 my essay on Haydn's compositions for the baryton may have
opened up new vistas; but today, with the bulk of this music published in the edition of the Haydn Institute, it has served its purpose, as foreseen, and retains only an historical interest. Among the
more recent items, however, there are some that call for a word or
two of comment—a correction, an amplification, or an account of
the present state of the research. Where such comment seemed
called for, I have elected to make it here, taking up the essays in
the order in which they appear in the volume itself.

Since 1950, when I attempted to establish the dates of his principal writings, we have learned a good deal about Marchetto da
Padova. In 1955 and 1956 two essays, one by Nino Pirrotta for
Musica Disciplina, the other by Giuseppe Vecchi for *Quadrivium,*
identified and assembled biographical data on Rainaldo dei Cinzi,
the citizen of Cesena in whose house Marchetto wrote his
Pomerium. Named governor of Padua in 1324, Rainaldo returned
later in the same year to Cesena where, following an abortive
attempt to seize political control, he was imprisoned and, on March
2, 1327, beheaded. With this, even those who had hesitated to
accept my early date for the *Pomerium*—1318 or, at the very latest,
1319—were confronted with an incontrovertible *terminus ante*

quem. To Vecchi we are also indebted for critical texts of the *Brevis Compilatio* (1956) and *Pomerium* (1961), texts far superior to those on which I was obliged to rely in translating a chapter from Marchetto for my *Source Readings.* And as the present volume goes to press, my friend Alberto Gallo tells me of two recent discoveries of his on which he will be reporting in a forthcoming issue of the *Archiv für Musikwissenschaft:* (1) documents in the archives of the Biblioteca Capitolare in Padua establish that Marchetto held the post of singing master to the boys at the cathedral from the spring of 1305 to 1307; (2) he is the composer of a double motet with Latin text preserved in a manuscript at the Bodleian Library, one of whose upper voices incorporates the acrostic "Marcum Paduanum."

Had I supposed in 1949 that with the publication of my postscript to Manfred Bukofzer's essay the problem of the canonic pieces in the Old Hall Manuscript was settled once and for all, I could not have been more mistaken. In 1958, in his *Music in Medieval Britain,* and again in 1960, in a chapter for the third volume of the *New Oxford History,* Frank Harrison drew attention to still another unspecified canon, the Sanctus by Pycard numbered 117 in Barclay Squire's list, a piece the more remarkable in that its leading voice paraphrases a plainsong melody. Correctly transcribed, Byterring's canonic Gloria and the two unspecified canons by Pycard can now be studied in the new edition of the Old Hall Manuscript edited by Andrew Hughes and Margaret Bent.

Like the Old Hall postscript, its companion piece, published in the same year, deals largely with the early history of the polyphonic Mass in England, this time with what is perhaps its first important landmark, Leonel Power's *Missa Alma Redemptoris Mater.* Here, again, the last word remains to be said. Years after my review was printed, while re-examining with a group of students the perennial problem of Mass movements based on antiphons, I took a closer look at what I had described in my review as "an anonymous but almost certainly English Kyrie and Gloria in Trent 87" and discovered, to my considerable astonishment, that the tenor of the two movements is laid out in such a way that its dependence upon the layout of Leonel Power's tenor is unmistakable.

In 1947 I had concluded my essay "Guglielmo Gonzaga and Palestrina's *Missa Dominicalis*" by asking whether some Italian colleague would not renew the search for the lost Masses Palestrina had written in 1578 and 1579 for the court chapel of St. Barbara in Mantua, whose archives, Gaetano Cesari had informed us, were divided between the library of the Liceo Musicale in Bologna and that of the Conservatorio "Giuseppe Verdi" in Milan. For an Italian colleague nothing could be simpler, I had thought at the time: Cesari had told him where to look and I had told him what sort of Masses to look for.

What I did not know was that the Danish scholar Knud Jeppesen had already been occupied with this search for some years, that he had visited Bologna only to learn that no part of the Mantuan archives had ever reached there, and that his plan to go on to Milan had been upset by the outbreak of the Second World War. This I learned from Professor Jeppesen himself when I met him for the first time at the International Congress for Sacred Music, held in Rome in May, 1950. During the war, he told me, the Mantuan archives at the Milan conservatory had been evacuated and the building itself bombed out; on revisiting Milan in 1947 and 1948 the manuscripts in which he was interested were still inaccessible. Immediately following the congress Jeppesen paid a third visit to Milan, and this time, by special permission, he gained access to the Mantuan archives and found what he had been looking for.

There were ten Palestrina Masses in all—one four-part Mass for men's voices, freely composed, and nine five-part Masses, composed on plainsongs, in which, apart from the Kyrie, Palestrina had set only alternate lines, leaving the rest to be supplied by an organist or by a second choir singing in unison. Jeppesen published a first report of his discovery, preliminary and tentative, in the *Acta Musicologica* for 1951. In this he expressed the opinion that the Mass for men's voices was probably the one commissioned by Duke Guglielmo in 1568, and I quite agree that this view is far more plausible than my earlier conjecture that one of the Masses on motets by Jacquet da Mantova might have been the work involved. At the same time, while accepting my interpretation of Don Annibale's enigmatic reference to "the second parts," he rejected the rest of my argument, thinking it improbable that the five-part Masses he had found had any direct connection with the correspondence of 1578 and 1579.

In a second report, supplementary and definitive, published in the *Acta* for 1953, Jeppesen took an entirely different stand. He had visited Mantua in the meantime and had discovered there several documents, until then overlooked, bearing on Palestrina's work for the ducal chapel. The most important of these, found among the minutes of the Mantuan chancellery for 1578, was a secretary's draft of a reply to Don Annibale's letter of October 18, emended by the duke himself. To paraphrase Jeppesen's comment, this draft showed unmistakably that Palestrina's Masses were to be polyphonic, that they were to be composed upon plainsongs the duke had revised or caused to be revised, and that these plainsongs had at first been sent to Palestrina in an incomplete form—in short, that the Masses were to be composed as "alternatim" masses and designed only in part for a many-voiced choir. Then there was a draft of a letter to Pompeo Strozzi, the duke's ambassador in Rome, bearing on the payment Palestrina was to receive, with letters from Strozzi in which there were references to two additional Masses, making nine in all, rather than seven, as had previously been supposed. Using as a foreword what is in effect an abridged Italian translation from the German of his second report, Jeppesen published the newly discovered Masses in 1954 as volumes 18 and 19 of the edition of the *Opere complete* begun by Raffaele Casimiri.

Strangely enough, the disputed *Missa Dominicalis* is not among the Masses contained in the choir books from St. Barbara, although these do contain the five similar works by Mantuan composers that were published with it in 1592 by the Mantuan Carmelite Giulio Pellini. Yet it is composed on Mantuan plainsongs and, like its fellows, it is clearly a Mantuan Mass. I still look on it as genuine, and Jeppesen is at least less certain about it than he was in 1925 when he pronounced it spurious. Noting that Pellini dedicated his publication to Duke Guglielmo's brother-in-law, Alfonso II d'Este, duke of Ferrara, Jeppesen suggests that the Mass may have been contained in one of the two choir books Guglielmo sent to Ferrara toward the end of his life. Unfortunately, these choir books appear to be no longer extant.

Here, in this same connection, is the place to correct an inaccurate and essentially absurd observation of mine. In calling Duke Guglielmo "the living embodiment of the teachings of Castiglione" I fell into one of those traps that await the unwary scholar who ventures into a field not properly his own, relying chiefly on

the data found in general encyclopedias and allowing his imagination free rein. A gentleman he certainly was and a skilled musician,
but I rather doubt that Castiglione would wholly have approved of
him. To begin with, he was a hunchback, and to this humiliating
deformity may be attributed both the strength and the weakness of
his character. "One governs with the spirit, not the body," he had
said on succeeding to the title, and to prove this he brought peace,
justice, and increased prosperity to Mantua and returned to Mantuan domination the disputed duchy of Monferrato. Charitable
where his own subjects were concerned, passionately devoted to
their welfare, he did his best to shield them from the terrors of the
papal Inquisition. At the same time, as though possessed, he was
stubborn, relentless, and so intent upon having his own way in all
things that, in 1583, after having reluctantly approved the use at
St. Barbara of the private breviary and missal the duke had designed, Gregory XIII is reported to have remarked, with some
bitterness, that if he were to have two such individuals to contend
with, he would resign. But Guglielmo's greatest weakness, perhaps, was his inability to establish and maintain a harmonious relationship with his son and heir, Vincenzo Gonzaga. Here the father's avarice and his tenacity in asserting himself led only to
resistance and rebellion on the son's part, and it is difficult to avoid
concluding that, as a result of this, Guglielmo was in some measure
to blame for the subsequent decline in Mantuan power and pres-
tige. To give the reader a livelier impression of the man with whom
Palestrina dealt I have supplied, as an illustration, a photograph of
the strikingly realistic effigy of the duke from the Mantuan basilica
of Sant'Andrea.

The general essay on Joseph Haydn, printed in this volume
before the one on his music for the baryton, was actually written
a year later. Its summary of Haydn's production during the 1790s,
while in general agreement with what was believed at the time,
is no longer acceptable. The three last piano sonatas, as we now
know, were written for Mrs. Therese Bartolozzi, the daughter-in-
law (not the wife) of the London engraver; the piano trio, composed in London in 1795 but later dedicated to Madame Moreau
in a version stripped of its cello part, is in E♭ minor; to the major
works of the first five years one needs also to add the piano trio in
G, formerly believed to have been written as a sonata for piano and

violin. On the other hand, the summary mistakenly lists as belonging to the first five years the three piano-trios dedicated to Mrs.
Bartolozzi, composed in Vienna during the later 1790s; to this
same period belongs also an important work not listed in the summary—the piano trio in E♭ major, composed in Vienna in 1796.
Aside from this, the two paragraphs on Haydn's first fifteen years
in Eisenstadt and Esterház, packed with specific detail, were lifted
bodily from my essay of 1932; in 1933 it had seemed to me useless
and more or less impossible to rewrite them, restating their contents in another form.

A recent inquiry from the Library of Congress enables me to
correct a minor inaccuracy in the essay with which this volume
ends. In the library's full orchestral score of Verdi's *Battaglia di
Legnano* (1849), a manuscript copy with Italian text and the title
"Patria," fourteen pages (441 to 454), with text in French, were
not written by the copyist who turned out the rest of the score, and
it had been suggested that these pages might be in Verdi's own
hand. I was confident that they were not, but at the same time
puzzled when I noticed that the aria involved did not belong to the
Battaglia and had evidently been inserted in place of one that did.
The interpolation was placed at the end of act 3, scene 2, and was
to be sung by "Roger," a baritone; the text began

> *O rage, ô transports de fureur,*
> *de sang ma haine est ivre.*

Its original proved to be the cabaletta of Stankar in act 3, scene 3,
of Verdi's *Stiffelio* (1850), "Oh gioia inesprimibile." In *Aroldo*
(1857), his later revision of *Stiffelio*, Verdi retained this piece, and
when this revision was published in Paris by Escudier, with French
text by Edouard Duprez, the translation began

> *O joie, ô transports de bonheur,*
> *de sang mon coeur est ivre.*

The text found in *Patria* is simply a paraphrase of this translation,
retaining most of its rhymes. The interpolated aria replaces Rolando's "Ahi! scellerate alme d'inferno," a highly conventional
piece, even for 1849.

The history of this adaptation of the *Battaglia* is indeed a curious
one. It had been prepared for the opening of the Théâtre de

Château d'Eau in 1889, the date of the Centennial Exposition. Verdi's original had been drastically curtailed, and while the scenes of the action remained Milan and Como and the plot still centered about the Battle of Legnano, the names of many of the characters had been changed, Arrigo becoming Lorédan, Rolando Roger, Marcovaldo Herman, and Imelda Anita. Perhaps it was thought that this rousing celebration of a crushing German defeat, which had not been previously performed in France, might appeal to the Parisian public of those days. A vocal score, with French text by Maurice Drack, was published by Choudens père & fils, but no public performance ever took place, for the production was withdrawn after a single dress rehearsal for the press. Under these circumstances the full score in Washington, labeled "No. 1," may very well be the only copy that ever existed. In any case my entry for it ought to have read: "For Choudens, Paris, with title 'Patria.' An abbreviated adaptation of Verdi's original, interpolating in French translation an aria from his *Stiffelio.*"

This running commentary on a part of the contents of the present volume should serve to underscore one of the points Professor Lockwood has made in his foreword—"No topic can be thought of as being exhausted." Most of these essays seek to answer a question or to solve a problem. But with the possible exception of the one on Haydn's work for the piano during his London years and after his return to Vienna, none can be said to have exhausted its topic. In this single case—although the shadowy figure of "the wife of the engraver Bartolozzi" continues to haunt Haydn criticism—the revised chronology I attempted to establish has been generally accepted and has long since passed into the public domain. For the rest, as the commentary reveals, the answers have sometimes proved to be only partial answers, while at other times the solutions have served also to uncover fresh problems. The study of the history of music is still far from having reached the point of diminishing returns; indeed, it has been my experience that no matter what corner of the field one chooses, one invariably finds that much has remained unexplored.

OLIVER STRUNK

Grottaferrata, Italy
October, 1973

ESSAYS ON MUSIC
IN THE WESTERN WORLD

ERICH HERTZMANN†

[*December 14, 1902–March 3, 1963*]

S PEAKING in December of last year about Erich Hertzmann to
members of the American Musicological Society, I could say,
with perfect truth, that I was speaking as a friend of Erich's to an
audience solidly made up of his friends. A native of Germany,
Erich had spent the best twenty-five years of his life in the United
States and had come to occupy a unique place in the affections of
his American colleagues. I have now only to widen the circle, for
thanks to the associations of his early years, later renewed and
strengthened, Erich was as well known and as well liked abroad as
he was at home. No one ever encountered this cheerful, animated,
intensely human being, radiating friendliness and sympathetic interest, without surrendering at once to the spell of his magnetic and
stimulating personality.

I suppose that I must be the first American whom Erich came to
know. Our acquaintance began as long ago as 1927, when we met
as fellow-students in Berlin, and I still retain a lively mental picture
of him as he was in those days, sitting absorbed for hour after hour
in the Musikabteilung of the old Staatsbibliothek, poring over the
Opere of Zarlino or reading villanelle from the separate part-books,
following a strange method of his own invention which involved
marking the place in two of the part-books with two fingers of one
hand while one finger of the other marked the place in the third.
As everyone knows, students often learn more from one another

†From *Acta Musicologica*, XXXVI (1964), 47–48. Reprinted by permission of
Acta Musicologica.

than from their teachers, and I am persuaded that, during that memorable year in Berlin, I learned quite as much from informal conversations with Erich as I did from my more formal meetings with Blume, Sachs, Schering, and Wolf.

These friendly exchanges were resumed, beginning in 1938, when Erich came to the United States and established himself in New York. During the early years of the war, he spent two summers with me in Princeton. Here we worked together on subjects of common interest, and this collaboration continued uninterrupted for two further summers in New York, where I was his guest at the old Hotel Regent. These summers spent together were enormously profitable for me, and I should like to think that Erich too gained something from them.

If Erich was not a particularly productive scholar, this was due in some measure to his rigorous self-criticism, perhaps also, though to a lesser degree, to the liveliness of his intellect, which led him on relentlessly from one problem to another and caused him to lose interest in a question once he had found the answer. In compensation, he was uniquely productive in another sense, for he was an extraordinarily gifted teacher whose influence has already had a powerful impact on the American scene, one that for years to come will continue to make itself felt. No teacher I have known has been more skillful in arousing and holding the interest of his students. Nor has any teacher I have known been as successful in winning the respect and affection of those he taught, as witness the album humorously entitled the "Festmann Hertzschrift," presented to him on the occasion of his fiftieth birthday by his students at Columbia.

Erich had begun as a critic and as a student of the French and Italian Renaissance, but it was not to be expected that he would for long remain content with these limited horizons. As time passed, he sought to broaden them, first in one direction, then in another. During his first years in the United States he worked his way back, step by step, through the fifteenth and fourteenth centuries to Notre Dame, Saint Martial, and the vast territory beyond. Turning then to the dominant personalities of the eighteenth and nineteenth centuries, above all to Beethoven, he immersed himself in textual criticism and in the creative process, as revealed in the phenomenon of the sketch book. One by-product of these later interests is his exemplary edition of the *Rondo a capriccio;* another is his study of the Diabelli sketches, not finished at the time of his death. His latest and most ambitious undertaking, the critical edition of the Attwood studies for the *Neue Mozart-Ausgabe,* to which he gave so much of himself and with which he was occupied in California during the last and in some respects the happiest months of his life, is now nearing completion, thanks to the generous intervention of an old student, Alfred Mann, and a more recent friend and admirer, Daniel Heartz. It will be Erich's enduring monument.

THE HISTORICAL ASPECT
OF MUSICOLOGY†

THE program of this session was planned, I take it, with a view to providing for the members of our two societies a broad view of the relations—as President Kinkeldey has it in the title of his concluding paper, of the *changing* relations—within the field of musicology as a whole. To this end the field has, as you see, been subdivided, and I need scarcely tell you that the particular plan of subdivision represented in outline by this morning's program is simply one of the several plans that have at one time or another been proposed. Musicologists will recognize in it the plan put forward by Hugo Riemann in his *Fundamentals of Musicology* (1908), familiar, surely, to every one of you through the critical examination of it by Waldo Selden Pratt in the first article of the first number of our first—and only—musicological journal, *The Musical Quarterly*. Whatever its logical defects, the Riemann scheme has at least the very practical merit of simplicity. I know no other that would have lent itself as readily to the purpose at hand. Let us accept it, then, as it stands. Let us take, as points of departure, Riemann's formulations of the general task of musicology and of the special task of musical history. They will help us, I think, to fix a little more precisely than we might otherwise the peculiar relation of musical history, on the one hand, to musicology; on the

†From *Proceedings of the Music Teachers National Association*, XXXI (1936), 218–220. Reprinted in *Papers Read at the Annual Meeting of the American Musicological Society, December 29, 1936, Chicago, Illinois*, 14–16. Permission for reprint granted by Music Teachers National Association.

other hand—and this is not less important—to the great body of historical knowledge.

To begin with (Riemann says), musicology has the general task of determining the psychic expression-value of the primitive elements in musical creation; of formulating the physical characteristics of musical sounds and the mechanical requirements of their production and prolongation; of demonstrating by simple, basic facts the effect of these sounds on the organ of hearing, and through its agency on emotion and intelligence, that is, on inner consciousness; and of tracing the employment of these sounds in the complex musical structure.

It is not difficult to see in this orderly and carefully considered progression of Riemann's a statement of the dependence, one upon the other, of four of his five musicological disciplines: Acoustics, psychophysiology, aesthetics, and theory. Where, you may well ask, does history come in? Apart from conceding that the single parts of his system appear sometimes to stand quite unrelated to one another, Riemann does not give us the answer. Despite their seeming lack of relationship, he says, their common aim—the explanation of music's wonders and the tracing out of its natural roots —combines them all in higher unity.

Commenting on Riemann's scheme, Pratt objects that it confuses logical categories, that musical history ought not to have been ranked as coördinate with such disciplines as acoustics and physiology. Here, surely, is the crux of the matter. Musical history is at once less and more than these—less, in that it is not in itself a distinct field within a system of fields; more, in that as a point of view, as a way of looking at the subject, it comprehends all fields, embraces the musical fact as a whole. It is, in short, an aspect—not a part—of musicology, and the author of this morning's program has in this one word admirably expressed its special and peculiar function. To remind you that the first musicologists—Chrysander, Adler, and Riemann too—were in fact historians is simply another way of bringing out this basic, simple truth. Of all musicians, it is the historian whose broad view of the art leads him most naturally to this sort of thinking.

Turning now to the second question proposed at the outset of this paper—the peculiar relation of musical history to the great body of historical knowledge—I draw again on Riemann, this time for his expression of one of the commonplaces of modern music-historical method.

The history of an art (he says) must obviously rest primarily on investigation of the existing art-works themselves; only where these are lacking ought it to fall back, for further motivation and to complete the picture, on contemporary and later reports and theoretical formulations.

This is, of course, the familiar antithesis common to all fields of historical research in which the worker is privileged to deal more or less directly with the historical fact. Just as the literary historian is concerned, not with literary men but with literature; just as the art historian is concerned, not with artists but with art; so the musical historian, relying for his knowledge on scores, not on books, must write the history of music, not of musicians. Can these analogies be pursued further? They cannot, and this is precisely my point, self-evident, to be sure, but none the less fundamental. For the musical historian, unlike his colleagues working in literature and the fine arts, does not have the actual art works before him. What he has are simply more or less faithful and intelligible directions for performance. Follow them he may, but the result is at best an approximation. His position, indeed, is something like that in which the student of classical architecture might find himself if, instead of dealing with the fragmentary remains of an ancient structure, he had only a ground-plan—and a ground-plan leaving much to the experience and taste of the artisan—to work with. Here, then, lies the special problem, the special difficulty, of musical history, here the special reason for the existence of its three so essential auxiliary disciplines—the history of musical performance *(Aufführungs-Praxis)*, the history of musical instruments *(Instrumentenkunde)*, and the history of musical notation *(Notationskunde)*. Here, too, its special relation to comparative musicology *(Vergleichende Musikwissenschaft)*, the field about which Miss Roberts is to tell you something later on. For it is to the comparative musicologist that the musical historian must look for a reconstruction, through analogy, of those early beginnings from which no records have come.

SOURCES AND PROBLEMS
FOR GRADUATE STUDY
IN MUSICOLOGY†

SOURCES are the historian's raw material. In the language of
historical method they are the surviving evidence of man's past
activity. One class of sources is intended from the first to convey
information; evidence of this kind the historian calls "tradition."
Another class of sources, while not so intended, is none the less
favorably adapted to this end; evidence of this kind the historian
calls "remains." To collect, criticize, arrange, and interpret such
raw material is the historian's task; the systematic formulation of
the processes involved is historical method.

Whatever the field of research—whether the particular side of
human activity singled out for investigation be social, political,
intellectual, or artistic—historical method remains very much the
same. That branch of musicology which deals with musical history
employs historical method as a matter of course. The musical historian, like his colleagues working in other fields, is concerned with
the collection, criticism, arrangement, and interpretation of
sources. But in classifying his raw material he follows a plan of his
own. For him the essential characteristic of a source is not the
purpose for which it was originally intended but the degree of
directness with which it bears on the historical fact. He distinguishes, accordingly, between direct and indirect evidence, be-

†From *Proceedings of the Music Teachers National Association,* XXVIII (1933),
105–116; read at the annual meeting of the association, Lincoln, Nebraska, December 30, 1933. Permission for reprint granted by Music Teachers National Association.

tween "monuments" and "documents," between the evidence of
the music itself and the literary, pictorial, or material evidence that
merely contributes to an understanding of the music. Such, at all
events, is the classification proposed by Guido Adler, whose *Method
of Musical History* is the one attempt that has been made thus far to
adapt historical method to the special needs of musical science.

If I have dwelt at some length on these theoretical distinctions
it is because I wished to emphasize that the distinction between
primary and secondary sources is in the main a practical one. Original manuscripts and contemporary editions are not in themselves
very much more trustworthy than facsimiles and historical reprints.
Neither the one nor the other can be taken on faith; neither the
one nor the other obviates the necessity for criticism or precludes
the possibility of misinterpretation. Where absolute accuracy is
essential, primary sources must be consulted; where relative accuracy will suffice, secondary sources, if such exist, have the obvious
advantage of being at once more accessible and more serviceable.
They bring the evidence to the student who is not in a position to
examine it at first hand; they bring it to him in a form that saves
time-consuming editorial drudgery; in a word, they remove a part
of the mechanical difficulty in the way of historical research, simpli-
fying the collection of evidence without interfering with criticism,
arrangement, or interpretation.

Musical scholarship in this country is inevitably and peculiarly
dependent on secondary sources. In the field of medieval music the
combined holdings of our libraries in the way of original material
are neither comprehensive nor representative enough to alter the
situation; to a lesser extent the same is true of the music of the
sixteenth and seventeenth centuries. In these fields the superiority
of the European libraries is absolute. As Oscar Sonneck pointed
out, in addressing the members of your Association just twenty-five
years ago, it is where the community of historical interests ends that
competition begins.

American resources, then, are less extensive than European; they
are also less accessible. The concentration of these resources in a
relatively small number of libraries, the natural reluctance of these
libraries to risk the loan of irreplaceable material, the tremendous
distances between one research center and another: all these things
make it imperative that working collections of facsimiles and his-

torical reprints be developed at every American university where graduate work in musicology is offered.

I have made the point that secondary sources have the two-fold advantage of being accessible and serviceable, and I have tried to show the connection between the first of these qualities and the conditions peculiar to musical scholarship in this country. There is a similar connection between the second of these qualities and the special aim of graduate study. No one who has not actually worked with original sources can have any conception of the mechanical difficulties they involve. Indeed, there are fields of research in which they cannot be studied at all until they have been recast in a more serviceable form: obsolete notations may have first to be translated into current symbols, separate parts may have first to be put into score. And, in the end, the material may not prove to be worth the time and effort its preparation has cost; not infrequently the sources available are found at length to have little or no bearing on the problem in hand. Research of this kind is always laborious and often unprofitable. Where the aim is the discovery of new knowledge, mechanical difficulties may have to be faced, but they are more likely to prove unnecessary and even undesirable distractions where the aim is what I take the aim of graduate study to be —training in the method of research.

The movement for the publication of secondary sources that began in 1850 with the founding of the Bach Society has been carried on with so much energy and enterprise in recent years that the present supply of such material actually exceeds the demand. Some of it invites critical reëxamination; some of it has never been examined in a critical way; there is no reason to believe that any of it has been worked over to the point of diminishing returns. In the hands of students trained in historical method it can still be made to yield new and valuable results.

What an experienced scholar can do with material of this kind is well illustrated in Dr. Glen Haydon's recently published monograph on the evolution of the six-four chord.[1] The problem, like all problems in the evolution of musical form and technic, involves

[1]Berkeley, Calif.: University of California Press, 1933. Another excellent example is Professor George S. Dickinson's essay, "Foretokens of the Tonal Principle," in *Vassar Mediaeval Studies* (New Haven: Yale University Press, 1923).

the examination of a chronologically arranged series of representative works. The existence of a sufficient quantity of suitable material in secondary sources makes the assembling of such a series a relatively simple matter and permits emphasis to be placed where it belongs in a study of this kind: on interpretation. Dr. Haydon found all the material he needed in secondary sources; to look further was superfluous. His thesis happens to have been written in Vienna; it could just as well have been written in Washington or New York or Chicago. It has been called "a significant step in the right direction"; other equally significant steps remain to be taken. A whole series of minor problems will have to be solved before a comprehensive history of dissonance treatment can be written. And I can think of no single group of problems in musicology that might more profitably be investigated by American students.

Further inquiry into the history of dissonance treatment will presumably follow along the lines already laid down: the works of one composer will be studied with reference to all types of dissonance, or the works of a series of composers will be studied with reference to one type of dissonance. Professor Jeppesen follows the first plan in his study of the dissonant element in the Palestrina style; it can be applied only to those composers whose works are more or less completely accessible in modern editions and whose style differs sufficiently from Palestrina's to warrant special study. Dr. Haydon follows the second plan; this can be applied only to those types of dissonance that have what Professor Jeppesen has called "idiomatic vitality." Specific problems that suggest themselves are:

1. The treatment of dissonance in the works of Obrecht, Byrd, Gibbons.
2. The evolution of the cambiata and other stereotyped forms of ornamental dissonance in representative works by masters of the First, Second, and Third Netherland Schools.
3. The trend from free to strict treatment of the suspension during the period 1450 to 1550.

It is perhaps best that investigations of this kind be limited for the present to the polyphonic period, and concentrated in so far as possible on the music of the fifteenth century. Certain characteristic elements of the *a cappella* style represent survivals of earlier practice; as such they deserve to be studied in their full vigor as well as in their decline.

Another group of problems in the music of the polyphonic period has to do with style-criticism. This involves the application of what I may call the "comparative method." When we compare one work with another we detect differences in style, the nature of which depends primarily on the relationship of the composers concerned. A comparison of works by representatives of different periods brings out differences in period conventions. A comparison of works by representatives of different groups within a period brings out differences in group conventions. The isolation of the individual element in musical style is possible only when we compare a composer's work with that of other members of his own group.

In any case, the presence of a natural basis for comparison is a real advantage. The ideal material for comparative study is obviously that in which the influence of the extraneous factors involved remains constant. The more closely these factors agree, the more nearly constant their influence becomes, and the more distinctly the essential characteristics of the material itself stand out. In accordance with this general principle we compare similar, analogous, commensurable works—interpretations of a single subject, settings of a single text, variations on a single theme. At the same time, by making not one, but several comparisons, or by comparing the works chosen for comparison with other works by the same composers, we avoid the obvious error of deriving a composer's individual style from a work not typical of his style as a whole. And by a systematic search for evidence of direct relationship, we guard against the further error of drawing false conclusions from a comparison of works between which such a relationship exists.

The tendency of the fifteenth- and sixteenth-century composer to build on borrowed foundations—his dependence, in short, on certain traditional and quasi-traditional *cantus firmi*—creates a condition peculiarly favorable to the application of the comparative method. Almost any two composers of this period will be found to have placed themselves, at least once, on common ground; often the use of a single *cantus* has been so widespread and long continued that a whole series of works has grown up about it. To distinguish individual style traits from conventions common to a group, a generation, or the period as a whole, we have only to select a sufficiently comprehensive series. And in some cases it is even possible to select such a series from the material available in secondary sources alone. A fair example is the series of masses developing one of the melodies of the Gregorian Ordinary, that in honor of the Blessed Virgin. There exist complete modern editions of no less than six of these compositions: one by Brumel, one by Morales, two by Palestrina, one by De Kerle, and one by Vittoria. A comparative examination of this series, representing the developments of an entire century, would be a worthwhile undertaking, a contribution not only to style-criticism, but to the history of form as well. I do not mean to imply that the practical application of the comparative method is limited to the field of the *cantus firmus* mass. Cecie Stainer applies it to the part-song in her paper on "Dunstable and the Various Settings of *O Rosa bella.*" Alfred Orel has applied it to the motet, Otto Gombosi to all the forms typical of the polyphonic period. The problems belonging to this group fall, accordingly, into three main classes:

1. Comparative problems in the field of the part-song.
2. Comparative problems in the field of the motet.
3. Comparative problems in the field of the *cantus firmus* mass.

And in any case the aim of the research may be either the definition of individual style-traits or the exposition of a particular formal development.

Historically related to this group, though not strictly part of it, is the problem of the evolution of the so-called "parody" mass, in which the borrowed foundation is not a melody, but a full-fledged composition, usually a motet, madrigal, or chanson. In this field, too, a wealth of secondary source material is available, the principal exponents of the form—Hassler and Lassus—being well represented in modern editions.

Still another group of problems in the music of the polyphonic period has to do with the part played by English musicians in the early development of musical style. While it is generally recognized and well supported by contemporary evidence that the force of English example effected a profound and even decisive style-change at a critical moment in musical history, the precise nature of the English contribution is still imperfectly understood. "Peculiarly embarrassing," says Jeppesen, "is the absence of adequate material to explain the important process of harmonic stabilization that took place in England about the year 1400." This unsatisfactory situation is to some extent corrected in recent publications of the Plainsong and Mediaeval Music Society at Nashdom Abbey. In *Worcester Mediaeval Harmony* (1928) Dom Hughes makes a notable addition to the material published years ago by Wooldridge and Stainer. And with the appearance of the first fascicle of the Old Hall MS (1930) the most important of all the musical monuments of medieval England becomes at least in part accessible. The publication of new evidence sometimes creates new problems; in this case it revives old ones, compelling reëxamination of the whole question of English influence on Continental developments. Some aspects of this question are:

1. The origin and development of *fauxbourdon* to the time of its acceptance by Continental musicians.
2. The definition of a specifically English melodic type and its identification in the music of the First Netherland School.
3. The formal characteristics of the English motet and mass and their reflection in Continental polyphony.

That these problems have already been (and are still being) studied by European scholars need not deter ambitious Americans from studying them on their own account. It appears unlikely that the possibilities of this particular field of investigation will be exhausted for some time to come.

What is true of these publications of the Plainsong and Mediaeval Music Society is also true of other recent publications. I need only name a few of the most important: in the general field, Arnold Schering's *Musikgeschichte in Beispielen* (1931) and Nagel's *Musik-Archiv* (since 1927), both so reasonably priced that no library can be excused for not owning them; in the field of early polyphony, Charles van den Borren's *Polyphonia Sacra* (1932), the facsimile of the Petrucci *Odhecaton* (1932), and Friedrich Blume's *Das Chorwerk* (since 1929); among national publications, *Tudor Church Music,* Henry Expert's *Monuments de la musique française au temps de la renaissance* (1924–29), and the first volumes of the *Istituzioni e monumenti dell'arte musicale italiana* (1931), of the *Mestres de l'esco-lania de Montserrat* (since 1930), and of the series published by the Music Department of the State Library at Barcelona (since 1921); among publications devoted to individual masters, the first volumes of the works of Guillaume de Machaut, Ockeghem, Philippe de Monte, Marenzio, Praetorius, Lully, Couperin, Weber, Bruckner, and Moussorgsky. If university and conservatory libraries do their share, the student limited to secondary sources has surely little reason to complain.

As regards original sources, I think it is fair to say that we suffer less from want of what we do not have than from want of students experienced enough to make proper use of what we do have. Those of you who attended the meeting in Washington last December and were able to visit the exhibit prepared at that time by the Music Division in the Library of Congress will probably not be disinclined to agree with me. Indeed, the Library of Congress has already realized in some measure what Sonneck urged on the occasion of your first meeting in Washington twenty-five years ago: the development of a collection of music and books on music sufficiently comprehensive to release the American scholar from the necessity of consulting European libraries except for research in fields that an American library cannot (or should not) be expected to cover. The development has in fact reached the point where an occasional European scholar finds himself obliged to apply to us.

Typical of such applications is an inquiry received not long ago from Cologne, relative to certain early opera librettos, among them one of the group of Mozart librettos in first editions exhibited last year—the first edition of the *Marriage of Figaro*. When I say that this group is unique, I speak advisedly. Not only was our correspondent, Dr. Anheisser, unable to locate any other copy of the original *Marriage of Figaro*, but on having located ours he discovered what had previously passed unnoticed: that it is undoubtedly a copy used by someone actively connected with the first performance of the opera. A contemporary hand has recorded the original cast, marked cuts in the recitatives, and indicated the omission of entire arias. Photostats of the libretto in Washington enabled Dr. Anheisser to establish the original text of the work for the first time and to determine which of the several existing manuscripts of the music is the ultimate authority.[2]

Another group of material exhibited last year was designed to suggest the comprehensive character of our collection of operas in full score and included dramatic music by Caccini, Marco da Gagliano, Vitali, Landi, and Marazzoli in original seventeenth-century editions; illustrated scores of operas by Lully; contemporary manuscripts of representative Italian works of the eighteenth century; first editions of Gluck and Weber; and transcripts of scores in European libraries, made expressly for Washington. Comparative figures will bring home to you what this exhibit could only imply. In locating manuscript copies of operas by Alessandro Scarlatti, Dent credits the British Museum in London with eight scores, the Royal Library in Brussels with six, the Brussels Conservatory with five: the Library of Congress has transcripts of sixteen. Eitner credits the Naples Conservatory with eleven scores by Leonardo Leo, the Paris Conservatory with seven, the Milan Conservatory with four: the Library of Congress has transcripts of twelve. Abert credits the Naples Conservatory with thirty scores by Niccolò Jommelli, libraries in Brussels, Paris, and Stuttgart with twelve each: the Library of Congress has transcripts of sixteen. Small wonder that a German critic (Dr. Alfred Heuss), in reviewing the preliminary catalogue of dramatic music published in 1908, should have intimated that at some future date the historian of opera might more profitably undertake a journey to Washington than gather his information from the four corners of Europe! Thanks to Sonneck's special interest in operatic history and to his expert and systematic collecting of material bearing on it, the Library of Congress is in a peculiarly favorable position to further research in this field, one as yet inadequately covered by secondary sources.

Other fields singled out in Washington for intensive cultivation include musical literature to 1800; first and early editions of the great masters from Bach and Handel to Debussy and Fauré; lute, guitar, and organ tablature, printed and manuscript. These special collections were all represented in last year's exhibit; to review them here would lead too far. Among materials not exhibited last year I mention only the contemporary manuscript sources in the

[2]See his article "Die unbekannte Urfassung von Mozarts Figaro," *Zeitschrift für Musikwissenschaft*, XV (1932–33), 301–317.

field of eighteenth-century instrumental music: chamber music and orchestral music, some of it unpublished and as yet unstudied, by Carl Philipp Emanuel, Johann Christian, and Wilhelm Friedemann Bach; Boccherini; Brunetti; Dittersdorf; Gossec; Carl Heinrich and Johann Gottlieb Graun; Joseph and Michael Haydn; Johann and Carl Stamitz; and a host of others.

How much use is actually being made of this material? By scholars in general, considerable, if less than it deserves; by graduate students, almost none at all. Disregarding for the moment the use made of it by writers on the history of music in America, I need only recall to you the work of Engel, Kinkeldey, Carleton Sprague Smith, and Sonneck himself, in articles outside the American field, to indicate the variety and interest of the problems on which it can be brought to bear. Yet I can cite only one recent instance of a graduate student's having based his research primarily on sources in the Music Division of the Library of Congress: Alfred Iacuzzi's *The European Vogue of Favari* (1932), a publication of the Institute of French Studies at Columbia University. The use of this material ought not to be confined to the few students who are in a position to consult it in Washington. A far wider use should be, and can be made of it. Unless full advantage is taken of photostat and interlibrary loan facilities, the resources of the National Library are national resources in name only.

Without proposing specific problems in the history of music since 1600 I name a few of the neglected, or at best insufficiently cultivated areas that might be explored on the basis of original source material in Washington:

1. The history of opera, especially in the seventeenth and eighteenth centuries.
2. The history of English music, especially between 1650 and 1800.
3. Catholic church music to 1800.
4. Lute and guitar music.
5. The decline of the *basso continuo.*
6. The treatment of individual forms by contemporary theorists.

Such forms as the *Choral-Vorspiel,* the Italian opera of the eighteenth century, the German *Lied,* invite the application of the "comparative method." Some problems best dealt with on the basis of secondary sources are:

1. The history of individual forms, especially the variation, the fugue.
2. The history of individual harmonic and contrapuntal devices, especially pedalpoint and modulation, harmonic and enharmonic.

In speaking of original sources I have limited myself to those in the Library of Congress. To cover a wider field was manifestly impossible. Yet I would remind you that the Library of Congress, though it stand in a class by itself, is only one of a number of American libraries whose combined holdings make possible the investigation of many problems that could not be investigated on the basis of Library of Congress material alone.

In your *Volume of Proceedings* for the year 1916 there is a paper by Sonneck on "The History of Music in America." He chose an ambiguous, two-edged title—and chose it deliberately. He might have spoken, as an American, on the history of music; he might also have spoken, as a historian, on music in America. Actually he did both. I have occasion now to remind you of some of the things he said. And I can think of no more fitting conclusion to this discussion of the sources and problems of musicology in America today than the words with which Sonneck, in 1916, concluded his plea for the recognition of musical research as a university subject.

> Initial steps toward this goal have been taken [he says], but they are too tentative and too few. The movement is as yet sporadic, not general. That ultimately it will become general is my firm belief. The development is likely to come, as most reforms do in our country, either with exasperating slowness, or with a rush. When it does come, studies in the history of music in America ought not to be neglected.
>
> Are there subjects enough [he asks] to make this plea for an extensive and intensive study of the history of music in America more substantial and solid than so many other pleas which have turned out to be mere soap-bubbles of specialists?

And having asked this question, Sonneck answers it, listing some thirty distinct fields of investigation that seemed to him worthy of serious attention. After seventeen years that list still stands. I do not presume to add to it. The systematic exploration of the history of music in America is the special task of musical scholarship in this country. Of all the problems that confront us, those in this field are the most pressing. If we do not solve them for ourselves, no one will solve them for us.

VERGIL IN MUSIC[†]

F OR the musician, the name of Vergil is inseparably associated
with that of the romantic composer of *Les Troyens,* "l'huomo più
'Vergiliano' dell' Ottocento," as he has been very justly called.
"The Latin poet," Berlioz writes, "telling me of epic passions of
which I had already a presentiment, was the first to find the way
to my heart, the first to appeal to my awakening imagination." In
an early chapter of the *Mémoires* Berlioz describes the unusually
vivid impression he received from his first reading of Vergil and
tells how, on one occasion, when translating orally from the *Aeneid,*
he became so affected by the poet's account of Dido's tragic death
that he was obliged to stop abruptly to avoid making a display of
his emotion before his father. "I ran from him," he concludes,
"and, in secret, gave myself over to my Vergilian despair." Again
and again, in the pages of the *Mémoires,* the figure of Vergil reappears. In Rome as a student, Berlioz felt himself irresistibly attracted by the associations of the Italian countryside.

> Sometimes [to quote from one of his accounts of his many excursions],
> when I had my guitar with me instead of my gun, a passage from the
> *Aeneid,* which had lain dormant in my mind from childhood, would
> suddenly rise to my recollection, aroused by some aspect of the sur-
> rounding scenery; then, improvising a strange recitative to a still
> stranger harmony, I would sing the death of Pallas, the despair of the
> good Evander, of his horse Aethon, unharnessed and with flowing mane
> and falling tears, following the young warrior's corpse to its last resting-

†From *The Musical Quarterly,* XVI (1930), 482–497. Reprinted by permission
of G. Schirmer, Inc.

place; of the terror of good King Latinus; the siege of Latium, which had stood on the ground beneath my feet; Amata's sad end, and the cruel death of Lavinia's noble lover. This combination of the past—the poetry and the music—used to work me into the most wonderful state of excitement; and this intensified condition of mental intoxication generally culminated in torrents of tears . . . I mourned for poor Turnus, whom the hypocrite Aeneas had robbed of his state, his mistress, and his life; I wept for the beautiful and pathetic Lavinia, forced to wed the stranger-brigand, bathed in her lover's blood. I longed for the good old days when the heroes, sons of the gods, walked the earth, clad in shining armour, hurling slender javelins at targets framed in burnished gold.' [From the translation by Rachel and Eleanor Holmes.]

Throughout his life Berlioz retained, undiminished, his youthful enthusiasm for the *Aeneid* and its author, and it is both appropriate and natural that the work which many regard as Berlioz's masterpiece should have been suggested, and, as the composer himself acknowledges, inspired by Vergil. "At the head of the vocal score of *Les Troyens* you will read these two words: *Divo Virgilio,*" Berlioz writes in December 1863 to the Princess SaynWittgenstein; "it is as if I had written there this motto of consecration: *Sub invocatione Divi Virgilii.*"

Remarkable though it was, this preoccupation of the musician Berlioz with the poet Vergil is by no means unique. Other musicians, in other days, have felt Vergil's influence and have expressed their veneration for him in other forms. An almost uninterrupted sensitiveness to Vergil on the part of musicians may be traced through nearly ten centuries of musical art. During certain periods, indeed, Vergilian music was decidedly in vogue. So numerous and so varied have been the tributes paid to Vergil in music that it is a little surprising that, save for Vladimiro Zabughin's valuable, though scarcely exhaustive survey of the subject,[1] no attempt to treat this aspect of Vergil's influence for its own sake appears to have been made. Within the confines of this article we propose to enumerate certain representative examples of Vergilian music, singling out a few particularly typical specimens for more detailed discussion.

Among the early evidences of the musician's regard for Vergil,

[1]In his *Vergilio nel rinascimento italiano da Dante a Torquato Tasso* (Bologna, 1921–24), v. 2, pp. 383, 432.

interest has centered in that afforded by the tenth-century *Aeneid* Ashburnham 23 of the Laurenziana in Florence, a manuscript once the property of the notorious Libri. Musical notation in neumes, of a somewhat later date than the text, is found on seven of its one hundred and eighty-two folios. The passages distinguished in this way, far from being random selections, include some of the most dramatic moments of the epic: Laocoon's warning, the apparition of Hector to Aeneas, Dido's appeal to Anna on discovering the Trojans in flight, and the last words of the dying Queen of Carthage. Jules Combarieu, who has made a careful study of the manuscript in his *Fragments de l'Enéide en musique d'après un manuscrit inédit* (Paris, 1898), shows that there is reason to believe that its provenance may have been the monastery of St. Gall. "We regard these melodies as having been copied at St. Gall by a Benedictine musician," he concludes, "a musician transcribing from a manuscript that has since disappeared; they are a part of that repertory of secular melody which the Middle Ages produced *simultaneously* with the music of the liturgy, and of which the manuscript of St. Martial of Limoges [to be referred to presently] has conserved for us some still earlier examples." Rejecting Coussemaker's suggestion that these melodies may be those to which Vergil's contemporaries sang his verses, Combarieu insists that they are none the less important when considered as products of Christian art. Fleischer, in a review of Combarieu's monograph, dismisses them, on the other hand, as "the scribbling of an idle monk." We are inclined to accept Combarieu's estimate of their significance, for it appears that they may have had a more than local importance. This is indicated by the musical notation found in Ms. 239 of the Stadtbibliothek in Bern, a ninth-century *Aeneid;* comparison of the two codices leads Friedrich Ludwig, in his contribution to the Adler *Handbuch,* to conclude that, though their melodies "are at times distinctly different, they have, nevertheless, so much in common that there is probably a connection between them." Combarieu's conjecture that the manuscript in Florence is of Swiss origin thus acquires a new importance. Whether the musical notation in the Bern manuscript antedates that in Florence has not been determined.

Thus far we have dealt only with Vergil the poet. Now he is to

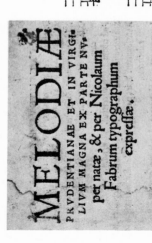

Title page and Sebastian Forster's Vergilian ode Daphnis ego in silvis *(Eclogues V, 43–44, and II, 17–18) from Nicolas Faber's* Melodiae Prudentionae et in Virgilium *(Leipzig, 1533).* (COURTESY OF THE LIBRARY OF CONGRESS.)

appear again in a medieval musical setting, this time in a role more characteristic of the period. Codex 1139 of the Bibliothèque Nationale, a twelfth-century manuscript[2] from St. Martial of Limoges, includes the liturgical music-dramas *The Wise and the Foolish Virgins* and *The Prophets of Christ*, together with the familiar organum *Mira lege* and other important monuments of medieval musical art. Coussemaker has published *The Prophets of Christ*, the section of the manuscript with which we are concerned, in facsimile, with transcription and comment. Unlike *The Wise and the Foolish Virgins*, the text of which is partly Latin, partly Provençal, *The Prophets of Christ*, based on a pseudo-Augustinian sermon, is in Latin throughout. Coussemaker regarded its melodies as plainsong and has given his transcriptions in modern choral-notation, but the regular rhythm of the Latin rhymes suggests that the music, too, is rhythmic, as Ludwig has held. After the opening song of thanksgiving in honor of the Nativity, sung perhaps by a chorus, perhaps by a precentor, thirteen prophets foretell the coming of the Messiah. Vergil is the eleventh to appear. To the exhortation: "*Vates, Maro, gentilium, da Christo testimonium,*" Vergil replies, "*Ecce polo dimissa solo nova progenies est*" (paraphrasing *Eclogue* IV, 7: *Iam nova progenies caelo demittitur alto*). A *Benedicamus* brings the little drama to a close.

The medieval musician's interest in Vergil does not appear, however, to have been very great, for if there exist early examples of Vergilian music other than those few isolated specimens just described, they have eluded the scholars specializing in this field. The composers of the Early Renaissance are even more disappointing. Not until the close of the fifteenth century do we find musicians turning once more to Vergil; then, and during the century which followed, his lines seem to have had an extraordinary fascination for the composers, who, aroused no doubt by the widespread revival of interest in the art and literature of Antiquity, vied with one another in their settings of favorite passages from the *Aeneid*.

Naturally enough, the lines which appealed most strongly to the Renaissance composer were the same which, centuries before, had stirred the imagination of the musician of the Middle Ages. Dido's

[2]According to Ludwig. Coussemaker assigns the manuscript to the eleventh century.

last words, *Dulces exuviae, dum fata deusque sinebant,* were now, as then, in especial favor. Without attempting to account for all the fifteenth- and sixteenth-century settings of this passage, no less than fourteen may be named. Heading the list is a motet by Josquin de Près; his example was followed by Jean Mouton, Mabriano de Orto, Jean Verbonnet, Derick Gerarde, Adrian Willaert, Stefano Rossetti, and Orlando di Lasso *(Sämtliche Werke,* v. 11), and in six anonymous compositions, one in Rhaw's *Symphoniae jucundae* (1538) and *Tricinia* (1542), and five in the British Museum Ms. Royal 8 G. vii.[3]

The settings of Josquin[4] and Mouton have a peculiar interest. The soprano parts of the two motets are identical, and Mouton's

composition has every appearance of being an elaboration of Josquin's. Making the utmost of the opportunities offered by the *cantus firmus,* Mouton has succeeded in introducing a number of very agreeable contrapuntal refinements; the conduct of the lower voices is, for the most part, entirely new, and the motet actually presents a rather striking contrast to Josquin's unassuming, straightforward composition. Quotation of the closing bars of the two settings will make this more clear.

Here Mouton's part-leading (the antiphonal opening-phrase, the effective canon between the soprano and tenor, and the imitations in the alto and bass just before the final cadence) is infinitely more sophisticated than Josquin's; yet, perhaps because of its very simplicity, the Josquin original, with its strange though very characteristic close, has an equal, if not a greater charm.

---

[3]An anonymous setting in Ms. 228 of the Bibliothèque de Bourgogne (Brussels, Bibliothèque Royale) was published by Maldeghem in the *Trésor musical (Musique religieuse,* 1882) as the work of Pierre de La Rue. The attribution is apparently unfounded; according to Burbure *(Etude sur un manuscrit du XVIe siècle),* the composition is identical with de Orto's setting in the Codex Basevi (now Ms. B. 2439 of the Biblioteca del R. Istituto, Florence).

[4]Ambros questions Josquin's authorship.

Ambros calls de Orto's setting of these lines "a composition well worthy of its text, with something of a suggestion of tragic, antique

(Aeneid, IV, 654)

Josquin de Près

(After Berg's NOVUM ET INSIGNE OPUS MUSICUM, Nuremberg, 1558-59.)

(Aeneid, IV, 654)   Jean Mouton

(After Berg's NOVUM ET INSIGNE OPUS MUSICUM, Nuremberg, 1558-59.)

dignity in its impressive declamation." In Willaeert's composition
the same writer sees an evidence of that master's classical training.
"Why," he asks, "were composers so attracted by this particular
passage, setting it again and again? Not only because, when taken
from the epic, it was, like the text of a motet, complete in itself;
the solemn pathos of the lines, the situation, and the poetic figure
of the dying queen appealed to them. Willaert's music, in which the

declamatory principle is more than usually prominent, makes all this felt. Nominally a motet, the composition is almost a tragic monologue."

Other fifteenth- and sixteenth-century settings of passages from the *Aeneid* are those of lines 305 ff. of Book IV *(Dissimulare etiam sperasti)* by Philippo de Luprano (in Book VIII of the Petrucci *Frottole,* 1507) and Cipriano da Rore (in the 1567 edition of Striggio's *Il cicalamento delle donne al bucato); the Oeglin Liederbuch* (1512)[5] and the British Museum manuscript already referred to include anonymous settings of lines 174 ff. of Book IV *(Fama, malum qua non aliud velocius ullum).* The beginning of the first Eclogue was set to music by Orlando di Lasso *(Sämtliche Werke,* v. 19), lines 6 ff. of the second by Stefano Rossetti.

At the same time German musicians were providing Vergil's lines with settings cast in an entirely different mold. Italian and Flemish composers, oblivious to learned speculation concerning the antique meters, and animated solely by artistic considerations, had conceived their music to the Latin verses in the traditional style and in the most appropriate of the established forms, that of the motet; the compositions of their German fellows, on the other hand, prompted by literati preoccupied with the problems of classical prosody, and written for the literary fraternities at the universities or for use in the schools, were deliberate attempts to supply a modern substitute for the lost music of the Ancients. At Ingolstadt in the fourteen-nineties, students of Conrad Celtes, distinguished German humanist and poet, sang odes of Horace, set to music by a certain Petrus Tritonius (Treybenreif), one of their own number. These compositions, published in two editions by Oeglin in 1507 as *Melopoiae, sive Harmoniae tetracenticae,* and reprinted with additions in 1532 and 1551–52 by Egenolf, soon attained an extraordinary popularity (Judenkünig included arrangements for the lute in his *Utilis et compendiaria introductio,* published in Vienna about 1515) and led to further experimentation. The first collection of Latin odes in which Vergil is represented seems to have been Nicolas Faber's *Melodiae Prudentianae et in Virgilium* (Leipzig,

[5]Publications of the *Gesellschaft für Musikforschung,* v. 9. The composition in question is also included in the Brussels Ms. 228; following this source, Maldeghem has published it in the *Trésor musical (Musique religieuse,* 1883), ascribing it to Pierre de La Rue.

1533), with contributions by two local composers, Sebastian Forster and Lucas Hordisch. In addition to the settings of the hymns of Prudentius, many of them designed for the use of the *Thomaner* at particular hours or on particular days, the collection contains a setting of lines 43 ff. of the fifth Eclogue by Forster and an anonymous composition to the opening of the *Aeneid*. A year later, at the request of the Basel scholar Simon Minervius, Ludwig Senfl made new harmonizations of the Tritonius tenors, adding twelve original compositions to Latin texts, among them Vergil's *Arma virumque cano*. Further settings of this passage appeared in 1539 in a collection by Benedictus Ducis (Herzog), intended for use in the schools of Ulm, and in Paul Hofhaimer's posthumously published *Harmoniae poeticae*. An anonymous setting of the beginning of the first Eclogue was included in the final edition of the Tritonius odes (Frankfort, 1551–52).

It would be difficult to imagine a style more homely than that which distinguishes this group of compositions. Neither harmonic simplicity nor formal severity could well be carried further. The ode, mechanically reproducing the rhythm of the text and scrupulously avoiding even the appearance of polyphony, is, indeed, the absolute antithesis of the motet, with its quasi-dramatic declamation and involved counterpoint. The possibilities of the style are extremely limited. There is, consequently, a rather depressing uniformity about its literature, and one doubts whether composers as distinguished as Hofhaimer and Senfl would have cared to submit to its restrictions had they not been bound by ties of friendship to men prominent among the exponents of Humanism in Germany. It is amusing to note that what a sixteenth-century critic found most tolerable in these pieces was precisely that which irritated his eighteenth-century *confrère*. Glareanus observes that "aside from the *concentus* (concord), one discovers no trace of an even moderate talent"; Forkel, on the other hand, complains particularly of the awkward heaviness of the harmonizations.

The anonymous *Arma virumque cano* of 1533 is quoted (in part) in the first volume of Wustmann's *Musikgeschichte Leipzigs* (Leipzig and Berlin, 1909); its companion piece, Forster's *Daphnis ego in silvis,* is reproduced in the accompanying facsimile. Though no copy of the odes of Benedictus Ducis has been preserved, his *Arma virumque cano* was reprinted in the *Erotemata musicae practicae* of Lucas Lossius (Nuremberg, 1563). The composition is so short that it may be given here in its entirety.

BENEDICTO DUCE: *MELODIA CARMINIS HEXAMETICI*
(Aeneid, I, 1-4)

ADVICE TO THE READER

A line of text was inadvertently dropped between pages 31 and page 32 of this volume, rendering the resulting paragraph unintelligible. Please note:

p. 31   style of composition introduced by Peri, Caccini, and their fellow
add   modernists was one scarcely congenial to Latin meters; partly as a
p. 32   result of the almost universal acceptance of this style, partly as a . . .

result of the almost universal acceptance of this style, partly as a result of a more general reaction from Renaissance values, secular compositions to Latin texts became from thenceforward more and more infrequent. Though Horace, to be sure, never quite ceased to interest musicians, later-day settings of his lines, such as Philidor's *Carmen saeculare* (1787) or Loewe's *Fünf Oden*, Op. 57 (1836), are distinctly irregular phenomena, curious, but hardly representative. Vergil's characters and situations, if not his lines, continued, however, to invite musical treatment, and we shall find the composers of the seventeenth and eighteenth centuries interpreting the *Aeneid* in the musical language of their day, producing Vergilian cantatas and operas to Italian, French, German, and English librettos.[6]

The *Dialoghi e sonetti* (1638) of the Roman composer Domenico Mazzocchi contain what are probably the earliest specimens of the Vergilian cantata, two dialogues, *Dido furens* and *Nisus & Euryalus*, the first from the fourth, the second from the ninth book of the *Aeneid*. These compositions, for three and four voices with *basso continuo*, may be said to represent the transition from the Latin motet to the Italian and French cantata, for though the style and spirit of the music are new, Vergil's original lines are retained. Mazzocchi's Vergilian dialogues are selected for special commendation in a contemporary defense of the new music, Pietro della Valle's *Della musica dell'età nostra* (1640). Addressing the reactionary Lelio Guidiccioni, an Italian translator of Vergil, della Valle writes, "Sir, you tell me of the delight which the playing of Correggio [Claudio Merulo] occasioned you in Parma many years ago, but more recently, as I hear, and as you yourself will perhaps deign to remember, you were unable to conceal your pleasure when certain passages from Vergil, in a most attractive musical setting by the elder Mazzocchi, were sung at the house of Signor Raimondo in Rome."

Early in the eighteenth century the Vergilian cantata came into its own, and its vogue, once established, was remarkable. In Italy

---

[6]Compositions to poems in the vernacular, paraphrasing Vergil's lines or suggested by his situations, were not unknown to the musical art of the Renaissance. Compare, for instance, the anonymous *La nocte aquieta ogni animali* in Book IV of the Petrucci Frottole, 1505 (paraphrasing *Aeneid*, IV, 522 ff.), and Palestrina's unusual madrigal *Dido, chi giace entro quest'urna?* (*Werke*, v. 28).

Vergil was celebrated in Alessandro Scarlatti's *Alle Trojane antenne,* in Benedetto Marcello's *Didone,* in Antonio Tozzi's *Dunque il perfido Enea,* and, later, in Nicola Antonio Zingarelli's *Didone;* in France in the *Didon* (1708) and *Enée et Didon* (1714) of André Campra, in the *Didon* (1723) of François Colin de Blamont, in the *La mort de Didon* of Michel de Monteclair, in the *La mort de Didon* of Jean Joseph Mouret, and in the *Enée et Didon* (1764) of La Garde.

Among the Italian examples, that by Scarlatti is easily the most interesting. Dent has not dated this cantata in his catalogue of Scarlatti's compositions; the bold harmonies implied by the *continuo,* particularly in the recitatives, suggest, however, that the work belongs among Scarlatti's later productions, perhaps among the cantatas written at the time of his correspondence with Gasparini in 1712. Quotation of the opening of the second recitative will give an idea of the dramatic quality of this music and of the character of Scarlatti's mature harmonic writing.

Tozzi's Vergilian cantata is cited by Eugen Schmitz in his *Geschichte der Kantate und des geistlichen Konzerts* (Leipzig, 1914) as a typical specimen of the great dramatic monologue cultivated in the opera by the masters of the Second Neapolitan School; its subject, the complaint of the abandoned Dido, was, he adds, a favorite one. Marcello's *Didone* is available in a modern edition.[7]

Most of the French cantatas enumerated above must have been heard, at one time or another, at the *Concerts spirituels,* where, beginning in 1727, secular compositions in French were admitted to the repertory. Colin de Blamont's *Didon,* in fact, was sung there on December 20, 1727, as part of the program which inaugurated this change in policy.

Descriptive music plays an important part in the French cantata. Colin de Blamont begins, for example, with an instrumental *"Tempeste,"*

Campra, in his *Enée et Didon,* with an *"Orage";* the same composer's *Didon* includes the air

>Que les vents déchaînés, que les flots en colère,

Monteclair provides a similar piece,

>Tyrans de l'empire de l'onde,
>Grondez, volez, vents furieux.

[7]Edited by Malipiero as No. 67 of the *Raccolta nazionale delle musiche italiane* (Milan, 1919).

Apparently only one section from this group of compositions has been reprinted, a recitative and air from Campra's *Didon*.[8]

The favor with which Italian music and the Italian style were regarded by the German aristocracy during the first half of the eighteenth century did not encourage native production. There were but few German contributions to the literature of the Vergilian cantata, and these exceptional compositions, written to Italian texts, are scarcely to be distinguished from those provided by Italian composers in German service. The entire activity centered about the Saxon court in Dresden, where the Elector's music-loving consort, Maria Antonia Walpurgis, had gathered round her a group of notable musicians and literati. Shortly after her marriage to the Elector, the Princess, who occasionally turned her hand to musical and literary composition, amused herself by writing two Italian cantata-librettos, *Didone* and *Lavinia e Turno*. Metastasio's *Didone abbandonata* served as a model for the first of these, but we are told that the Princess was dissatisfied with Metastasio's poem and endeavored to improve on it by following Vergil more closely than had her predecessor. Subsequently the two librettos were submitted to Metastasio for criticism; in replying to the Abbé Pasquini, who had acted as intermediary, Metastasio piles compliment upon compliment, protesting, at the same time, that he has not been taught "the language of adulation." "Oh poor Pasquini! and poor me!" he concludes; "if sovereigns write such excellent poetry, what is to become of us wretched plebeian bards" (Burney). In 1748 both librettos were set to music by Giovanni Alberto Ristori, composer of church music to the Saxon court and, after 1750, Vice-Capellmeister under Hasse; later settings were provided by Johann Gottlieb Naumann, associated with music in Dresden from 1764 until his death in 1801. Gennaro Manna, of Ferrara and Naples, is also credited with having set both poems to music.

Two further compositions to *Lavinia e Turno,* by Giovanni Placido Rutini of Prague and Carl Heinrich Graun of Berlin, were published in 1756 and 1762 by Breitkopf. The printed scores do not mention Maria Antonia; the authorship of the poem was, however, an open secret. "The graceful Italian verses are the creation

[8] As No. 27 of *La cantate au XVIIe et au XVIIIe siècles,* edited by Mme. Jane Arger (Paris, 1912?).

of an exalted hand," writes Marpurg, reviewing the Rutini cantata in his *Historisch-kritische Beyträge*.

Despite this intensive cultivation, however, the role of the cantata in the Vergilian music of the seventeenth and eighteenth centuries appears relatively insignificant when compared with that of the opera. Librettists and composers were not slow to recognize the operatic possibilities of certain portions of the *Aeneid,* and it was not long before Dido, Aeneas, Lavinia, and Turnus became familiar operatic figures. The earliest dramatic composition on a theme from the Aeneid is Monteverdi's *Didone,* an intermezzo composed in honor of the marriage of Odoardo Farnese and Margherita Medici and performed in Parma, December 13, 1628. In 1641 followed the first operas on themes from the *Aeneid,* Monteverdi's *Le nozze d'Enea con Lavinia* and Cavalli's *La Didone,* both performed in Venice. Neither of the Monteverdi scores has been preserved; the libretto of his *Didone,* by Ascanio Pii, is reprinted, however, in Solerti's *Musica, ballo e drammatica alla corte Medicea* (Florence, 1905). In Germany priority belongs to Johann Wolfgang Franck's *Aeneas des trojanischen Fürsten Ankunft in Italien* (Hamburg, 1680), in England to Purcell's *Dido and Aeneas* (London, ca. 1689), in France to the *Enée et Lavinie* of Colasse (Paris, 1690).

A detailed account of the history of the Vergilian opera would be a formidable undertaking, and it is a question whether such an account would contribute anything of genuine importance to our appreciation of Vergil's relation to music. It will perhaps suffice to say that the total number of Vergilian operas is so great that it cannot even be conveniently estimated. One libretto alone, Metastasio's *Didone abbandonata,* was set to music more than forty times; from 1724 (Sarro) to 1824 (Reissiger) it dominated the entire field of operatic composition for a century. It must be remembered, too, that Vergil is one of the principal sources for the Orpheus legend; a thoroughgoing survey of the Vergilian opera will need, then, to consider the innumerable compositions on this theme in addition to the operas dealing with Dido, Aeneas, and the other heroes and heroines of the *Aeneid.*

There will, perhaps, be the objection that Vergil's Dido and Aeneas have little or nothing to do with the Didone and Enea of Metastasio and his contemporaries, and that the phrase "Vergilian opera" is something of a misnomer. One has but to turn, however,

to the prefaces and dedications which are so characteristic a feature
of the seventeenth- and eighteenth-century opera-libretto and one
will find, here and there, an acknowledgment of the Vergilian
source of an author's inspiration, accompanied, perhaps, by a Vergilian quotation. Hinsch, for instance, writes as follows in the
preface to his libretto for Graupner's *Dido, Königin von Carthago*
(Hamburg, 1707): "We are obliged to the excellent Latin poet
Virgilius for the content of this drama." There follows a seven-
page dissertation on the historical inaccuracy of the *Aeneid*, with
appeals to the authority of Menander, Justinus, Solinus, Macrobius,
Josephus, and a host of other writers, ancient and modern. In the
original edition of Calsabigi's libretto for Gluck's *Orfeo ed Euridice*
(Vienna, 1762) the reader is expressly referred to *Georgics*, while
on the fly-leaf appears the following quotation:

> *Te, dulcis coniunx, te solo in litore secum,*
> *Te veniente die, te decedente canebat.*
> *(Georgic IV, 456–66.)*

Cramer prefaces the German edition of his libretto for Naumann's
Orpheus and Euridice (Kiel and Hamburg, s. d.) by complete translations of the passages dealing with Orpheus in the *Georgics* and in
Ovid's *Metamorphoses,* followed by a very sensible discussion of the
theory of dramatic poetry in its relation to his own poem (previously published in his *Magazin der Musik* for 1786).

Non-operatic Vergilian music since 1800 need not detain us
long. Rossini's cantata *La morte di Didone*, composed in 1811 for
Ester Mombelli, waited until May 2, 1818, for a hearing. A contemporary critic, quoted by Radiciotti in his biography of the composer (Tivoli, 1927–29) reported "the poetry beneath criticism,
the music of no consequence, and the performance indifferent."
Two French cantatas, Berlioz's *La mort d'Orphée* and Gustave Charpentier's *Didon,* were *morceaux de concours*. The fate of the Berlioz
cantata is a familiar story; rejected as impossible by the jury of the
Académie des Beaux-Arts, it was performed at a concert given by the
composer in May 1828. The score, which Berlioz was believed to
have destroyed, was recently discovered in the Library of the Conservatoire and has just been published by the *Réunion des Biblio-
thèques nationales.* Charpentier was more fortunate; in the competition of 1887 his cantata won him the *Prix de Rome.* Much more

significant are the instrumental compositions written to Vergilian programs or bearing Vergilian mottoes. Clementi's piano sonata *Didone abbandonata,* Op. 50, No. 3 (1821), is an isolated early example. More recent and more ambitious essays in this field are the third movement from Edward MacDowell's *Erste moderne Suite* for the piano, Op. 10 (1883), with a motto from Book II of the *Aeneid;* Paul Gilson's *Suite pastorale* for orchestra; Henri Rabaud's *Eglogue (Poème Virgilien,* for orchestra, Op. 7 (1898), with a motto from the first Eclogue; Charles Martin Loeffler's *A pagan poem* for orchestra with piano, English horn, and three trumpets obbligati, Op. 14 (1909), suggested by the eighth Eclogue; and Gabriel Pierné's *Sonata da camera* for piano, flute, and violoncello, Op. 48 (1927), a memorial to Louis Fleury with a motto from the fifth Eclogue. One assumes that Mario Castelnuovo-Tedesco's unpublished *Madrigali a Galatea* for four voices (1914) are an anticipation of the Neoclassicism which has distinguished so much of the Italian music since the war. At the moment of writing (May 1930) comes the report that Riccardo Zandonai is at work on a Vergilian "sinfonia," commissioned for the September Bimillennial Festival in Mantua.

There is a temptation to recognize in this vast and varied repertory a reflection of men's constantly changing attitude, not only toward Vergil, but toward antique culture in general. Some few of the compositions enumerated here are, to a certain extent, the products of a combination of accidental circumstances; these compositions, however, represent the exception rather than the rule. That Vergilian music has flourished in one period and declined in another is neither accidental nor due entirely to variations in musical style and technique. It is rather that these variations themselves are to be interpreted as phenomena attendant upon changes in the broad cultural background.

ON THE DATE OF
MARCHETTO DA PADOVA[†]

As our familiarity with the music of the Italian Trecento in-
creases and we draw nearer to the point from which we will
be able to take a comprehensive view of the whole development,
our uncertainty as to the date of the theoretical writings of Marchetto da Padova becomes more and more of an embarrassment.
Until we know this date we shall not know when Piero and Giovanni da Cascia began their activity, for the musical notation described by Marchetto is substantially the same as that found in the
MS which contains their earliest works (Rome, Vat. Rossi 215).
And until we know whether Marchetto precedes or follows Jean de
Muris and Philippe de Vitry, we cannot properly estimate the
extent to which Italy was at first dependent upon France.

A re-examination of the evidence indicates that a specific date
can be satisfactorily established. This being the case, it will be
unnecessary to review in detail the various conjectures advanced
by Muratori, Burney, Gerbert, Zacco, Ambros, Fétis, Balbi,
Favaro, Wolf, Cesari, and Torri, particularly since Ludwig has
already demonstrated that the dates once generally accepted—
"1274" for the *Lucidarium* and "1309" for the *Pomerium*—are
altogether without foundation and wholly untenable;[1] as Ludwig
has plausibly suggested, the date "1274," a later interpolation in

†From *Rassegna musicale*, XX (1950), 312–315. Reprinted by permission of
Giulio Einaudi Editore.

[1]*Archiv für Musikwissenschaft*, V (1923), 289.

the Milan MS of the *Lucidarium,* is perhaps due to the *explicit* of the preceding treatise, the *Scientia artis musicae* of Elias Salomonis. The present state of the question is accurately summarized by Reese[2] and Apel.[3]

From the first it has been generally recognized that the dates of the two writings could be inferred from the unusually circumstantial letters of dedication which accompany them if only the various persons and events referred to could be positively identified. Let us begin with the dedication of the *Lucidarium.* This reads as follows:

> To the magnificent soldier and his powerful Lord Ranieri, vicar general in the province of Romagna, son of Lord Zaccaria of Orvieto and servant of the illustrious prince Lord John, Count of Gravina and Lord of the Honor of Mount Sant Angelo, glorious son of Lord Chárles, King of Jerusalem and Sicily, of illustrious and distinguished memory, Marchetto da Padova presents himself prepared for every sort of command.[4]

The treatise was accordingly written after the death of Charles II, King of Naples, which occurred in 1309; it was written after August 19, 1310, when Charles's successor Robert was appointed vicar and rector in Romagna by Clement V;[5] it was written during the lifetime of Robert's brother John, Count of Gravina, who died in the spring of 1335;[6] it was written before July 11, 1318, the date of John's marriage to Mathilda of Hainaut, for through this marriage John acquired a claim to the contested title of Prince of Achaia and Morea, a title which he proceeded to use from this time until 1333, when he renounced his claim to it and began to style himself Duke of Durazzo and Lord of the Kingdom of Albania.[7]

---

[2]*Music in the Middle Ages* (New York, 1940), p. 340.

[3]*The Notation of Polyphonic Music,* 4th ed. (Cambridge, 1949), p. 368.

[4]Magnifico militi et potenti domino suo Raynerio domini Zacharie de Vrbe veteri illustris principis domini Johannis clare & excelse memorie domini Karoli regis Jerusalem & Sicilie gloriosi filij comitis Grauine et honoris montis Sancti Angeli in provintie Romandiole vicario generali. Marchetus de Padua se ipsum paratum ad omnia genera mandatorum. (Text of the Library of Congress MS ML 171.J6, "Scripsit dominus Johannes Franciscus de Papia monachus venerabilis cenobij sancti Georgij de Venetijs. 1465.")

[5]Romolo Caggese, *Roberto d'Angiò e i suoi tempi* (Florence, 1921–1930), I, 118.

[6]*Ibid.,* I, 649; II, 321.

[7]*Ibid.,* I, 647–649: II, 303–304, 309–322.

The *Lucidarium* must accordingly have been written sometime between August 19, 1310, and July 11, 1318. To obtain a more precise date we shall need to determine when John's servant, Ranieri di Zaccaria of Orvieto, was Robert's vicar general in Romagna. Two dates for Ranieri are given by Caggese in his biography of Robert of Anjou: in 1315 he was Robert's vicar in Florence; in 1329 Robert appointed him to a corresponding post in Rome.[8] The date of his vicariate in Romagna is supplied by Scipione Chiaramonti in his history of Cesena, under the year 1318:

> In this year the jurisdiction of King Robert over our province came to an end. . . . There were six vicars: . . . Niccolò Caracciolo, Gilberto de Santillis, Simone Bedocco . . . Simone Bedocco was succeeded by Didacus Rattus, whom the chronicle calls Diego de La Rat; the fifth was Anfuso, whom the chronicle calls Simon the Fearless; the last was Ranieri of Orvieto, the son of Lord Zaccaria (as the chronicle says), who governed the province in the year 1318.[9]

With the date of the *Lucidarium* established, the events referred to in the dedication of the *Pomerium* can be readily identified. The epistle begins:

> To the most eminent of princes, Lord Robert, by the grace of God King of Jerusalem and Sicily, Marchetto da Padova humbly and devoutly commends himself.[10]

Toward the end of the epistle Marchetto also lets us know that the king is currently occupied with a military undertaking:

> Hence it is that devoutly considering what would be fitting to offer to your exalted majesty, I have decided to compose, by searching through my poor knowledge, a little work on the art of music, which by reason

---

[8]I, 217: II, 135.

[9]Hoc Anno cessauit Regis Roberti in Prouinciam nostram iurisdictio. . . . Vicarij sex fuere . . . Nicolaus Caracciolus, Gilbertus Santillus, Simon Bedoccus . . . Simone Bedocc successit Didacus Rattus vocat Chronicon Diegum de Larat, quintus fuit Anfusus, quem Simonē sine timore vocat Chronicon; postremus fuit Rainerius Vrbeuetanus Domini Zachariae (vt dicit Chronicon) filius, qui anno 1318. Prouinciae praefuit.—*Caesena historia* (Cesena, 1641), pp. 492–493.

[10]Praeclarissimo Principum domino Roberto Dei gratia Ierusalem & Siciliae Regi Marchetus de Padua recommendationem humilem & devotam.—Gerbert, *Scriptores*, III, 122.

of its novelty may sometimes divert your royal mind in the camp of your present expedition, while the fortune of war hangs in the balance.[11]

And in his *explicit* Marchetto at least implies that he began work on his second treatise not long after having finished the first:

> I, Marchetto da Padova, after composing a book on the understanding of plainsong, have gone on to compose this book treating of measured music.[12]

The *Pomerium*, then, was written sometime between 1318, the date of the *Lucidarium*, and 1343, the year of Robert's death. In view of what Marchetto says in his *explicit*, it was almost certainly written in 1318 or shortly thereafter, the more so since it was written in Cesena, the city in which the *Lucidarium* was begun, and with the help of the same Dominican who had worked with him on the *Lucidarium*, Brother Syphans of Ferrara.

Now it so happens that in 1318 Robert was indeed occupied with a military undertaking. On July 10 of that year, "with 46 transports, 25 light galleys, and many other ships and vessels laden with provisions," and with 1,200 men at arms, Robert set sail from Naples for Genoa, where he arrived on July 21. The Ghibelline forces, under Marco Visconti, promptly withdrew to the lower valley of the Bisagno, leaving Robert and the Guelfs encamped in the city. The inevitable conflict, which took place on February 5, 1319, proved a crushing defeat for Marco Visconti and his allies. On April 29, 1319, following this encounter, Robert went on to Provence,[13] where he remained, for five years the peaceful guest of John XXII at Avignon, until his return to Genoa on April 22, 1324.[14]

Thus, unless we are to suppose that Marchetto was occupied with the composition of the *Pomerium* for more than five years—and this would seem to be excluded by what he says himself and by every-

---

[11]Hinc est, quod devota mentis intentione considerans, quid per me dignum foret vestrae celsitudinis offerendum, decrevi quoddam meae exilitatis indagine musicae artis opusculum condere, quod regium animum in campo praesentis militiae & Marte bellorum ancipite laborantem interdum suae novitatis ordine delectaret.—*Ibid.*, III, 123.

[12]Ego Marchettus de Padua post librum a me conditum sapientiam planae musicae, addidi componere librum istum musicae mensuratae.—*Ibid.*, III, 187.

[13]Caggese, *op. cit.*, II, 31–36.

[14]*Ibid.*, II, 71.

thing that we know about the circumstances connected with the composition of the *Pomerium*—this second treatise must belong to the latter part of the year 1318 or at the very latest to the beginning of the year 1319.

To draw only the most obvious conclusions, we now know that, however much the early Trecentisti may have been indebted to France, they were certainly not in any way dependent upon the theory of the Ars Nova as first formulated by Jean de Muris in 1319 and later developed by Philippe de Vitry. We now know also that we owe to an Italian our clearest account of the transitional notation used in France at the turn of the century and our earliest theoretical presentation of perfect and imperfect time as equally privileged varieties of measure. There is now nothing to prevent our placing the MS Rome, Vat. Rossi 215, in the 1320's, which would mean that Piero and Giovanni da Cascia began their activity some ten to twenty years earlier than was formerly supposed. Finally, since of these two at least Giovanni is known to have been with Jacopo da Bologna at the court of Mastino della Scala, ruler of Verona from 1329 to 1351, and since Marchetto tells us himself that it was in Verona that he completed the *Lucidarium*, it is of decided interest to be able to place this brief stay of Marchetto's in Verona within the lifetime of Mastino's predecessor, Cangrande I.

CHURCH POLYPHONY
APROPOS OF A NEW FRAGMENT
AT GROTTAFERRATA†

D EDICATED from the first to the rule of Saint Basil and to the celebration, in Greek, of the Byzantine rite, the Badia greca di Grottaferrata remains today the last flourishing outpost of Italo-Greek monasticism. Its collection of manuscripts is of necessity a collection of Greek manuscripts, many of them products of its own scriptorium, and as the Greek-rite monasteries of Sicily, Calabria, and the Basilicata were one by one abandoned, secularized, or absorbed by the Latin orders, the library of the Badia became the sanctuary within which some part of their collections found refuge. Inevitably, a considerable fraction of the manuscripts at Grottaferrata is devoted to the liturgical music of the Greek rite, and as a natural result of this the library of the Badia has in our day become the principal center for the study of an important chapter in the history of music in Italy—the survival and preservation of the Byzantine musical tradition in what was once part of the Byzantine Empire.

Yet, like most other special libraries, Grottaferrata has sometimes found itself harboring manuscripts wholly foreign to its limited and legitimate interests. A case in point is the set of six small volumes (E.beta.x to xv) with *cantate* and *duetti da camera,* some of them by a certain Agostino Dante, in the outlandish format familiar

†From *L'Ars Nova italiana del trecento, Secondo convegno internazionale 17–22 Iuglio 1969* (Certaldo, 1970), 305–313. Reprinted by permission of Centro di studi sull'Ars nova italiana del Trecento.

to every student of seventeenth-century music. Another is the little parchment fragment (E.beta.xvi) with music of the French and Italian Ars nova, recently described by Giuseppe Corsi[1] and Kurt von Fischer.[2] Far from being newcomers to Grottaferrata, these two items were already listed in Antonio Rocchi's *Codices Cryptenses,* published as long ago as 1883.

By contrast, the fragment in which I have interested myself is a recent acquisition. It has received the designation "Collocazione provvisoria 197" and in his inventory of supplementary manuscripts Father Marco Petta, the librarian at the Badia, has described it as follows:

> Questi 13 fogli di musica sono stati donati alla Biblioteca della Badia dal signore Giorgio Liguori, studente in medicina alla Università di Roma e abitante in via Gregorio XIII, 125, Roma. A lui furono lasciati in eredità dallo zio, ch'era un appassionato collezionista di stampe e libri.
>
> I fogli suddetti erano stati incollati tra di loro per formare i cartoni nella rilegatura di un libro.
>
> Donazione fatta insieme con altre carte di archivio e pergamene il 4 luglio 1966.
>
> I fogli sono stati lavati e restaurati nell'ottobre 1968 presso il Gabinetto di Restauro di questo Monastero.

The folios are of paper, uniform in quality and texture. Where a water-mark can be made out, it is one of the earlier forms of the popular "Three Hills with a Cross," as used in Italian mills from a little before until a little after the year 1400, the wire-marks distinctly coarse, the chain-lines running at right angles to them approximately six centimeters apart.[3] Like the paper itself, the ruling of the staves is also uniform. Originally, each page was ruled in red with ten five-line staves, sometimes enclosed between verti-

---

[1]"Frammenti di un codice musicale dell' 'Ars nova' rimasti sconosciuti," *Belfagor,* XX (1965), 210–215.

[2]"Ein neues Trecentofragment," *Festschrift für Walter Wiora* (Kassel, 1967), pp. 264–268.

[3]C. M. Briquet, *Les filigranes,* 2nd ed. (New York, 1966 = Leipzig, 1923), pp. 588–600. For these forms of his "Monts, montagnes ou collines" Briquet uses the designation "Trois monts surmontés d'un trait en croix." "Cette marque," he adds, "devenue banale en Italie, y a été employée par plusieurs battoirs." While the specific form seen in the Grottaferrata fragment does not agree exactly with any those he reproduces, it closely resembles his No. 11675.

cal rules setting off the left- and right-hand margins. Four of these ruled pages are blank. On the remaining twenty-two one finds entered, arranged as in a choir-book, twelve three- and four-voiced compositions—five Glorias, five Credos, a motet in honor of the Venetian Doge Marco Cornaro, hitherto known only through the preservation of a single voice in another fragment, and the familiar virelai "Par maintes foys" by Joannes Vaillant; with these are two additional items—an isolated contratenor for a ballade, without identifying text, and the solemn plainsong for the Magnificat in the eighth tone. One has only to consider the uniformity of the paper and ruling to recognize that the thirteen folios constitute the remains of a single manuscript, and noting then that two of the compositions it contains—the virelai and the motet—date from the 1350's and 60's and that none of its other items suggests a date of composition later than about 1425, one may conclude that in its original state the manuscript must have been an important one. It is tempting to suppose that it may once have contained a repertory comparable in extent to those of the somewhat later manuscripts in Bologna at the Biblioteca Universitaria (2216) and the Civico Museo (Q15), but all that one can actually claim for it is that there must once have been at least six additional folios, with the missing voice or voices of compositions now represented by one or two voices only, with the beginning of a composition now represented only by its Secunda pars, and with the ending of another for which the Prima pars is all that remains.

Before being glued together, the thirteen folios were ruthlessly trimmed to their present size—roughly 31.4 by 21.8 centimeters. No folio has been spared at the top, with the result that no upper margins remain and that there has been a further loss of anywhere from two to ten staff-lines; at the sides, to the left and right, the first and last few centimeters of the staves below have usually been sacrificed. But from those folios that have retained, on the recto side, their right-hand margins and from those that have been so severely trimmed at the top that the margin at the bottom has been left more or less intact, one may estimate that in their original state the folios must have measured somewhere in the neighborhood of 45 by 28 centimeters. The manuscript thus exemplifies the new format whose earliest appearance Besseler places near the end of the fourteenth century[4]—the folio format, physically arranged as in a choir-book, but differing from the true choir-book in that it is not adapted for use by more than three to four musicians, the note-heads and other details of the notation being too small to be read by anyone not standing close by. The height of the staves is only 1.7 centimeters.

As one consequence of the merciless mutilation to which the folios have been subjected, no single item among the fourteen that they transmit has been perfectly preserved. There are other consequences, equally serious. All titles and composers' names that may once have been recorded have been trimmed off, and if the folios were originally numbered, all traces of this have disappeared. Since every recto page has lost its left-hand margin it is quite impossible to determine whether any pair of folios was originally conjunct. There are no visible numerals or letters marking the beginnings and endings of gatherings. That the folios had been trimmed and incorrectly assembled before being glued together is evident from the mirror impressions that the ink from certain pages has left on those that happen to have been laid next to them—two of these mirror impressions are actually upside down. And before being brought to Grottaferrata the folios had already been separated. Three folios are consecutive and there are four pairs; two folios are independent. Their original order can no longer be determined. Any order one gives to them now is more or less arbitrary. One possibility would be to assume that the Glorias should come first with the Credos following, as they do in most manuscripts of this sort. Another would be to begin with the entries of the principal hand, going on then to those of the two hands ranking next in importance. With either plan, the incidental entries in other hands will fall into place of themselves, for the positions of the isolated contratenor, the motet, and the virelai are given.

This ought to be the place to offer an inventory, listing the single items in the order adopted, with indications of any concordances that may exist and comments on the fragment's deviations from concordant sources wherever these are significant. Such an inventory would need also to distinguish among the several scribes who

[4]See his "Neue Quellen des 14. und beginnenden 15. Jahrhunderts," *Archiv für Musikwissenschaft*, VII (1926–27), 167–252, especially 174.

Badia greca di Grottaferrata, Collocazione provvisoria 197, folios 1 verso and 2.

have made the entries and to tell us whether any of these have been encountered elsewhere. Professor Pirrotta has already recognized in the Lowinsky fragment the hands of the two scribes responsible for the manuscript Paris 568 and has shown further that one of these hands occurs also in the little fragment at Lucca.[5] Something of the same sort can easily have happened here. Until we know more about its concordances and about its scribes, it will be only prudent to forego all discussion of date and provenance.

But if this ought to be the place to offer an inventory, it is also the place where the ice is beginning to become a bit thin for an avowed Byzantinist. A really useful inventory can be made only by a scholar with an intimate, first-hand knowledge of all the sources potentially involved, and it is for this reason, and in the best interests of the fragment itself, that I have invited the collaboration of Ursula Günther. I am more than grateful to her for having taken up the challenge. Confident that I am entrusting it to the most competent hands, I leave to her the lion's share of our common task —the more exacting share, perhaps, but surely the more rewarding.[6] For myself, however, I have reserved the exploration of the one concordance that concerns me directly and calls, as it were, for some comment from me.

In September 1968 my good friend Nino Pirrotta published, as a compliment to me, a carefully thought-out and persuasively worded essay entitled "Church Polyphony apropos of a New Fragment at Foligno."[7] I read and reread this with the keenest interest, relishing its savor to the full, and studied with rapt attention the facsimiles and transcriptions it included. Some days passed, a light finally dawned, and to my astonishment I perceived what I ought certainly to have perceived at once—the first of the three Glorias in the Foligno fragment and the only one it preserves in anything like completeness, Pirrotta's Gloria No. 1, is essentially identical with the first of the five Glorias in the fragment at Grottaferrata,

---

[5] *Paolo Tenorista in a New Fragment of the Italian Ars Nova* (Palm Springs, 1961), p. 18 and n. 24.

[6] For the inventory, see her contribution to the proceedings of the congress, "Quelques remarques sur des feuillets récemment découverts à Grottaferrata."

[7] Harold Powers, ed., *Studies in Music History* (Princeton, 1968), pp. 113–126. Since the publication of Professor Pirrotta's essay, the fragment has been transferred from Sala A of the Biblioteca Comunale to the Archivio di Stato in Foligno.

my own Gloria No. 1. When I informed Professor Pirrotta of this spectacular coincidence he was not less astonished than I had been myself, for although I had written to him about the Grottaferrata fragment as soon as it was received at the Badia, I had not supplied him with a set of photographs until long after his essay had gone to press. Thus I am indebted to Professor Pirrotta, not only for the graceful compliment he has paid me, but also for having unwittingly supplied me with an essential piece of my puzzle. The compliment invites a *risposta,* and now that I have that essential piece, it is my duty to show how it fits in.

If I begin my exploration by considering the version found in the Grottaferrata fragment, it is because it is simpler than the one at Foligno, more complete and more readily understood.[8] A line-by-line setting of the Gloria text, simultaneously declaimed by the three voices, note against note and syllable against syllable, the single lines set off from one another by rests of two tempora affecting the whole complex, the notation—except for a single minim—in longs, breves, and semibreves throughout, the little piece might almost have been made to order as an illustration of what Besseler has called "der freie Fauxbourdonstil."[9] It makes little difference that the tenor is incomplete, breaking off with the word "Suscipe," for while there are some gaps in the two upper voices, they are easily filled in, and in the free fauxbourdon style it is the relationship of the contratenor to the cantus that is decisive. Whether we consider this relationship in terms of semibreves or of progressions is immaterial—in our Gloria, the fourth is beyond any doubt the dominant interval. Six and seven consecutive progressions from one fourth to another are by no means uncommon, and in the line "Domine deus, agnus dei, filius patris," which concludes what is often treated as the first main division of the Gloria text, the two upper voices are at the fourth almost throughout. With minor modifications the setting of this line occurs again at "Jesu Christe: cum sancto spiritu, in gloria dei patris," the concluding line of the second main division, involving in its modified form an unbroken

[8]A transcription of the Gloria accompanies the contribution by Ursula Günther. A facsimile of the version found at Foligno is published by Pirrotta in the volume referred to in n. 7, figs. I and II, facing pp. 114 and 115.

[9]*Bourdon und Fauxbourdon* (Leipzig, 1950), pp. 158–159.

succession of eighteen progressions at the fourth and at the same
time imposing a degree of formal organization on the composition
as a whole. In view of its lack of harmonic variety one might call
the little piece artless, even inartistic, but as an extreme example
of the free fauxbourdon style, as tangible evidence that the harmonic possibilities of the first inversion were clearly recognized at
the time it was written, one cannot ignore it or deny its historic
importance.

The last significant word we have had on the continental fauxbourdon comes from Heinrich Besseler, and in Besseler's view the
free fauxbourdon style derives from what he calls "das Fauxbourdonstück," that is, from a type of piece in which two written voices
carry or imply the direction *au fauxbourdon,* prescribing that the
intervals formed by the written voices are to be filled in by a
contratenor moving throughout at the fourth below the cantus.[10]
Again in Besseler's view the beginnings of the free fauxbourdon
style on the continent are to be placed after the year 1430—in the
1420's, he adds, the attractive sound of this kind of writing would
have been inconceivable.[11] There is no conflict between these
views and Pirrotta's tentative date for the Foligno fragment—
"within the first third of the fifteenth century." But how are we to
reconcile them with his bold conjecture that the date of our Gloria,
at least its notational date, is to be placed "about one century earlier
than the fragment itself"?

At this point we shall need to turn to the Foligno fragment and
to its notation, which—as Pirrotta observes—is far from being
flawlessly accurate. Particularly in our Gloria it is indeed so consistently inaccurate, not to say confused, that it is often impossible to
divine what the scribe had in mind. To Pirrotta it suggests that the
writing down of the piece was "a sort of gratuitous gesture." To
me it suggests also that the scribe's grasp of the *ars notandi* can at
best have been rudimentary. But that he was copying—and copying carelessly—from a fourteenth-century *Vorlage* is only too obvious. After some hesitation Pirrotta transcribes the first two lines of
the piece in accordance with the rules given by Marchetto da
Padova for the tempus imperfectum *modo gallico.* In the light of the

---

[10] *Bourdon und Fauxbourdon,* p. 2.
[11] As above, pp. 158–159.

Grottaferrata concordance, this interpretation seems rather less than plausible. But even if we abandon it, the archaisms remain—for example the writing of from four to six semibreves within a single tempus, the frequent use of the punctus divisionis where it is superfluous, the occasional resort to the descending breve plica as a substitute for a descending ligature. No one, surely, will care to maintain that these are practices characteristic of the first third of the fifteenth century. Even in the last quarter of the fourteenth they would have seemed out of place and anachronistic.

In the simpler version of the Grottaferrata fragment, the time relationships are those of the tempus perfectum and the notation is unambiguous and straightforward throughout. The sorry state of this source prevents our controlling all the anachronistic details of the Foligno concordance, but where controls are possible, we often find that the anachronisms have been suppressed. Thus at "Qui sedes ad dexteram patris," where Foligno has nine semibreves in a cluster as though they were to fill a single tempus only, Grottaferrata clearly forbids this interpretation, inserting puncti divisionis and spreading the nine semibreves over three measures. At "Hominibus bone voluntatis," on the other hand, Grottaferrata appears to support Foligno's division of the tempus into six semibreves in that it substitutes for Foligno's six the equivalent of three. And in its old-fashioned predilection for the superfluous punctus divisionis, the Grottaferrata version, being the more consistent of the two in its notation, carries matters to extremes. For this single entry the rule appears to be that, excepting where three semibreves stand between two breves, the punctus divisionis shall mark the end of every tempus in which a semibreve is involved. Not only does this depart from the normal practice of the later fourteenth and earlier fifteenth centuries, it even departs from the normal practice of the scribe responsible for the entry. How can we avoid concluding that both versions of our Gloria—Grottaferrata and Foligno—descend from an old *Vorlage,* or from several of them, and that the composition itself is distinctly earlier than the manuscripts that contain it?

This brings us back to Besseler's views and to the contradiction between them and Pirrotta's, a contradiction that will prove to be more apparent than real. Besseler's contention that "das Fauxbourdonstück" is a purely continental phenomenon first encountered shortly before the year 1430 is not affected in any way by Pirrotta's earlier date for our Gloria. But in contending further that the beginnings of the free fauxbourdon style on the continent are to be placed after the year 1430, Besseler is arguing from the absence of evidence to the contrary, always a hazardous procedure, particularly so in a case of this kind, and the moment conflicting evidence is produced, his contention falls of its own weight. And with it, of necessity, falls also his contention that the free fauxbourdon style on the continent stems from pieces like Dufay's "Vos qui secuti estis" and Lymburgia's "Regina celi letare." In the light of what we have seen, Pirrotta's view that it stems rather from improvisational practices, that it is a style of composition "reminiscent of the style of improvised polyphony," seems the only one possible.

THE MUSIC OF THE
OLD HALL MANUSCRIPT
—A POSTSCRIPT †

PROFESSOR Manfred F. Bukofzer's exhaustive and penetrating study of the Old Hall MS will have served to reawaken general interest in this crucial insular document whose interpretation is decisive for the interpretation of subsequent Continental developments. With the settling of the controversy over the date of the Old Hall MS it at last becomes possible to relate it to the general scene. Particularly helpful from this point of view are the additional concordances with Continental MSS, which show that the Old Hall repertory was rather more widely diffused than formerly supposed, and the demonstration that the MS itself contains at least one additional piece of Continental origin. Significant, too, is the bearing of the date of the MS upon the date of Leonel Power's removal from England to Continental Europe.

Early in the first installment of his study Professor Bukofzer disclaimed any intention of dealing with all aspects of the Old Hall repertory. The purpose of this brief postscript, which Professor Bukofzer has encouraged me to prepare for publication, is to draw attention to a group of pieces discussed only briefly in what has gone before. This seems worth doing, not only because the pieces are in themselves important, but also because they are imperfectly and incompletely represented in the published edition.

As published in the edition brought out by the Plainsong &

†From *The Musical Quarterly*, XXXV (1949), 244–249. Reprinted in Manfred Bukofzer, *Studies in Medieval and Renaissance Music* (New York: W. W. Norton, 1950), pp. 80–85. Reproduced by permission of G. Schirmer, Inc.

Mediaeval Music Society, the Old Hall MS contains five canonic
settings of texts belonging to the Ordinary of the Mass—three
Glorias by Pycard (I, 76, 84, and 119) and two anonymous Credos
(II, 82 and 101). For the solution of the canons in all but one of
these pieces the MS itself gives explicit Latin directions. In the one
case remaining (II, 82) there is no direct indication that canonic
writing is involved, but an attempt to score the three voices found
in the MS shows unmistakably that something is missing. Mr. H.
B. Collins offers a brilliant and altogether convincing solution of
this piece—as a three-part canon with two accompanying voices—
in the second volume of the Plainsong and Mediaeval Music Society's edition, and in a note printed with his transcription he remarks
that at several points within the piece the written cantus part has
two sets of words—at *Genitum non factum* the second set begins with
Qui propter nos, while *Et in Spiritum* is similarly combined with *Qui
cum Patre,* and *Confiteor* with *Et expecto.* At the corresponding points
in his transcription, Collins adapts the upper lines of text to the
voice beginning the canon and to the first of the two voices that
follow it, leaving the lower lines to the second of the consequent
voices. In effect, the result is not unlike that seen in the familiar
"telescoped" settings of Gloria and Credo.

Thanks to Mr. Collins and his remark about the double set of
words in his anonymous Credo, it is not difficult to add a new item
to the list of canonic settings in the Old Hall MS and to show that
another item, already on this list, is not a simple canon, as indicated
in the MS, but a double one. For, once it is recognized that a single
voice-part provided with a "telescoped" double text may in itself
be an indirect indication of the presence of canonic writing, the rest
is easy and the surprising thing is that the obvious conclusions were
not drawn long ago.

The first of the two pieces in question is a Gloria by Byttering
(I, 47)—No. 15 in Barclay Squire's thematic list of contents. This
is a setting in three written parts, with vocal cantus and instrumental tenor and contratenor. Here the "telescoped" double text runs
without a break from the first measure of the cantus part to the last,
the upper line giving the beginnings of the successive clauses, the
lower line the endings. If one approaches this piece with the possibility of unspecified canonic writing in mind, the solution leaps to
the eye—in the first section *(tempus imperfectum cum prolatione*

EX. 1 BYTTERING: GLORIA NO. 15 with canon.

majore) the consequent voice enters at the unison after four measures (Ex. 1). Not only does the consequent voice fit perfectly with those given in the MS, it also supplies the missing fifths and thirds for a number of incomplete triads and fills in occasional gaps in the texture. With three voices only, the sudden cessation of movement in measures 5 and 6 of the tenor and contratenor has an awkward appearance; with four voices, it is seen to be a deliberately calculated refinement. Indeed, it is no exaggeration to say that without the fourth voice the piece makes no real sense at all.

In the second section of Byttering's Gloria *(tempus perfectum,* with the contratenor in *tempus imperfectum* at the beginning) the entrance of the consequent voice is again at the unison; a nice stroke is the reduction of the time interval from four measures to three for this, the final section of the piece (Ex. 2).

EX. 2 BYTTERING: GLORIA NO. 15, second section.

A particularly attractive feature of Byttering's little piece is the carefully planned co-ordination of words and music. As a result of the canonic structure, the first section falls into periods of four measures, the second into periods of three. In dividing the liturgical text between antecedent and consequent, Byttering follows this over-all periodization exactly, with the result that in each period the consequent voice completes the clause left unfinished by the antecedent, echoing the notes that have just been sung, while the antecedent voice is simultaneously propounding the first half of the clause that follows. A further result, characteristic of many canonic and quasi-canonic settings of the Gloria text, but unusually well worked out in this one, is the symbolically simultaneous declamation of the appeals to Father and Son: while the consequent voice is singing *Deus Pater omnipotens,* echoing the *Domine Deus Rex caelestis* that has just been heard, the antecedent voice is already beginning the *Domine Fili unigenite.* Similarly, but with another shade of meaning, *Domine Deus, Agnus Dei,* and *Jesu Christe* are heard at the same time.[1]

We ought now to be ready to assume that any voice provided with a "telescoped" double text is a potential canonic antecedent, and meeting with one more such voice among the Glorias of the

---

[1]Compare the comments of Friedrich Ludwig on a similar treatment of the Gloria text in Modena 568 ("Die mehrstimmige Messe des 14. Jahrhunderts," in *AMW,* VII [1925], 423).

Old Hall MS we shall naturally put it to the test. This time (I, 84) the composer is Pycard, by whom we have two other canonic Glorias (I, 76 and 119) and—if Professor Bukofzer's attribution is accepted—a canonic Credo (II, 101); his piece is No. 24 in Barclay Squire's thematic list. There are two vocal parts, one with a "telescoped" text that is alternately single and double (as in the Credo transcribed by Mr. Collins), the other with the complete text in the usual form. Accompanying them is an instrumental tenor with the direction: *Tenor et contratenor in uno, unus post alium fugando quinque*

EX. 3 PYCARD: GLORIA No. 24 with double canon.

temporibus. The manuscript has also a "solus tenor" part which may
be substituted for the canonic tenor and contratenor if a reduction
in the number of voices is desired. As it stands, then, the piece
appears to be for four voices (or for three, if the "solus tenor" is
used). But the "telescoped" text below the one cantus part suggests
that it is actually for five voices (or for four), and an attempt to
apply the tenor's rule to the cantus confirms this. In Ex. 3 (four
five-measure periods from the concluding "Amen"), the alternative "solus tenor" is omitted. As in the Gloria by Byttering, the
added consequent voice fills out a number of incomplete triads.
What is more striking, it also completes the hockets: the construction of the antecedent voice, which sings alternately after and on
the beat in the corresponding measures of the successive five-
measure periods, is now seen to be a deliberate and ingenious
calculation. Once again the piece becomes fully intelligible only
when the unspecified canon is resolved; it is this canon that is the
truly essential one—not the specified canon of tenor and contratenor, whose omission the composer expressly sanctions. Pycard's
canonic Gloria is doubtless somewhat earlier than Dufay's familiar
Gloria ad modum tubae and is in any case one of the very few
multiple canons that we have from the time before Josquin and the
later Okeghem.

* * *

Surely it is significant that of the six canonic pieces in the Old
Hall MS four are Glorias while only two are Credos. Throughout
the earlier fifteenth century the Gloria text is the preferred text for
canonic treatment: we have no Credos to offset the canonic Glorias
of Modena 568,[2] of Arnold and Hugo de Lantins,[3] of Trent 90,[4]
of Dufay. It is also significant that of the six canonic pieces in the
Old Hall MS only the two Credos involve three-part canonic writing. For their time, these six pieces constitute the largest-known
group of their kind. And they follow too closely on the heels of the

[2]An anonymous dialogue-like setting with accompanying instrumental canon
(fol. 2ᵛ), published in part by Jacques Handschin in *Zeitschrift für Musikwissenschaft,*
X (1927/28), 552–55, and an accompanied canon ("Fuga," fol. 9ᵛ) by Matteo da
Perugia, cantor at the Milan Cathedral from 1402 to 1414.

[3]Charles van den Borren, *Polyphonia sacra* (Nashdom Abbey, 1932), pp. 10 (the
canon broken off at "Laudamus te") and 118.

[4]Nos. 925 and 927 of the thematic catalogue.

pair in Modena 568 to justify the assumption of a direct borrowing from Italy; it is at least equally possible that the application of the canonic principle to the Ordinary of the Mass began independently and more or less simultaneously on both sides of the Channel.

THE *ORDINARIUM MISSAE*
IN SETTINGS BY
DUFAY AND POWER

Documenta Polyphoniae Liturgicae S. Ecclesiae Romanae.
Serie I. Ordinarium Missae. 1. Guillaume Dufay. Frag-
mentum Missae. 2. Leonel Power. Missa super "Alma
Redemptoris Mater."†

S TUDIES in the sacred music of the later Middle Ages have
prospered since the end of the war. The discovery of two new
MSS (Egerton 3307 and the Aosta MS) and the publication of a
whole series of important texts—the Machaut Mass (Machabey),
the Dufay motets (De Van), and the second volume of the masses
of Ockeghem (Plamenac), this last brought out by our own Society
—are encouraging signs of renewed activity in an area that continues to promise rich returns. The series of parallel publications
announced by the Saint Cecilia Society in Rome through its editor,
Father Laurence Feininger of the Music Division of the Vatican
Library, may well prove to be the most significant of all these
undertakings, for it is boldly conceived on a scale so broad that if
it can be carried to completion it will fill in nearly every major gap
in our present resources. Briefly stated, the plan calls for the publication of four series (I: The Ordinary of the Mass; II: The Proper
of the Mass; III: The Divine Office; IV: The Motet) in two parallel
editions, the one scientific *(Monumenta)*, the other practical *(Documenta)*. Thus far, Father Feininger has found it possible to bring out
two complete volumes of the *Monumenta;* reviews of these will
appear in later issues of the *Journal*. The present review covers only
the first two installments of the *Documenta,* all that has been published to date.

†From *Journal of the American Musicological Society,* II (1949), 107–110. Reprinted by permission of the American Musicological Society.

Dufay's "Fragmentum Missae" consists of three short movements—Kyrie, Gloria, and Credo—found in immediate succession
in the MS Bologna 37 and again, widely separated, in the recently
discovered Aosta MS, fully described by Guillaume de Van in the
current issue (II, 1/2) of *Musica Disciplina*. The little work is
chiefly interesting in that it shows us Dufay using for his paired
Gloria and Credo an old-fashioned technique not to be found in
any other example of his work thus far published: the two upper
voices declaim the text alternately in a sort of dialogue over a
supporting instrumental tenor. In this and other respects these
movements faithfully reflect the musical environment in which
Dufay grew up. Particularly striking are the resemblances between
Dufay's Gloria and Credo and a similar pair by Richard de Loqueville, choirmaster at Cambrai from 1412 until 1418, the year of his
death (Loqueville's Gloria is published by Van den Borren, *Polyphonia Sacra,* no. 20); it has been repeatedly suggested that Loqueville may have been one of Dufay's first teachers. In general, the
style of the whole Mass fragment is that of the older generation of
French musicians whose music Dufay must have heard and sung as
a boy; one can only suppose it to have been written prior to his first
impressions of Italy or at the time of his stay in Paris during the
mid-'twenties.

So far as sacred polyphony is concerned, the period 1415 to
1445 is one relatively well represented in the sources. For the
Ordinary of the Mass, to say that we have from this time several
hundred settings of the single texts Kyrie, Gloria, Credo, Sanctus,
and Agnus Dei would be a conservative estimate; the Bologna MS
alone, covering only the earlier part of the period, contains well
over a hundred. Yet among all these settings, the cyclic tenor-mass,
later to become the central and all-important variety, is represented
by exactly two examples: a *Missa Alma Redemptoris Mater,* transmitted anonymously in Trent 87, and a *Missa Rex saeculorum,* attributed in Trent 92 to the English Leonel Power. A third example,
likewise from Trent 92, was published some years ago by Rudolf
Ficker, but its supposed continuity, once regarded as an established
fact, begins to look very dubious indeed as the music of the first
half of the century becomes better known. With the discovery of
the Aosta MS a second source for the *Missa Alma Redemptoris Mater*
has come to light and with it the identity of its composer; once

again it is Leonel Power. Ficker's principal thesis—that the cyclic
tenor-mass is of English origin—is thus confirmed in the most
positive way. Father Feininger's publication of the *Missa Alma
Redemptoris Mater* has accordingly made accessible a highly significant music-historical monument, one that demands a more extended and more careful examination than is possible in a mere
review, which cannot attempt to do more than to single out a few
points of obvious interest.

Surely the first point to be made about Power's Mass—it is for
three voices and without Kyrie—is that it is one in which the first
formulation of the given melody is retained throughout without
essential change and that it is thus the starting point for a line of
development that leads through Dufay's Mass on "Se 'la face ay
pale" and Josquin's masses on "L'Homme armé" *(Super voces musicales)* and "Hercules dux Ferrariae" to Palestrina's six-voiced
Missa Ave Maria and perhaps beyond. The exact correspondence
of the several movements extends even to the measures of rest that
separate the tenor-periods; the only liberties that Power allows
himself are the free setting of the first half of the second Agnus Dei
(for divided cantus without tenor and contratenor) and the free
duos of the upper voices that open the Credo and Sanctus. Inasmuch as the *Missa Rex saeculorum* is constructed in just the opposite
way (to judge from the facsimile of the Gloria published by De Van
and the thematic incipits of the Trent catalogue), the absolute
rigidity of the *Miss Alma Redemptoris Mater* is the more striking. It
is now evident that both types of tenor-mass—the strict and the
free, the symmetrical and the asymmetrical, the one type variation-
like, the other *durchkomponiert*— go back to the very beginning of
the development, just as they also continue to the very end. Likewise striking is the bipartite structure of Gloria, Credo, and Sanctus
—only the Agnus Dei, by virtue of its inner duo, is in three sections; each movement brings one exposition of the given melody
and one only; no section of the Sanctus is for reduced voices.

The familiar antiphon upon which Power has based his Mass is
one frequently used as a tenor by his contemporaries, particularly
by his contemporary fellow-countrymen. Thus one finds it fulfilling
this function in a Credo by an "Anglicanus" (*Denkmäler der Tonkunst in Oesterreich*, XXXI, no. 49), in the motet *Ascendit Christus,*
variously ascribed to Dunstable and to Forest (*ibid.*, XL, 53), in an

anonymous but almost certainly English Kyrie and Gloria in Trent 87 (nos. 133 and 134 of the thematic catalogue); one finds it also as the tenor of a Credo by Jean Franchoys of Gembloux (Aosta 31 and other MSS). Like the "Anglicanus" of the Trent MS and the composer of the motet *Ascendit Christus,* Power follows the Sarum version of the plainsong, and a comparison of his tenor with this version will show that, so far as the mere notes are concerned, he takes it over quite literally [see example]. What he does with the structure is another story. In view of his over-all plan, Power needs a tenor divided into two sections roughly equal in length. And to allow for two-part interludes he wishes to break each of his two sections into three periods, with measures of rest after the first and second periods of each section. Nothing, surely, could be more arbitrary than the way in which he goes about this. Not only does he proceed with the most complete disregard for the inner logic of the given melody, systematically avoiding its natural stopping points by running over or stopping short; he even destroys its tonal balance by beginning and ending his second section with the second step of the mode. Up to a certain point, his method resembles that used by the musicians of the 13th and 14th centuries in laying

ANTIPHONALE SARISBURIENSE, p. 529 (original a fifth higher, without flat in signature)

out the tenors of their motets. But whereas the intention behind
the older method is clear, Power's intention is not likely to become
so until other masses in this style are available for study. For the
present, all one can say is that Power's tenor is obviously the
product of some sort of scholastic speculation and that in terms of
sound in time it is a pure abstraction. For if we disregard the final
measure (or measures) in each of the two sections—and this is
always necessary in dealing with motetlike compositions—the first
section of Power's Gloria runs to 56 measures, the second to 84.
Thus the two sections appear to stand in the relation 2:3. But in
actual time two measures of the first section will have precisely the
same duration as three measures of the second, so that the two
sections are exactly balanced, standing in the relation 1:1. The
same applies, of course, to the remaining movements, for the first
half of the second Agnus Dei and the opening duos of the Credo
and Sanctus lie outside the scheme. One cannot suppose this harmonious structure to be a mere accident: similar things occur in
other English works of the time, for example in a paired Gloria and
Credo by Dunstable (*Denkmäler der Tonkunst in Oesterreich,* XXXI,
nos. 60 and 61), where in either movement—both have the same
tenor—the proportions are 6:4:3:2.

Father Feininger's edition of the *Missa Alma Redemptoris Mater* is
intended as a practical one and his brief foreword, addressed to the
general reader, is silent on many points about which the historian
would have welcomed information. For example, it fails to tell us
what we can learn from the thematic incipits of the Trent catalogue
—that in the first section of each movement the two upper voices
imply one time signature (O) while the tenor indicates another
(C) and that to put these sections of the work into score it is
necessary to double the note values of the tenor part. Until about
the middle of the 15th century, this is a peculiarly English convention; we find it, for instance, in four numbers of the Old Hall MS
(I, 65; II, 93 and 185; and III, 58—three of these by Power
himself), in the Credo by Forest published by Ficker, in Dunstable's Credo and Sanctus on "Da gaudiorum premia" (Aosta 166
and 167), and in various anonymous compositions whose English
origin can be at least surmised (Trent 133 and 134, Aosta 159).
That we find it here, in every movement of a work attributed to
an English musician, is a further and an emphatic confirmation of

its English origin. And when we consider the importance of this convention for the later history of the Mass—its frequent and systematic use by Ockeghem and Josquin and above all by Busnois and his Burgundian imitators—the decisive character of the role played at the outset by the English school becomes very evident indeed.

In his foreword to the *Missa Alma Redemptoris Mater,* Father Feininger makes the interesting suggestion that the omission of the Kyrie in this and other masses of the period is due to liturgical considerations—to the close connection in plainsong between Introit and Kyrie and to the traditional association of particular plainsong Kyries with particular classes of festivals. This suggestion commends itself, and it is strongly supported by the evidence of a number of early MSS (the earlier fascicles of Trent 92, fascicles 2 and 3 of the Aosta MS, the greater part of Trent 90 and 93) in which the Introit is treated as though it were a regular component of the Ordinary. The practice is in any case quite as characteristic of Italy as it is of England.

In a sixteen-page pamphlet announcing the two editions and the plans for their continuation, Father Feininger makes an admirably concise statement of the editorial principles he has adopted and explains his reasons for adopting them. Full discussion of these principles must be deferred until the first volumes of the *Monumenta* are reviewed, for as Father Feininger has planned them the two editions are interdependent and do not lend themselves to separate treatment. But even at this stage one may say that to make a sharp distinction between the practical edition and the scientific one and to hold that the practical is necessarily unscientific and the scientific necessarily impractical is simply begging the question. In the last analysis, the requirements of the practical musician are identical with those of the musical scientist: like the scientist, he wants an edition that will answer every question he may wish to ask about the relation of edited text to original, and like the scientist, he will be satisfied with nothing less.

ORIGINS OF
THE "L'HOMME ARMÉ"
MASS†

IN a systematic comparison of more than twenty of the thirty-odd masses written between 1450 and 1600 on the tenor "L'homme armé," it was discovered—quite by accident—that the mass by Jacob Obrecht, published some years ago by Johannes Wolf, is neither more nor less than a colossal "parody" on the hitherto unstudied mass by Antoine Busnoys, still in manuscript in the archives of the Cappella Sistina. The parallelism between these two works goes much further and is far more striking than the mere dependence upon one another of the several "Caput" masses: Obrecht's tenor and Busnoys's are identical, Obrecht's formal structure is accordingly dependent to the last detail on Busnoys's, and a familiarity with Busnoys's mass is of course essential to an understanding of Obrecht's. Even the free (tenorless) sections have been made to correspond, and as one result of this perfect parallelism the two works are of exactly the same length. On the other hand, the Obrecht mass is much more than a slavish imitation of its model: new canons replace those of the original, a new harmonic scheme is employed, and the use of imitation is at once more fluent and more extensive. The mass of Busnoys, cited by Ramis in 1482 and by Tinctoris at a still earlier date, belongs in all probability to the year 1475 or thereabouts; it is only reasonable to suppose that Obrecht's mass dates from about the year 1490, when the two

†From *Bulletin of the American Musicological Society*, II (1937), 25–26; read at a meeting of the Washington-Baltimore chapter of the society, Washington, April 15, 1936. Reprinted by permission of the American Musicological Society.

masters were together in Bruges, Busnoys at the church of St. Saviour, Obrecht at the church of St. Donatius.

In the light of this discovery we shall do well to reconsider Aron's statement, in the *Toscanello* (1523), that Busnoys was thought by some to have been the "inventor" of the melody "L'homme armé." This tradition, as Aron reports it, would appear to be to some extent supported by what we may call the "authority" of Busnoys's mass, which evidently occupied, in its day, the place later occupied by the Josquin mass "Ad voces musicales," and still later by the five-part mass of Palestrina. The existence of Obrecht's parody is a further and striking indication of this, for there is little reason to doubt that it represents a tribute, on Obrecht's part, to the "authority" of his model.

The case for Busnoys becomes still clearer when we examine the chanson-setting of "L'homme armé" by his Burgundian associate Robert Morton, which bears, like the Obrecht parody, an easily recognized relation to our mass—appears indeed to have been directly inspired by it or by the hypothetical chanson-setting by Busnoys on which the whole series may have rested. The Morton setting, presumably a quodlibet, is actually little more than a combination of the three lower voices of the "Tu solus altissimus" section of Busnoys's "Et in terra" with an independent discant. The conclusion is obvious. Either the Morton setting borrows directly from the Busnoys mass, or both compositions go back to the hypothetical original, by Busnoys, to which Aron alludes. And it is only from the "Tu solus altissimus" section of Busnoys's mass that we may conclude with any certainty what this hypothetical original may have been like.

RELATIVE SONORITY AS A FACTOR IN STYLE - CRITICAL ANALYSIS

[*1450–1550*]†

Conciosiache è necessario . . . che nella Compositione perfetta si ritrouino sempre in atto la Quinta, &
la Terza, ouer le loro Replicate (III, xxxi). Douemo per
ogni modo . . . cercare con ogni nostro potere, di fare
vdire nelle nostre Compositioni queste due Con-
sonanze, più che sia possibile, ouero le loro Replicate
. . . Osseruarà adunque il Compositore questo, accioche
la sua cantilena venghi ad esser sonora & piena, &
accioche contenghi in se ogni perfettione di harmonia
(III, lix).

IN these and in many, many other passages of the *Istituzioni
armoniche,* Zarlino speaks of the complete triad as though it were
a sort of Summum Bonum. He has this in view when he makes his
basic distinction between "perfect harmony," as in the singing of
many parts, and "imperfect harmony," as in the singing of two
parts only (II, xii). He has this in view when he says that musicians
speak of the four usual parts as containing in themselves every
harmonic perfection (III, lviii). Incomplete triads sound fragmentary and thin, he points out; they are inherently lacking in variety;
if we would imitate nature, we should avoid them, just as nature
avoids the incomplete and the unvaried. Only in three-part writing
is their use to be tolerated, for to try to avoid them here would be
to spoil the elegant, easy flow of the single voices and to ruin the
music with awkward progressions (III, lix). Evidently he thought

†From *Studi musicali,* II (1973), 145–153, reprinted by permission of the Ac-
cademia Nazionale di Santa Cecilia, Rome. Read at the annual meeting of the
American Musicological Society, New York, December 28, 1949.

it unnecessary to add that to use the incomplete triad, whether lacking the third or the fifth, would seem to him also to be sacrificing some part of music's power over the affections; as is well known, Zarlino believes this to depend to some extent upon the opposition of the major and minor triads, and it is actually in connection with this antithesis that he first formulates his rule (III, xxxi).

In summing up his recommendations on this point, Zarlino uses the word "sonorous" in a special and rather narrow sense. It is in this same sense that I have used the word "sonority" in the title of this paper. For my present purposes, accordingly, the expression "relative sonority," used with reference to the three- or four-part writing in a particular piece of music, is to be understood as meaning the frequency of the complete triad, or—more precisely—the ratio between the duration of the three- or four-part writing as a whole and the duration of that fraction of it during which the complete triad is, as Zarlino puts it, "actively present."

What Zarlino has in mind—the high "relative sonority" of the motet and madrigal of Willaert and Rore: this was an end-product, arrived at only after decades of trial and compromise. Broadly speaking, the winning of this full sonority was in some measure dependent upon other style-changes that were taking place at the same time: the expansion of the normal complement of voices from three to four and from four to five, the substitution of simultaneous conception for successive, the simplification of the rhythmic detail, the stylization of the dissonance. More narrowly, one might describe the historical process that led up to it as a gradual readjustment of the conflicting claims of the linear and harmonic principles; or, still more narrowly, as a progressively more and more elaborate realization, in free part-writing, of the ideal sonority achieved at one stroke in the fauxbourdon and similar three-voiced textures.

Now "relative sonority" is surely one of the least conspicuous of the many elements that, taken together, go to make up what we call a "style." Admittedly it has little or nothing to do with aesthetic value; to study it will not help us to understand the point of view that underlies the work of the artist and of his time. Yet, precisely because it is inconspicuous, it can tell us what more conspicuous elements cannot. It belongs among the involuntary—or shall I say "obligatory"—aspects of style; as an unconscious habit, a result of routine, a part of the composer's metier, it can be expected to remain relatively stable in the work of a particular individual at a particular time, little affected by the varying conditions of composition. And precisely because it is involuntary and relatively stable, it can provide a basis for comparing things otherwise scarcely comparable. It resembles what art-historians call a "Morellian" characteristic: since it contributes nothing to expression, it does not attract attention or invite imitation. Yet it is through studying what is not, or cannot, be imitated that questions of date, provenance, and authorship have ultimately to be answered. In some respects it resembles the element of the dissonance and its conventional treatment. But one can measure it readily and precisely, whereas one cannot measure the relative modernity of a dissonant situation.

The several questions to be answered can now be phrased quite simply. Can the measurement of "relative sonority" be made to yield trustworthy indications as to date, provenance, and authorship? With works of known authorship, can it be used to separate early works from late? With works of questioned authorship, can it be used to separate the spurious from the genuine? With works of unknown authorship, can it be used in connection with other evidence to determine date and provenance?

With a view to offering at least a partial answer to these questions and as a practical demonstration of the uses to which the measurement of "relative sonority" can and cannot be put, I have prepared, as illustrations for this paper, three tables. Table I presents in chronological order the frequencies for a series of works of known date, ranging from 1460 to 1559, the year following the publication of Zarlino's monumental treatise; Table II bears on a case of questioned authorship; Table III on two related works of uncertain date. Partly because it proved simpler and more convenient, but also to avoid seeming to class dissonant beats as deficient in sonority, I have preferred to use, for these tables, figures representing the frequency of the incomplete triad; the higher the figure, then, the lower the "relative sonority." In each case, my figures are based either upon the entire composition, the final measure or measures excepted, or, where larger works are involved, upon a fraction of it sufficient to assure a dependable result. In certain instances, however, so small a part of the composition is written for three voices or for four that the one figure or the other is necessarily inconclusive; this applies particularly to the figure given for three-part writing under 1536.

The compositions included in Table I are the following:

1. for 1460, the *Déploration* on the death of Binchoys, transmitted anonymously in the Dijon chansonnier but ascribed to "Oquegan" in the MS Montecassino 871;
2. for 1462, two sections from the *Missa L'homme armé* by Jean Regis, copied at Cambrai in that year;
3. for 1464 or thereabouts, the motet "In hydraulis" by Antoine Busnoys, a tribute to Ockeghem approximately dated through topical references in the text;
4. for 1470 or thereabouts, the motet "Omnium bonorum plena" by Loyset Compère, also to be dated approximately through topical references in the text;
5. for 1484, the *Missa L'homme armé* by Philippe Basiron, dated through the reference to it as "new" in a letter written by Ercole d'Este in that year;
6. for 1491, Obrecht's *Missa S. Donatiani,* dated through an archival reference;
7. for 1492, Isaac's elegy on the death of Lorenzo dei Medici:
8. for 1514, Mouton's elegy on the death of Anne of Brittany;
9. for 1521, the elegy by Benedictus on the death of Josquin Desprez;
10. for 1536, Willaert's madrigal "Amor mi fa morire," first published in that year; and
11. for 1559, Willaert's "Liete e pensose," a dialogue for seven voices printed among the madrigals of the *Musica nova.*

On the whole, the table bears out the foregoing conclusion that there was a gradual increase in "relative sonority" during the course of the century 1450 to 1550. At the same time it shows us that considerable variation may be expected, even in works that follow rather closely upon one another, a variation perhaps due in part to differences in the specific technical problem but surely not to be wholly accounted for in this way. Thus, for example, the discrepancies between the figures given for 1491 and 1492 or for 1514 and 1521 must certainly be due in some measure to environmental or individual differences: Obrecht is more restricted in his mass than Isaac in his elegy; with Mouton and Benedictus there is no real difference in the conditions of composition.

So far as I have been able to observe, however, discrepancies of

Table I

			à 3	à 4
1460	Ockeghem		.435	.10
1462	Regis {	Qui sedes	.515	.41
		Et iterum	.51	.33
1464?	Busnoys		.44	.30
1470?	Compère		.64	.23
1484	Basiron		.53	.13
1491	Obrecht		.32	.13
1492	Isaac		.49	.27
1514	Mouton		.40	.12
1521	Benedictus		.46	.25
1536	Willaert		.30	.07
1559	Willaert		.19	.00

Table II

		à 3	à 4
Josquin {	Qui tollis	.45	.19
	Et incarnatus	.45	.18
	Et in Spiritum	.36	.11

Table III

	à 3	à 4
Busnoys	.17	.45
Obrecht	.145	.41

this sort are not found when the compositions compared are written at the same time by the same individual. To bring this out, I
have compared the two madrigals by Willaert used in Table I with
two other madrigals of his, drawn from the same collections. "Liete
e pensose," the seven-voiced dialogue from the *Musica nova,* is a
special case: it is a setting of a sonnet in which the first half of the
octave is sung by four low voices, the second half by three high
voices, the sestet by various contrasted combinations of four voices;
only after the entire text has been presented does the full choir
begin its repetition of the final couplet. This was an ideal example
in that it yielded conclusive figures for the three-voiced texture as

well as for the four-voiced. No other madrigal from the *Musica nova* will quite do this. But to take another of the dialogues at random, "Che fai, alma? che pensi?" is fully sonorous throughout; in this case, however, the three-part writing is incidental and not sustained. "Amor mi fa morire," the madrigal cited in Table I under 1536, showed frequencies of .30 and .07; "Quando giunse," another madrigal of Willaert's from the same collection, shows .37 and .05. For a three-voiced ricercar by Willaert, first printed in 1543, I obtain the frequency .20, only a shade higher than the comparable figure for the *Musica nova* of 1559, distinctly lower than the admittedly inconclusive figures for 1536. Considering that the madrigals of the *Musica nova* are known to have been written some years before the date of their publication, it should be safe to conclude that by about 1540 Willaert had already attained a maximum sonority, both in three- and in four-part writing. Apart from this, we might also conclude that the madrigals of the *Musica nova* cannot possibly date from the 'thirties, at least in their published form, and that they are probably not older than about 1545.

Again with a view to showing the degree of stability, or instability, that can be expected in two works written by the same individual at the same time, I have broken down my figures for the *Missa L'homme armé* by Regis, giving one set of frequencies for the Qui sedes of the Gloria, another for the Et iterum of the Credo. The two sections are ideally comparable. The tenor parts are identical; the same is largely true of the contratenor altus parts, occupied after the opening measures with quasi-canonic anticipations of the tenor and toward the end with the exposition of an independent plainsong; the two sections differ only in their cantus and contratenor bassus parts and in the contratenor altus of the opening measures. In this instance, only the "relative sonority" of the three-part writing remains stable; the marked discrepancy between the two figures obtained for the four-part writing is perhaps to be explained as due to insufficient evidence—in each of the two sections, less than thirty per cent of the whole is actually for four voices. But aside from this it may be said in general that, wherever the "relative sonority" of the three-part writing could be measured satisfactorily, it has proved to be more stable and a more dependable guide than the figure obtained for the four-part writing.

Table II, the table bearing on the case of questioned authorship, gives frequencies for three sections from Josquin's *Missa L'homme armé super voces musicales,* for the Qui tollis of the Gloria and for the Et incarnatus and Et in Spiritum of the Credo. The work is perhaps the most familiar example of that variety of tenor mass in which a single formulation of the given melody is retained throughout, subject only to such systematic modifications as are, or might be, indicated by canonic directions or changes of time-signature. As is usually the case with works of this kind, certain sections of the successive movements are wholly commensurable: they have the same number of measures, with a measure-for-measure correspondence, they have the same time-signatures, their tenors have the same notes and the same rests. In this particular instance, the wholly commensurable sections are the openings of the Sanctus and Agnus, the Et in terra and the Patrem, the Qui tollis and the Et incarnatus. Smijers's edition of the mass rests upon a collation of 15 sources—8 MSS and 7 printed editions. In all but one of these sources the Credo is incomplete in that it skips over a whole series of clauses, beginning with Et in spiritum and ending with Et in unam sanctam. The one source to contain a setting of this part of the official text, the MS Cappella Sistina 154, is a comparatively late one, copied during the pontificate of Julius III, or between 1550 and 1555. Quite properly, Smijers publishes this section with the rest of the mass, although not without expressing his doubts as to its authenticity. A few moments spent in studying the score will, I think, be sufficient to persuade anyone at all familiar with Josquin's style that these doubts are fully justified. It is even quite easy to name the composer probably responsible, for the same MS contains also an ad libitum quintus part for the final Agnus, signed by a certain Joannes Abbate, an alto singer who began his seventeen years of service in the Papal Choir in July 1535, only a few weeks before the admission of Morales. But however this may be, the composer of the interpolation very naturally accommodated himself to the formal scheme of Josquin's mass and made his Et in Spiritum wholly commensurable with the Et incarnatus that precedes it. All three sections accordingly show a measure-for-measure correspondence; the only differences in the conditions of composition are that in the Et incarnatus and Et in Spiritum the given melody is taken a step higher than in the Qui tollis, and that in the two genuine sections the given melody is presented in a retrograde exposition, while in the Et in Spiritum it returns to its original shape. This curious situation offers us a unique opportunity to test the validity of our procedure. Unless the frequencies for the undoubtedly genuine sections are in substantial agreement, and unless there is a distinct discrepancy between these figures and those obtained for the undoubtedly spurious interpolation, we shall have to abandon the use of "relative sonority" as a stylistic criterion. The figures speak, I think, for themselves. But I may add that in this case a further revealing difference can be brought out by comparing the extent of the four-part writing in the genuine sections with that in the spurious one. On the one hand the percentages are .44 and .465, on the other .585. This difference is the more striking in that the conditions of composition set .80 as a maximum.

Table III, the table bearing on the related works of uncertain date, gives frequencies for the "L'homme armé" masses of Busnoys and Obrecht and is based in either case upon three sections—the Qui tollis, the Et incarnatus, and the Osanna. Some years ago, in a paper read before two of the local chapters of this Society, I was able to show that the Obrecht mass is actually an elaborate tribute, built from beginning to end upon the tenor of the mass by Busnoys. Here again, as in the Josquin mass, the various sections used for comparison are ideally commensurable, differing only in their modality and in the modality chosen for the given melody. Since Obrecht is evidently in close sympathy with Busnoys and his music —it might be said that he draws on it also for the model of his *Missa Je ne demande*—the near agreement between the two pairs of figures may be significant and would in any case suggest that the younger work cannot have been written very much later than the older. This, in turn, appears to be borne out when the two pairs of figures are compared with those given for Busnoys and Obrecht in Table I. Busnoys's mass is evidently somewhat later than his motet for Ockeghem, yet the differences are not so great as to be incompatible with the reference to the mass in the *Proportionale* of Tinctoris, written not long before 1476. I should have been pleased to find, upon comparing the "relative sonorities" of the two masses by Obrecht, some confirmation of my earlier conjecture that his *Missa L'homme armé* belongs to the time of his residence in Bruges at the beginning of the nineties. The evidence seems, however, to point once more in the other direction and to a somewhat earlier date, perhaps in the early 'eighties. Here again, comparisons of the extent of the four-part writing in these works by Busnoys and Obrecht will prove instructive: for the motet and mass by Busnoys the figures are .21 and .37, for the masses by Obrecht .40 *(L'homme armé)* and .61 *(S.Donatiani)*.

To attempt now to answer the several questions raised at the outset, it may be said, I think, that with works of unknown authorship, the measurement of "relative sonority" can be used only to confirm conclusions reached by other means. With works of questioned authorship, it can be used effectively to separate the spurious from the genuine, although even here it cannot be expected to be of much help when the actual author of the questioned work is, as often happens, a member of the supposed author's immediate circle. But with works of known authorship it should prove a useful and reasonably dependable means for establishing a rough chronological sequence.

A CYPRIOT IN VENICE†

IN the spring and summer of 1958, at the time of my first visit
to Copenhagen, Carsten Høeg spoke to me more than once
about his long-standing interest in a unique and thoroughly exceptional treatise on music contained in one of the MSS belonging to
the library of the monastery of St. Catherine on Mount Sinai.
During the course of his brief stay at the monastery in 1931, he had
studied the text of the treatise on the spot and had immediately
recognized it as something quite out of the ordinary. At his request,
I myself took another look at it during the course of my own stay
at the monastery in May and June of 1958. By that time, through
the courtesy of the Library of Congress in Washington, Høeg had
obtained complete photographs of the text and it was his intention
to prepare and publish an account of it. This intention was never
carried out. Thus, when Professor Sørensen invited me to contribute to this collection of essays, it seemed to me that I might most.
appropriately fulfil a debt to Høeg by carrying out his plan and, in
so doing, offer to my old friend Knud Jeppesen the story of a
strange meeting between the music that interests him and the music
that interested Carsten Høeg, between the music of sixteenth-
century Italy and the music of Byzantium.

The MS in question, Sinai 1764, is briefly described by Bene-

†From *Natalicia musicologica: Knud Jeppesen septuagenario collegis oblata* (Copenhagen, 1962), 101–113. With the permission of Wilhelm Hansen, Musik-Forlag,
Gothersgade 9–11, 1123 Copenhagen K, Denmark.

šević in the third volume of his catalogue of the Sinai library.[1] It
runs to 102 folios, and like most MSS of its class, contains a number
of independent theoretical writings on music, copied by several
hands. Benešević assigns it to the seventeenth century, but—as we
shall see—this assignment, no doubt correct for the bulk of the
contents, is rather too late for the first item (folios 5–31), the one
in which we are interested. This is the treatise Περὶ χρείας
μουσικῆς γραικῶν χαρακτήρων (On the Need of Characters
for the Music of the Greeks) and its author is Hieronymus Tragodistes of Cyprus.

Preceding the preamble and text of the treatise itself is an extended letter of dedication, full of learned allusions and rhetorical
phraseology. It is addressed to a Cardinal whose name is not mentioned, and in the course of this dedication Hieronymus gives some
account of his life and of his purpose. "All men by nature desire
knowledge," he reminds his patron, and persuaded of the truth of
this dictum of Aristotle's, he has left his native country for Italy,
where he has now spent nine years in study, three of them in
Venice under the tutelage of Gioseffo Zarlino, the rest at the
Gymnasium in Padua. Believing that his compatriots have begun
to misunderstand the notation of their own music, often confusing
one sign with another, believing indeed that this misunderstanding
had already begun a little before his own time, he has determined
to set down his own observations on the subject. At first he had
planned to publish these observations, but on learning that this
would be both time-consuming and expensive, not so much because of the Greek text but rather because of the lack of suitable
type for the music, he has abandoned this scheme. At the end of
the dedication he promises to conclude his treatise with an original
setting of a liturgical text in Greek.[2]

[1] *Catalogus codicum manuscriptorum graecorum qui in monasterio Sanctae Catharinae
in Monte Sina asservantur.* III, 1 (Petropoli, 1917), 186.

[2] According to present plans, the full text of the treatise will eventually be
published by the Monumenta Musicae Byzantinae as a part of the series Corpus
Scriptorum. In the meantime, to permit the identification of further copies, if such
exist, I supply the incipits of the letter of dedication (1) and of the treatise itself (2):

1. Πολλῶν καὶ διὰ μακρῶν πολλάκις τῶν καθ᾽ ἡμᾶς τε καὶ πρὸ ἡμῶν
περιφανεστάτων ἐν τοῖς μαθήμασι χρόνων . . .
2. Μέλλοντας ἡμᾶς περὶ μουσικῆς χαρακτήρων . . .

Hieronymus must have hoped that the Cardinal would offer to defray the expense of publication. But in this he was disappointed: the only known copy of his treatise is the one at Sinai, and of the modified notation it sets forth, the only known practical example is the one with which the treatise itself concludes. As a contribution to the theory of Byzantine music, it scarcely deserves our notice, remaining, as it were, an idle and somewhat quixotic speculation. Nevertheless it has a decided interest. It tells us how the notation of Byzantine chant looked to an intelligent and cultivated Greek who had become thoroughly familiar with the theory and practice of Western music as it was taught in the Venice of Zarlino's day. Since it makes systematic use of Western terminology, it answers for us several questions not answered by other writings on its subject. Finally, it throws an unexpected light on a series of observations made by Zarlino himself. But before he can evaluate these several points of interest, the reader will need some understanding of what Hieronymus sought to teach.

Like the modern Greek notations devised early in the nineteenth century by Chrysanthus of Madytos and George of Lesbos, the notation taught by Hieronymus is at once a drastic simplification and a radical departure. It presupposes a diatonic system, and—true disciple of Zarlino that he is—Hieronymus makes it quite clear that this system is the diatonic system of Zarlino, with its distinction between the major and minor tones. As in the notation he has set out to reform, the neumes used to represent melodic progressions are interval-signs, not signs of pitch, but these neumes are now made to stand for precisely measured intervals, not for steps or leaps whose measurement will vary with their position in the system. Thus, of the ascending step-signs he retains, Hieronymus equates the *oligon* with the ascending semitone, the *oxeia* with the ascending tone, and to offset this in descent, he is obliged to add to the simple *apostrophos,* which he equates with the descending semitone, a new sign for the descending tone—the *oxeiapostrophos,* formed by writing the *oxeia* and *apostrophos* in a single stroke. Beyond this, in order to distinguish between the major and minor tones, he is obliged to recognize two forms of the *oxeia* and two of the *oxeiapostrophos,* these differing from one another in either case only in rising more or less sharply from the horizontal.[3] Hieronymus also retains the traditional sign for the unison (the *ison*) and the four leap-signs, or *pneumata,* all of which have for him the same meaning that they have in the classical practice. To distinguish in ascent between the minor and major third, he has only to combine the *kentema* now with the *oligon* and now with the *oxeia.* In descent, however, he adds to the simple *elaphron,* which he equates with the descending minor third, a new sign for the descending major third—the *elaphroxeia,* formed by writing the *elaphron,* which is normally rounded, as an inverted *V.* All of these signs, singly and in various combinations, are illustrated in the little exercise at the end of the treatise (Plate 1), and for this Hieronymus obligingly provides his own transcription.

In so far as it gives to the neumes representing melodic progressions a meaning in terms of precisely measured intervals, the notation of Hieronymus constitutes a radical departure. Not less radical are its provisions for the precise measurement of time. Each intervallic sign is accompanied by an auxiliary sign indicating its duration, and of these durational signs, the three that occur most frequently are signs taken over from the established practice and used in what is substantially the established way. The *argon* Hieronymus equates with the semibreve, the *tzakisma* with the minim, and the *gorgon* with the semiminim; then, building on the first and last of these three primary signs, he constructs a system of time-values ranging from the maxima *(oktargon)* to the semifusa *(oxydigorgon).* Used alone, that is, when not accompanying intervallic signs, these durational signs are understood as rests. In the more reasonable of these provisions, Hieronymus anticipates Chrysanthus by nearly three hundred years and—curiously enough—he anticipates him also in the invention of the signs *diargon* and *digorgon,* with their nomenclature. A few of these durational signs, together with the *bareia* and *diple,* which Hieronymus equates with the tie and fermata, are illustrated in the little exercise already mentioned.

For the rest, Hieronymus is content to devise equivalents for the

[3]As will be evident from the facsimiles to be given later on, it is sometimes impossible to determine which of the two forms is intended, while at other times the form used is not the correct one.

Western accidentals, clefs, and time-signatures. A composite sign whose elements, Hieronymus tells us, are the *ison,* the *phthora,* and the *oligon* represents the large enharmonic diesis in ascent; to obtain the same effect in descent, he has only to replace the *oligon* with the *apostrophos.* In ascent, a *hemiphthora* represents the small enharmonic diesis, and in descent the same effect is obtained by inverting the sign.[4] A genuine innovation is the substitution of clefs for the established modal signatures. The Greek letters K, Φ, and Γ are made to serve as equivalents for the Western C-, F-, and G-clefs, and the interval between the pitch implied by the clef and the opening pitch of the melody is then indicated in the usual manner by an interval-sign, or by several of them in combination. When a *phthora* follows a clef, the mode is transposed, just as in the Western music of Zarlino's day; untransposed modes are called diatonic or natural (φυσικόν), transposed ones "phthoric" (φθορικόν). For the tempus imperfectum diminutum Hieronymus prescribes a time-signature consisting of two parallel horizontal strokes (Plates 1 and 2); for the tempus perfectum diminutum his signature consists of one stroke only, surmounted by a *tzakisma* or *bracheia.*

As must have been evident from the foregoing brief and necessarily prosaic summary, what Hieronymus proposes is in effect that the notation of Byzantine chant be made capable of expressing everything that can be expressed in Western notation; in addition, it implies that to do this is in itself enough and that all aspects of the Byzantine notation that have no Western counterparts are superfluous and susceptible of elimination. From among the fifty to sixty simple and composite signs listed and described in the theoretical handbooks of his time, Hieronymus retains only fifteen, and although at one point he mentions in passing the existence of a few others—the *pestaste,* the *pelaston,* the *kouphisma,* the *hyporrhoe,* the *kratemohyporrhoön,* and the *kratemokatabasma*—he goes on to say that discussion of these signs and others like them is foreign to his purpose. No doubt the desire to simplify played some part in this; one has also to consider that, in a precisely measured notation,

---

[4]For these intervals, I retain the terminology of Hieronymus.

some of these signs are no longer essential, while others, like the Western ligatures and conjunctures, are resistant to measure and incompatible with it.

I come now to the original composition promised at the end of the dedication (Plate 2). It is a setting, for four voices, of the final troparion of the Easter canon, the words—as Hieronymus is at pains to point out—by John of Damascus, the music by Hieronymus himself. That three of the four voices, which are arranged on opposite pages as in a choir-book, should be written in the conventional Western notation of the sixteenth century, obviously by a practiced hand, is a compelling reason for supposing the Sinai copy of the treatise to be an autograph. For the Tenor, Hieronymus uses his own notation, and in one respect this voice is a distinct disappointment. Had he elected to treat, as cantus prius factus, the quasi-official melody for this text, or any of the later melodies for it current in his day, it would have been most interesting to see how he reduced it to measure and what he understood its harmonic implications to be. As it is, we must be satisfied to have his declamation of the text, for—like the other voices—the Tenor is freely composed. All that it has in common with tradition is its mode, the First Authentic, presented here in its transposed or "phthoric" form.[5]

Hieronymus has told us about his studies with Zarlino and we can see from the text of his treatise and from his composition that he has profited by them; on the other hand, he tells us also that he has devoted himself from childhood to the study of ancient and modern writings on the music of the Greeks—on "our music," to use his own phrase. Assuming for the moment that his background was equally solid on both sides, we may certainly infer from his observations that the Byzantine chant he knew was fundamentally diatonic, even though we may hesitate to understand the term "diatonic" in the precise sense in which it was understood by Hieronymus and his teacher. At no point in his treatise does Hieronymus as much as mention another possibility; the notation he advocates is wholly unsuited to the musical systems of later Byzantine theory and practice; and it is noteworthy that, having

---

[5]Strictly speaking, Hieronymus uses the plagal register, while tradition calls for the authentic one.

Ὤ Πά - σχα τό μέ - γα καί ἱ - ε - ρώ - τα - τον, Χρι - στέ

ὦ σο - φί - α καί Λό - γε, τοῦ θε - οῦ καί δύ - να - μις, δί - δου ἡ - μῖν

ἐκ τυ πώ - τε - ρον τοῦ με - τα -

σχεῖν ἐν τῇ ἀ - νε - σπέ - ρῳ ἡ - μέ - ρᾳ τῆς βα - σι - λεί - ας σου.

provided means for indicating chromatic alternations, he makes no use of them in his own Tenor, although his accompanying voices are liberally supplied with sharps and flats.

This much is inference. But on another point Hieronymus is as explicit as one could wish. Having found occasion to mention the solmization-syllables *ut re mi fa*, and anticipating that these may not be understood by his compatriots, he resorts to a form of notation often used in the elementary teaching of Byzantine chant, writing above each of the Latin syllables, each time it occurs, a Byzantine modal signature. Above the progression *ut re* he writes the signatures of the Fourth Plagal and First Authentic modes, above the progression *re mi* those of the First Plagal and Second Authentic, and above the progression *mi fa* those of the Second Plagal and Third Authentic. This need not mean, of course, that the pitches represented by these signatures are to be equated with the specific pitches C, D, E, and F, or with any other specific series of similar pitches. It does mean, however, that the pitches represented by these signatures form a series of this type, and although students of the problem have assumed from the first that this was the case, unambiguous supporting testimony is always welcome.

Less from what Hieronymus says in his letter of dedication than from what he does not say, we may draw two inferences about the date of its composition. Since he makes no mention of his teacher's death, we may conclude that the letter was written before 1590. And since he says nothing about the loss of Cyprus to the Turks, we may conclude that it was written before 1571—in a letter addressed to a Cardinal one might reasonably have expected at least a pious reference to this turning-point in the history of Cyprus, which brought with it the expulsion of the Roman clergy. But if we turn now to the text of Zarlino's *Istituzioni armoniche,* in its bearing on the text of the treatise itself, we shall find that the time of writing can be placed rather more precisely.

Chapter viii of the Fourth Book of the *Istituzioni* is entitled *"In qual maniera gli Antichi segneuano le chorde de i loro Modi."* After having commented briefly on the notations of classical Greek music, basing himself solely on the account found in Boethius, Zarlino goes on to speak of more recent developments in a curious passage that appears, with minor changes in wording, in every edition of his book. I reproduce it here after the first edition of 1558.

Ma tali cifere sono state lassate da un canto: imperoche Giouanni Damasceno dottore santo ritrouò altri caratteri nuoui, li quali accommodò alle cantilene Greche ecclesiastiche di maniera, che non significano le chorde, come faceuano li nominati caratteri, o cifere: ma dimostrano l'Interuallo, che si hà da cantare. La onde ogni interuallo cantabile hà la sua cifera; di maniera, che si come quella del Tuono è differente da quella del Semituono; & quella della Terza minore, da quella della maggiore, & cosi le altre, che ascendeno: cosi sono differenti etiandio quelle cifere di Tuono, di Semituono, et altri che discendeno, da quelle, che ascendeno; alle quali tutte si aggiungono i loro tempi, di modo che si può ridurre ogni cantilena sotto cotali caratteri, o cifere, con maggior breuità, di quello, che facemo adoperando li nostri; come posso mostrare in molte mie compositioni; & si può accommodare in essa ogn'uno di quelli accidenti, che concorreno alla sua compositione; sia qual si voglia: imperoche hò posto ogni diligenza di fare accommodare il tutto, secondo che torna al proposito.

But signs of this sort have been abandoned since John of Damascus, a sacred doctor, discovered other new ones; these he adapted to the Greek ecclesiastical melodies in such a way that, unlike the signs previously mentioned, which stood for the pitches, they stood for the intervals that were to be sung. Thus each interval has its own sign, and just as in ascending the sign for the tone differs from that for the semitone, the sign for the minor third from that for the major, and so on with the others, so also in descending the signs for the tone and semitone and so forth differ from one another and from the ascending ones; time-values are added to all of these signs, so that, using them, one can write out any melody with greater brevity than we can, using our own, a thing I can show in many of my compositions, and one can accommodate in such a melody all the accidents that occur in it, whatever they may be, for I have taken all care to cause everything to be accommodated, in so far as it is to the purpose.

As a survey of the notation of Byzantine chant, this is correct in principle, utterly misleading in detail. It is true that the signs used in the notation of Byzantine melody indicate intervals, not pitches, and it is true that ascending signs are distinguished from descending ones. But it is not true that the semitone is distinguished from the tone, or the minor third from the major, and it is not true that

PLATE *1*. *Sinai 1764, Folios 29 verso & 30.*

PLATE 2. *Sinai 1764, Folios 30 verso & 31.*

all interval-signs are supplied with auxiliaries indicating their duration.

Had we happened upon this passage unaware of its background, we would have been at a loss to account for its inaccuracies. As it is, we cannot fail to recognize in it a summary of the theories of Hieronymus, admirably concise and correct in every particular. We cannot know whether Hieronymus actually led Zarlino to believe that the views he expounded were identical with those generally held by his compatriots, or whether Zarlino, misunderstanding what he had been told, simply assumed this to be the case. Between these alternatives we may choose as we please—our main conclusion remains intact. For this one passage in the *Istituzioni,* Hieronymus was Zarlino's informant, and this means that he must have written his treatise before 1558, the year of Zarlino's first edition.

With this established, it becomes possible to identify—with some degree of assurance—the Cardinal to whom the treatise is dedicated. To Pierluigi Petrobelli of Padua, a former student of mine, I owe the suggestion that by far the most plausible candidate is Alvise Cornaro (1517–1584),[6] a member of that distinguished Venetian family whose connection with Cyprus extends from 1472, the year of Caterina Cornaro's marriage to the last of the Lusignan kings, to the capitulation of Famagusta in 1571 and the end of the Venetian sovereignty. Knight of St. John of Jerusalem, Grand Commander and Prior of Cyprus, Cardinal Alvise Cornaro was instrumental in persuading Pius V to join the League against the Turks, and to this cause he donated seventy thousand scudi from his own revenues.[7] His active interest in Cyprus and his ties to Venice would have commended him as an ideal patron to a

---

[6]I have also to acknowledge his helpfulness in verifying for me, with the aid of the copy of the first edition at the University of Bologna, the text of the passage quoted from Zarlino; he tells me, further, that he has found no trace of Hieronymus Tragodistes (or of Geronimo Cantore, as he may also have called himself) in Paduan or Venetian archives and that Professor Elpidio Mioni of Padua has located no copy of the treatise in any of the Italian libraries covered by his card-index of Greek incipits.

[7]For these details and further information, see Francesco Policini, *I fasti gloriosi dell'eccellentissima casa Cornara* (Padua, 1698), p. 21; Gaetano Moroni, *Dizionario di erudizione storico-ecclesiastica,* XVII (Venice, 1842), 143–144; *Hierarchia catholica medii et recentioris aevi,* III (Regensburg, 1910), 36.

Cypriot in Venice with an unpublished and as yet undedicated treatise on his hands. And if he is the man to whom Hieronymus addressed his letter, the treatise it introduced ought to have been written after 1551, for it was in that year that Julius III elevated Alvise Cornaro to membership in the Sacred College.

After this paper was already in proof, having occasion to consult Vogel and Gardthausen's *Griechische Schreiber*[8] in quite another connection, I learned to my considerable astonishment that Hieronymus had more than one string to his bow. Apart from his interest in music, he was a professional scribe from whom patrons might order copies of the Byzantine classics. His specialty, it appears, was the Chronicle of Constantine Manasses, beyond supplying copies of which he also filled orders for writings by Michael Psellus, by Symeon Metaphrastes, and by Symeon the Theologian. Specimens of his handiwork are preserved today in Paris and Munich and at the Biblioteca Vaticana. The earliest of these specimens —Paris, Bibliothèque Nationale, gr. 1770—was surely copied in Italy and is dated 1545. In 1558 and 1559 Hieronymus was working in Augsburg, evidently for a member of the Fugger family. These dates confirm my own earlier inferences in a most satisfactory manner, and if one makes allowance for the slight changes that may take place in a man's writing habits over a period of fifteen years, one cannot doubt that the copyist of the MSS now in Paris, Munich, and Rome was also the copyist of the first item in Sinai 1764.[9]

[8]Marie Vogel and Victor Gardthausen, *Die griechischen Schreiber des Mittelalters und der Renaissance*, (33. Beiheft zum Zentralblatt für Bibliothekswesen), Leipzig, 1909.

[9]My colleague Professor Lewis Lockwood was kind enough to compare a few photographs from Sinai 1764 with the MS at the Biblioteca Vaticana (Palatina gr. 397). I myself have made similar comparisons in Paris.

GUGLIELMO GONZAGA
AND PALESTRINA'S
MISSA DOMINICALIS[†]

I N July 17, 1881, in the course of a communication laid before the Royal Venetian Institute of Sciences, Letters, and Arts, the Abbate Pietro Canal made known the existence of a series of letters addressed by Giovanni Pierluigi da Palestrina to Guglielmo Gonzaga, Duke of Mantua.[1] German translations of a number of these letters were published by Haberl in 1886,[2] and in 1890 Bertolotti brought out the full Italian text of the entire series.[3]

There are twelve letters in all and they extend over a period of twenty years. By 1567, having published two books of masses, a book of motets, and a book of madrigals, Palestrina had already sufficient reputation abroad to have been offered the post of choirmaster to the Emperor Maximilian II, a post made vacant by the death of Jacob Vaet and subsequently filled by the appointment of Philippe de Monte: the earliest letter is dated February 2, 1568. The twenty years to which the correspondence actually belongs are also the years of Palestrina's greatest productivity: they saw the publication of the remaining books of motets and the composition

[†]From *The Musical Quarterly*, XXXIII (1947), 228–239; read at the annual meeting of the American Musicological Society, Detroit, February 23, 1946. Reprinted by permission of G. Schirmer, Inc.

[1] *Della musica in Mantova*, in *Memorie del Reale Istituto di scienze, lettere ed arti*, XXI, 655–774.

[2] *Das Archiv der Gonzaga*, in *Kirchenmusikalisches Jahrbuch*, I, 31–45.

[3] *Musici alla corte dei Gonzaga in Mantova* (Milan), pp. 47–55.

of all but a very few of the remaining masses. The series ends with the letter of July 6, 1587, written in the year of Guglielmo's death: in 1588 begins the publication of the "last works"—the books of Lamentations, Hymns, Magnificats, Offertories, and Litanies. In view of their number and of the period within which they fall, the letters to Guglielmo are biographical documents of the first importance. And they have an importance beyond that to which these considerations entitle them, for apart from the formal letters of dedication that accompany such works of Palestrina's as were printed during his lifetime, they are the only Palestrina letters we have.

Born in 1536, Guglielmo Gonzaga was a boy of fourteen when he succeeded to the family titles in 1550. Mantua was even then in possession of a rich musical tradition, a tradition that had begun in the time of Isabella d'Este and the frottolists Cara and Tromboncino and that was to continue unbroken into the 17th century—up to and beyond the performances of Monteverdi's *Orfeo* and Gagliano's *Dafne*. The young Duke will perhaps have been able to remember Jacquet da Mantua, court choirmaster during the thirties and forties; during the first years after his succession the choirmaster was Marenzio's teacher, Giovanni Contino, whose departure from Mantua in 1564 marks the end of a chapter in Mantua's musical history. A fresh chapter begins in 1565 with the opening of the new court chapel dedicated to St. Barbara. The building itself was the realization of a personal project of Guglielmo's, and the music and musicians at St. Barbara's now became his particular concern. The organ was an Antegnati and had been designed by Girolamo Cavazzoni, then organist at the local cathedral; the choirmaster was Giaches de Wert, who had come from Ferrara expressly to fill the post. It was for St. Barbara's that Palestrina composed the motets *Gaude Barbara beata* and *Beata Barbara,* and it was at St. Barbara's that a place was made for Rodolfo Palestrina, the composer's youngest son, shortly before his death on November 20, 1572. Earlier in this same year the composer and his patron may actually have met, for in May 1572 Guglielmo was in Rome for the coronation of Gregory XIII. It will have been at this time that Rodolfo's appointment was arranged and it will have been in recognition of this arrangement that Palestrina addressed to Guglielmo, later in the year, the dedication of his second book of motets for five voices, a dedication in which he expresses not only his own gratitude but also that of his entire house. In the years that followed, musicians were seldom appointed to the ducal service until Palestrina had been consulted. For a time Francesco Soriano held such an appointment, but this pupil of Palestrina's evidently failed to come up to expectations, for by 1583 the Duke was taking steps to replace him. Overtures were made to Annibale Zoilo and at one time Luca Marenzio was under consideration, but in the end it was to Palestrina himself that Soriano's post was offered. Nothing came of these negotiations, however, for Palestrina asked for more than the Duke was ready to pay, and when in 1586 the place was still unfilled, the Duke was content to let it remain so.

In a century conspicuous for its enlightened patronage of music Guglielmo Gonzaga stands out. But he was more than a patron of music—he was himself a musician. In 1570 he sends a motet and a madrigal of his own composition to Palestrina for criticism[4] and in 1574 a mass[5]; in 1583 he prints a book of madrigals—"not out of ambition, but simply in order that his former labors may not be lost entirely, some of them having already gone astray, and that he may enjoy from time to time the fruits of his past studies."[6] Guglielmo Gonzaga, whom Tasso calls "a prince of lofty intelligence, well lettered, most judicious, and most liberal,"[7] was the living embodiment of the teachings of Castiglione, who held that music was not only an ornament but likewise a necessity for the Courtier.

We can no longer know just what it was that first brought Palestrina to the Duke's attention. The simplest explanation is that the beginnings of the correspondence, in 1568, were simply a part of the wider recognition that had come to Palestrina with the publication of his second book of masses in the preceding year, the year of his appointment to the private service of Cardinal Ippolito d'Este and of his flattering offer from Maximilian II. Some importance might also be attached to the presence, in Cardinal Ippolito's *en-*

[4]Knud Jeppesen, "Über einen Brief Palestrinas," in *Festschrift Peter Wagner* (Leipzig, 1926), pp. 100–107.

[5]A Kyrie from a mass by Guglielmo is published by Gaetano Cesari in his "L'archivio musicale di S. Barbara in Mantova ed una messa di Guglielmo Gonzaga," in *Theodor Kroyer-Festschrift* (Regensburg, 1933), pp. 118–129.

[6]Canal, *op. cit.*, p. 685.

[7]*Ibid.*, p. 684.

Kneeling figure of Duke Guglielmo Gonzaga in the Basilica of Sant'Andrea, Mantua.

tourage, of Don Annibale Capello, a Mantuan agent. But the most attractive hypothesis is that Guglielmo's interest in Palestrina was actually first aroused by the inclusion, in Palestrina's second book of masses, of two compositions on motets by Jacquet da Mantua— the masses *Aspice Domine* and *Salvum me fac.*[8] This double tribute on Palestrina's part to an adopted Mantuan subject, the late choirmaster at St. Peter's, the Mantuan cathedral, cannot have passed unnoticed. In 1570, when Palestrina's third book of masses made its appearance, it again included two compositions on motets by Jacquet—the masses *Spem in alium* and *Repleatur os meum.* May we not see, in one or the other of these two works, the mass commissioned by the Duke through Giaches de Wert at the outset of his negotiations with Palestrina, the mass of which Palestrina writes in his first letters of February 2 and May 1, 1568?

All this is admittedly conjecture. These earliest letters of Palestrina's make it perfectly clear that the mass in question was his first work for Mantua; they do not really permit any inference as to the particular work involved. But with the important series of letters bearing on the masses commissioned by the Duke in 1578 the case is different. These later letters are detailed and circumstantial; they point unmistakably to a specific and unusual kind of work and thus invite, indeed demand, a positive identification. At the same time they take so much for granted and present so many difficulties of interpretation that Haberl, Bertolotti, Molitor,[9] Cametti, and the other writers who have studied them have given them up as hopelessly obscure. Palestrina and Don Annibale, the Mantuan agent, report to the Duke on the progress of work that he has commissioned. The actual terms of the commission are never stated. Each letter assumes on the part of its reader a knowledge of certain facts. This knowledge must be supplied from without. One set of facts, and one set only, will meet all the conditions. To simplify the presentation I shall begin by outlining what I take these facts to have been. The letters will then explain themselves.

Duke Guglielmo has commissioned Palestrina to write a number

---

[8]The Prima Pars of Jacquet's *Salvum me fac,* a motet for five voices first published by Gardano in the *Motetti del frutto* of 1538, is reprinted by Haberl as an *opus dubium* in his collected edition of Palestrina's works, XXXI, 58–62.

[9]*Die nach-tridentinische Choral-Reform zu Rom,* I (Leipzig, 1901), 229–234.

of masses for the private use of the choir at St. Barbara's in Mantua. These masses are to be written upon plainsongs personally selected by the Duke, who sends the melodies to Palestrina only after revising them (or causing them to be revised) in conformity with the taste of the time. This much is implicit in the letters themselves. Beyond this I infer that the melodies in question were plainsong masses, not hymns or antiphons, that Palestrina was to set only alternate lines, leaving the odd-numbered lines of the Glorias and Credos to be chanted in unison by a second choir, and that with this in view the Duke has sent him, not the complete plainsongs, but only those parts of them upon which he was actually to compose.

Don Annibale opens the correspondence on October 18, 1578, with a report that Palestrina has begun his work.

M. Giou. da Palestrina non seruendogli per l'indispositione graue hauuta di fresco la testa ne la uista per esercitare la gran uoluntà di seruire in quel modo che può V. A. ha cominciato a porre sul liuto lo Chirie et la Gloria della prima messa et me le ha fatte sentire pieni ueramente di gran suauita et leggiadria.

Et quando con buona gratia di lei potesse farlo hora che N. S. in San Pietro ha comandato che si canti con due chori di xij dodici per choro come ha trovato che ordinò Giulio ij quando lascio per tal effetto entrade bastanti a quel capitolo et ha per questo anche fatto mandar uia tutti i cantori conjugati salvo lui per priuilegio spetiale. Vorebbe anche le seconde parti et seruirsene nella detta chiesa in molte solennità in luogo dell'Organo perchè afferma che nel uero V. A. ha purgati quei canti fermi di tutti i barberismi e di tutte l'imper-

Having passed recently through a serious illness and being thus unable to command either his wits or his eyesight in the furtherance of his great desire to serve Your Highness in whatever way he can, M. Giovanni da Palestrina has begun to set the Kyrie and Gloria of the first mass on the lute, and when he let me hear them, I found them in truth full of great sweetness and elegance.

And now that His Holiness has commanded that there are to be two choirs at St. Peter's, each choir of twelve singers (for he has discovered that Julius II so ordered when he provided the chapter with revenues sufficient for this purpose), and has for this reason also caused the dismissal of all the married singers save only Palestrina by special privilege, if with the gracious permission of Your Highness it may be so, Palestrina wishes also to have the second parts and to use them in

fettione che ui erano.[10] Il che spero non farà senza sua licenza; ma quando prima dalla debolezza gli sarà permesso spiegarà ciò ch'ha fatto col liuto con tutto il suo studio.

the church in question instead of the organ on occasions of high solemnity, for he affirms that Your Highness has in truth purged these plainsongs of all the barbarisms and imperfections that they contained. I trust that he will not do this without your permission. And as soon as his infirmity permits he will work out what he has done on the lute with all possible care.

Don Annibale's references, in the second paragraph of his letter, to the division of the choir at St. Peter's and to Palestrina's wish to have "the second parts" to use "instead of the organ" remain meaningless and unintelligible unless the terms of the commission were substantially as I have described them. When this letter was written, the division of the choir had been in effect for less than three months.[11] For the first time Palestrina was in a position to offer at St. Peter's a mass designed for antiphonal performance, the two choirs singing alternately in parts and in unison. For festive use such a mass is obviously more appropriate than one in which the organ alternates with the unison chant. Recognizing this, Palestrina asks for "the second parts" in order that he may perform the mass himself. The Duke's commission has come at precisely the right time.

On November 1 of the same year Don Annibale makes a second report.

Mando ancho una messa del Palestrina con la sua lettra, il quale attendara a fugarle il più che si potrà: il quale spera non succedendo altro di mandarne ogni dieci giorni

I send also a mass by Palestrina with a letter of his; he will endeavor to hasten the others as much as possible, and unless something interferes, he hopes to send one every

[10]Molitor, who is persuaded that the revisions of the plainsongs were made by Palestrina and not by the Duke, translates (op. cit., I, 230: "Denn er versichert, dass Ew. Hoheit in Wahrheit nun diese canti fermi erhalten, rein von allen Barbarismen und Unvollkommenheiten, die darin waren."

[11]See Baini, Memorie (Rome, 1828), II, 79–80, and for the regulations of Julius II, Haberl, "Die römische "Schola cantorum," in Vierteljahrsschrift für Musikwissenschaft, III (1887), 249–251.

una et quanto a i canti fermi mostra desiderarli grandemente.

ten days. As to the plainsongs, he shows that he is most desirous to have them.

Palestrina's own letter makes it clear that "the second parts" have not yet reached him, suggests indeed that the Duke has flatly refused to send them on, for it ends by advancing a new reason for his wish to have them, this time one calculated to appeal to his patron's vanity.

Ser^mo Principe.

V^a Altezza haura l'inclusa messa da me fatta nella mia convalescenza, et lo sa Iddio se quando mi furono portati i canti fermi, più mi premeua il non poterla seruire che il mal ch'io hauea, hora attendero all' altre con ogni studio accio habbiano in se quelle parti che l'Altezza V^a desidera. Io nel comporre questa ho trasportato il canto fermo talhora una quinta più su talhora una ottava acciò uenisse più alegra che non porta di sua natura il quarto tono, quest'altra della Madonna non ne haura bisogno per esser da se stessa autentica hauro per grandissimo fauore poter hauere il remanente del canto fermo poiche così ben purgato da barbarismi et dai mali suoni et se l'Altezza V^a si contentara si mandaranno in stampa con il graduale che nostro signore mi ha comandato ch'io emendi, ne altro ocorrendomi baccio humiliss^te la mano a V. A. con desiderarele da N. S. Iddio ogni grandezza et lunghezza di vita.

Di V.A.S.humiliss. et devotiss. seruo
GIO. PETRO LOYSIO

Di Roma li 1 di 9bre 1578

Serene Prince:

I enclose the mass written for Your Highness during my convalescence, and God knows that when the plainsongs were brought to me I was more disturbed by my inability to serve you than by my illness. Now I shall attend to the other masses, taking every care that they may have those qualities that Your Highness desires. In composing the present mass I have transposed the plainsong, now to the fifth above and now to the octave, in order that the mass may gain in brightness, a quality not natural to the Fourth Mode. The mass of Our Lady will have no need of this since it is of itself authentic. I shall consider it a great favor if I may have the remainder of the plainsong, for as it stands it has been well purged of barbarisms and wrong notes, and if Your Highness is willing, the chants shall be printed with the Gradual that His Holiness has ordered me to amend. Having nothing further to say, I humbly kiss Your Highness' hand, praying Our Lord to grant you every distinction and a long life.

Your Highness' most humble and devoted servant
GIOVANNI PETRALOYSIO

Rome, November 1, 1578

In calling Palestrina's proposal to print the Duke's versions of the plainsong masses in the revised Gradual on which he was then at work an appeal to his patron's vanity, I do not mean to imply that it was in any way insincere. Elsewhere in the correspondence, in speaking of compositions that the Duke has sent him for criticism, Palestrina finds ways of expressing his polite disagreement. Surely it would never have occurred to him even to suggest the inclusion in the projected new Gradual of revisions with which he was not in sympathy. Apart from this, if Palestrina's request for "the remainder of the plainsong" can be understood only in the light of the interpretation already placed on Don Annibale's letter, his reference to a Mass of Our Lady contributes also to the general effect. By 1578 Palestrina had written and published two masses *De Beata Virgine*. Are we to suppose that the Duke would have asked him to write a third one unless it was to be distinctly different from the two already in print?

The remaining letters are of interest only in so far as they enable us to form an idea of the extent of the commission and of the length of time that it took Palestrina to execute it. On November 15 of the same year Don Annibale sends on the second mass, on December 10 the fourth. Palestrina himself dispatches "the last three" on March 21 of the following year with a letter acknowledging the receipt of the one hundred *scudi d'oro* that have been paid to him on the Duke's order. This would be the equivalent of about one half of the annual income that Palestrina was regularly receiving at this time.

That the masses commissioned in 1578 were written for antiphonal performance, with the successive lines of the Glorias and Credos to be sung alternately in parts and in unison, is a view quite different from those advanced by earlier students of Palestrina's music. I have tried to show that it is the view that agrees best with the actual wording of the documents. It is indeed the only view that wholly fits the facts. But it will be of little use to us unless it leads us to the identification of at least one of the Mantuan masses. To make such an identification we shall need, to begin with, a mass designed for antiphonal performance. Then there must be nothing about its tradition or its style that is inconsistent with the attribution "For Mantua in 1578 or 1579." Finally, if our identification is to be a positive one, we shall need to connect the mass with Mantua and to show that it has been written upon an emended plainsong. Among the ninety-four masses published by Haberl in his edition of Palestrina's works only one—the disputed *Missa Dominicalis*—will meet our first condition.[12] If it will meet the others it should be the mass for which we are in search.

The work in question, a mass for five voices, was published in Milan in 1592 under Palestrina's name as a part of the contents of a volume comprising six *Missae Dominicales* collected from various authors by a certain Giulio Pellini, a Carmelite friar who dedicates his book to Alfonso d'Este, Duke of Ferrara. Haberl regards the piece as "an authentic mass from Palestrina's youthful period."

> In Palestrina, his native town, Pierluigi often visited the Carmelite cloister which is today still standing in the neighborhood of the family house; here he may have become acquainted with Brother Giulio.

In short, Haberl asks us to believe that the *Missa Dominicalis* dates from the 1540's, that before leaving Palestrina for Rome the composer entrusted a copy of it to a friar who happened to be living nearby, and that this friar, after having carried the work about with him for nearly fifty years, published it in 1592 together with five similar works by other composers presumably obtained in the same manner. This is asking too much. And, in any case, no such elaborate explanation is necessary. For Brother Giulio does not describe himself simply as a Carmelite; he says "a Carmelite of Mantua." And aside from the mass that he attributes to Palestrina, his book contains works by Mantuan composers only. The first of the six masses is by Giaches de Wert, choirmaster at St. Barbara's from 1565 to 1582; following this are masses by Francesco Rovigio, the organist at St. Barbara's, by Giovanni Contino, choirmaster at St. Peter's in Mantua until 1564, by Giovanni Giacomo Gastoldi, the master of the *balletto,* choirmaster at St. Barbara's after the retirement of Giaches de Wert, and by Alessandro Striggio, the noble amateur who regularly styles himself, on the title-pages of his madrigal books, *gentilhuomo mantovano.* The mass attributed to Palestrina comes at the end, as befits a contribution from a distinguished outsider. The book then is above all a Mantuan collection and

---

[12]Collected edition, XXX, 28–34 (alto and bass parts only); XXXIII, 1–33 (in score).

doubtless represents the actual repertory of the ducal chapel.[13]

In a note bearing on Palestrina's treatment of the cambiata, Jeppesen rejects the *Missa Dominicalis* offhand, characterizing it as "undoubtedly spurious."[14] For this reason I have thus far refrained from calling it genuine. I need no longer hesitate to do so. The tradition of the work is now so clear that the burden of proof rests with its critics and not with its defenders.

Once accepted as belonging to the group of masses written for Mantua in 1578 and 1579, the *Missa Dominicalis* should hold a special interest for us. Palestrina tells us himself that the plainsongs upon which these masses were written had been "well purged of barbarisms and wrong notes." He even goes so far as to propose their inclusion in the Gradual that he has been asked to edit. His letters to the Duke have told us something of his attitude toward plainsong; his mass will tell us more.

In the Kyrie, Gloria, and Sanctus of the *Missa Dominicalis* Palestrina paraphrases the plainsongs brought together in the Graduale Vaticanum as Mass XI (*Orbis factor); for the plainsong of the Agnus Dei he turns to Mass XII[15] while for the Credo he uses a melody no longer current and wholly unfamiliar to me. It is not difficult to isolate these underlying melodies from their polyphonic context. Particularly in the Gloria, where the declamation of the melodic original is largely syllabic and its polyphonic treatment relatively simple, it is usually possible to determine from one voice, if not

[13]For Haberl's comments on the mass and a precise bibliographic description of Pellini's collection, see his collected edition of Palestrina's works, XXX, iii.

[14]*Der Palestrinastil und die Dissonanz* (Leipzig, 1925), p. 191.

[15]This is precisely the plan followed by Cavazzoni in his *Missa Dominicalis,* an organ mass published in Venice by Bernardino Vitali sometime after 1543 and reprinted by Giacomo Benvenuti in *Classici della musica italiana,* VI; see also Arnold Schering, "Zur alternatim-Orgelmesse," in *Zeitschrift für Musikwissenschaft,* XVII (1935), 19–32, and for the publisher and date, Claudio Sartori, "Precisazioni bibliografiche sulle opere di Girolamo Cavazzoni," in *Rivista musicale italiana,* XLIV (1940), 359–366. Victoria's *Missa Dominicalis,* a mass for four voices designed like Palestrina's for alternate performance and published by Pedrell after a MS belonging to the Cathedral of Tortosa (Victoria, *Opera omnia,* VIII, 5–14), draws on Mass XI for its Kyrie and on Mass XVIII for its Sanctus and Agnus Dei; there is no Gloria. The *Missa Dominicalis* (1607) of Viadana, a mass for solo voice and basso continuo likewise designed for alternate performance and published by Peter Wagner in his *Geschichte der Messe* (Leipzig, 1913, pp. 534–545), paraphrases Mass XI throughout. In all three of these masses the plainsong for the Credo is the "Credo Dominicalis" (Credo I).

Lansdowne **462**

Et in ter - ra   pax ho - mi - ni - bus   bo - nae vo - lun - ta - tis.

Palestrina

Be - ne - di - ci - mus te. | Glo - ri - fi - ca - mus te.

Do - mi - ne De - us, Rex coe - le - stis, De - us Pa - ter o -

mni - po - tens | Domine Deus, Agnus Dei, (= Domine Deus, Rex cœlestis.) | Fi - li - us Pa - tris.

Qui tol - lis pec - ca - ta mun - di, sus - sci - pe de - pre - ca - ti - o -

nam no - stram | Quo - ni - am tu solus san - ctus.

Tu so - lus Al - tis - si - mus, Je - su Chri - ste. | A - men.

from more than one, the exact reading of the melody that Palestrina had before him. In the example above, an attempt to reconstruct this reading is compared with the reading of the British Museum MS Lansdowne 462 (15th century) as published in facsimile by W. H. Frere in his edition of the Sarum Gradual,[16] a reading somewhat closer to Palestrina's model than that of the Graduale Vaticanum.

The character and extent of the Duke's revisions are now clear. These revisions are plentiful and they are drastic. As early as 1558 Zarlino had complained of what he took to be corrupt versions of the ecclasiastical melodies, attributing them to "the ignorance or carelessness of copyists" and to "the arrogance of persons of little understanding";[17] in another connection he complains of the "barbarisms" that he finds on every hand:

> Over and over again [he says] we hear length given to the penultimate syllables of such words as *Dominus, Angélus, Filius, miraculum, gloria,* and many others, syllables that are properly short and fleeting. To correct this would be a praiseworthy undertaking and an easy one, for by changing the melody a very little, one could make it most suitable, nor would this change its original form, since this consists solely of many figures or notes in ligature, placed under the short syllables in question and inappropriately making them long when a single figure would suffice.[18]

In his Brief of October 25, 1577, entrusting Palestrina and Zoilo with the revision of the chant, Gregory XIII seems almost to echo Zarlino's words.

Quoniam animadversum est, Antiphonaria, Gradualia et Psalteria . . . quam plurimis barbarismis, obscuritatibus, contrarietatibus ac superfluitatibus, siue imperitia siue negligentia aut etiam malitia compositorum, scriptorum et impressorum esse referta . . . Itaque vobis

Inasmuch as it has come to our attention that the Antiphoners, Graduals, and Psalters . . . have been filled to overflowing with barbarisms, obscurities, contrarieties, and superfluities as a result of the clumsiness or negligence or even wickedness of the composers, scribes, and printers . . . we charge

[16]London, 1894, pp. 9*–10*.
[17] *Istituzioni armoniche,* IV, xxx.
[18] *Ibid.,* IV, xxxii.

. . .purgandi, corrigendi et refor-   you with the business of purging,
mandi negocium damus.   correcting, and reforming them.[19]

It is in this spirit that Guglielmo has made his revisions. "Barbarisms" are suppressed by shortening the penultimate syllables of
Domine, omnipotens, suscipe, and *quoniam;* at *hominibus* the final syllable is taken a third lower in order to evade the rising inflection of
the original; at *glorificamus te* the position of the melisma is shifted
from the end of the distinction to the syllable bearing the logical
accent. "Wrong notes" are "corrected" at *Et in terra, Benedicimus
te, Deus Pater, Qui tollis,* and *Amen,* evidently on the theory that each
distinction ought to begin and end with the modal final or confinal.
It goes without saying that these changes are an expression of a
point of view diametrically opposed to that embodied in the original, whose logic they have nullified, whose equilibrium they have
upset, and whose symmetry they have destroyed. Yet it is not that
they reveal a lack of skill on Guglielmo's part; it is simply that the
two points of view—the medieval and the humanistic—are totally
irreconcilable. This is perhaps most evident in the original parallelism and subsequent divergence of *homínibus bóne, Dómine Déus,* and
quóniam tu.

Recalling that Guglielmo's revisions had Palestrina's approval
and that Palestrina actually proposed to print them in his projected
edition of the Gradual, we may conclude that they are substantially
the revisions he would have made himself. More than any other
work of Palestrina's, the *Missa Dominicalis* can tell us what this
projected edition would have been like. What has happened to the
six companion pieces of 1578 and 1579, among them a *Missa
Quarti toni* and a *Missa de Beata Virgine?* Perhaps an Italian colleague will undertake to renew the search for them in the archives
of the ducal chapel, divided some years ago between the Liceo
Musicale in Bologna and the Royal Conservatory "G.Verdi" in
Milan. Now that we know their character, the task should not be
difficult.

[19]Molitor, *op. cit.,* I, 297–298.

SOME MOTET-TYPES OF
THE SIXTEENTH CENTURY†

THIS paper aims to take a systematic and comprehensive but necessarily superficial look at the motet of the 16th century with a view to defining the general character and extent of the relationship between liturgical situation and musical style. To do this, we must begin with the motet texts, and, defining a liturgical text as one which the Church has sanctioned by prescribing its use in a particular connection, we must determine the extent to which these texts fall under our definition; in addition to this we shall want to know which varieties of liturgical text were actually used in the motet, what, from the standpoint of the motet, the relative importance of these varieties was, and whether or not these text-varieties correspond in any way to musical varieties. That such a correspondence exists for the liturgical chant itself is generally conceded. We know that the musical style of a particular chant turns less on text-content than on liturgical situation, that in different situations a given text is set in different ways, that in the same situation different texts are set in the same way. Is this true also of the polyphonic setting? If it is, we have that sorely needed tool—a means of classifying this enormous body of material.

On first consideration it would seem that such a correspondence must exist, that the century which saw the publication of the *Officia* and *Lectiones* of Lassus, the *Offertoria* of Palestrina, and the *Gradu-*

†From *Papers Read at the International Congress of Musicology, Held at New York, September 11 to 16, 1939* (New York, 1944), pp. 155–160; read on September 14, 1939. Reprinted by permission of the American Musicological Society.

alia of William Byrd cannot have been so unmindful of liturgical considerations as to reduce the variety of traditional forms to a common denominator. But on further consideration it is evident that a sort of leveling process did take place, that distinctions sharply drawn at the beginning of the century were at the end less marked, and that the general trend was toward the absorption of what had been specific varieties into a single "collective" or "neutral" type. In what follows I shall try to enumerate and to define a few of these varieties and to suggest, with the aid of examples drawn from Palestrina, that the leveling process, though real, was not complete, and that even with Palestrina there persists a sufficient correspondence between liturgical situation and musical style to justify a classification on this basis.

The distinctive motet-form for the Mass—at the same time one of the oldest motet-forms of all—is the Sequence. Throughout the 15th century this was the one large liturgical form in general use. And even after other forms arose and sequence poetry itself was losing favor, the peculiar adaptability of the form, which lends itself to a variety of treatments, prevented it from passing wholly out of use. Its chief characteristic is the parallelism inherent in its paired structure, a parallelism which invites a polyphonic treatment of alternate verses (as in the Sequences of the *Choralis Constantinus*), a setting as variation-chain (as in the Sequences of Josquin or Willaert), or an antiphonal harmonization (as in the typical Sequence of Palestrina). Not less important is its tendency to paraphrase the plainsong model, a tendency so marked that until well into the 16th century it is an absolute rule, evaded only in those Sequences which, like Josquin's *Stabat Mater,* are built upon an unyielding tenor not related to the principal text. These two conditions suffice to distinguish the Sequence-Motet from other types involving metrical texts and to stamp it with a character of its own, so pronounced that the type would be readily recognizable even were the text not present. Admittedly, the Sequence does not have for Palestrina and his time the importance that it had for the composers of Josquin's generation. Disregarding the cycle of Offertories, the settings of texts from the Song of Solomon, and certain posthumously published works, most of them questioned or spurious, I count in all for Palestrina 224 motets; only 12 of these are

Sequences, and of these 12, only one—the *Lauda Sion Salvatorem* of 1563—is built along classical lines. Yet on the whole these 12 motets have a physiognomy of their own which sets them apart from the rest of Palestrina's work. Even where no paraphrase is present (and it is present in only six) the characteristic parallel structure is as a rule maintained through alternations and combinations of two choirs. Of the 12 works, only two—the two settings of *Gaude Barbara beata*—could possibly be assigned to the "collective" or "neutral" motet-type. One sees, too, that Palestrina connects certain definite procedures with the form—that, generally speaking, it is for him a large form, calling for a large and divided body of voices (normally the eight-part chorus) and for homophonic rather than polyphonic treatment; that he relies for his effect less on complex combination than on beauty of line and accent; and finally that, following the tradition, he tends, more in this motet-type than in any other, to elaborate rather than to invent.

Beyond these 12 Sequences, the Offertories, and a half-dozen miscellaneous pieces, Palestrina sets as motets no liturgical texts intended specifically for the Mass. Insofar as it is liturgical at all, the great bulk of his motet-production falls, almost equally divided, into two main classes—Antiphon and Respond. Like the Sequence one of the oldest motet-types, the Antiphon owes its intensive development to the 16th century. In its 15th-century form it was limited in practice to a relatively small circle of texts—to the familiar Concluding Antiphons of Compline, together with a certain number of similar pieces of more or less general application; as indicated, the Antiphon-motet for the specific festival is a distinctly later development. For this reason, perhaps, but also because of differences in the liturgical situation, Palestrina makes a sharp distinction between the old established texts on the one hand and the texts for specific festivals on the other. In setting such texts as *Alma Redemptoris Mater,* for example, he carries paraphrase of the plainsong model even further than in the Sequence, going so far as to begin in some cases with the official intonation; when he sets the *Ave Regina coelorum* and *Salve Regina* the sequence-like structure of his originals induces a sequence-like structure in his motet and leads in half a dozen instances to the use of two choirs. As to the Antiphon motets for specific festivals—these being normally set-

tings of Magnificat and Benedictus Antiphons, exceptionally settings of Antiphons for the Psalms—no positive characteristics can
be enumerated. They are perhaps best summed up as representing
the hypothetical "collective" or "neutral" type toward which the
others tend—in any case, as small forms, preferably for a relatively
small body of voices.

For the Office, then, the Antiphon is, so to speak, the typical
small motet-form. The typical large form, occupying a position
analogous to that occupied in the Mass by the Sequence, is the
Respond. Its characteristic feature, when fully developed, is its
division into two sections, exactly reproducing the form of the
plainsong Respond from which it takes its text. The first section (or
Prima pars) sets the text of the Respond proper; the second section
(or *Secunda pars*) sets the text of the Verse and concludes with a
repetition of the concluding line or lines of the Respond; the
whole, then, exhibits the form AB *(Prima pars)*: CB *(Secunda pars)*.
The plainsong Respond from which this motet-type derives is a
musical reply to the reading of a Lesson or Chapter, an elaborate
and extended composition affording considerable opportunity for
soloistic display. In keeping with this, the motet-setting of the
Respond text is usually an elaborate, extended, and brilliant composition. Palestrina, while he occasionally begins an Antiphon with
full harmonies, the several voices reciting the text in unison, does
not use this technique in Responds for four and five voices, which
invariably open with imitations. What is more, he provides a sufficient number of examples to permit the generalization that, for him
at least, this motet-type calls in its full development for a relatively
large body of voices. Among the Palestrina motets for four voices
the Antiphon is the commonest type, among those for five it occurs
less frequently, among those for six to eight still less frequently; the
fully developed Respond occurs infrequently among the motets for
four voices, more frequently among those for five, still more frequently among those for six to eight. Or, to put it differently, the
Palestrina Responds for four voices are for the most part un-
developed, consisting then in settings of the Respond alone, without the Verse and Repetitio; as more voices are added, these un-
developed settings become less and less usual. If we may read in
this a tendency to reproduce in the motet not only the specific form

but also the general characteristics of the plainsong model, we may discover further evidence of this tendency in those admittedly exceptional examples in which there is a pronounced contrast between the settings of Respond and Verse, the Verse being set off from the genuinely polyphonic Respond by beginning with full harmonies and straightforward syllabic declamation. Particularly clear examples are the half-dozen Responds of Palestrina in which there is no formal division between Respond and Verse, the fully expanded text being set as a single movement:

> For five voices:
> *Orietur stella* (1584, 7)
> *Aegipte noli flere* (1584, 8)
> *Surge Petre* (1584, 11)
>
> For eight voices:
> *Disciplinam et sapientiam* (1876[a], 29)
> *Expurgate vetus fermentum* (1876[a], 32)
> *Dies sanctificatus* (1876[b], 29)

These works actually represent a distinctive type, widely cultivated during the second half of the century (notably by de Monte). The distinction turns less on the absence of formal division than on the reduced scale of the whole; in particular, the setting of the Verse is as concise as the context will permit, opening in each case with full harmonies and, in addition to this, set off from the Respond proper by the use of triple time or of anticipatory accent. Still another means of contrasting Respond and Verse may be seen in the Ingegneri Responds for Holy Week (once attributed to Palestrina); in this series, the Verses are set systematically for a reduced number of voices, as are the Introit Verses in the *Gradualia* of William Byrd. Similar to these, but further distinguished by plainsong repetitions, relieving the polyphony, is Palestrina's posthumously published funeral-motet *Libera me Domine,* the Respond proper for four voices, the successive Verses for three, three, and four. This last example is incidentally the one exception among the motets of Palestrina to the general rule that the Respond-motet does not paraphrase its plainsong model. With the Sequences such paraphrases are, as we have seen, normally present; the same is true of the concluding Antiphons, and one will find a few instances among the Antiphons belonging to other classes, for example:

Gaudent in coelis (1563, 32)
Veni sponsa Christi (1563, 35)
O sacrum convivium (1572, 5)

And the *Libera me Domine,* it will be noted, is exceptional in every respect—exceptional in its liturgical significance, exceptional in the structure of its plainsong model, exceptional in the structure of the polyphonic setting itself, exceptional in the close dependence of the one upon the other.

Motet-settings of the Psalms and Canticles (other than the Magnificat) call for still another mode of treatment. Here, as with the Sequence, the eight-part chorus is the norm, and the necessity for dealing with a relatively lengthy text without exceeding the usual bounds leads to the employment of a homophonic or at best quasi-polyphonic texture and to an emphasis on sonority and rhythmic declamation. At the same time the parallel structure of the Sequence is lacking and the melodic interest less sustained. Other text-varieties used by Palestrina—Gospel, Lesson, Chapter, Prayer —do not occur in sufficient number to permit discussion in general terms. If specific procedures are to be defined for these, it will be done by establishing a chronological series, not by examining the work of any one composer.

To deal effectively with any large body of evidence the historian must begin by putting it in order. In many instances, as in this one, several means of ordering will present themselves. Which one he begins with may in the end make very little difference; before he has finished he will probably have to use them all. In stating the case for this means I do not question the value, indeed great value, of others. But I am persuaded that the use of this means, a means in keeping with the spirit and intention of the works themselves, is the logical first step and, in any event, an essential one.

HAYDN[†]

I N Haydn's London diary, among the entries for 1791, there is
this note: "On December 5 there was a fog so thick that one
might have spread it on bread. In order to write I had to light a
candle as early as eleven o'clock." Could Haydn have known what
had happened in Vienna on that critical morning, he would not
have cared to write at all. As it was, he wrote on; two weeks later
he received news of Mozart's death. "I am as pleased as a child at
the thought of coming home and embracing my good friends," he
writes to Marianne von Genzinger on the 20th. "My one regret is
that the great Mozart will not be among them, if it be true, as I trust
it is not, that he is dead. Not in a hundred years will posterity see
such a talent again."

Though the Haydn who penned these lines was no longer a
young man, his vitality was unimpaired, his productivity unabated.
"I am still sprightly and in the full possession of my strength," he
had assured Mozart before leaving Vienna; early in 1792 he reports with evident satisfaction to Frau von Genzinger that he has
never written so much in one year as in that just passed. His
reputation, already distinguished, now assumed such proportions
that, in later life, he often insisted that he had become famous in
Germany only by way of England. Strangers stopped to stare at
him, exclaiming: "You are a great man!" Within less than a year

†From David Ewen, ed., *From Bach to Stravinsky, the History of Music by Its Foremost
Critics* (New York: W. W. Norton, 1933), pp. 77–87. Reprinted in ed. David
Ewen, *The World of Great Composers* (Englewood Cliffs, N.J.: Prentice-Hall, 1962),
pp. 91–102.

three fashionable artists had painted his portrait. Honored with a Doctor's degree conferred by Oxford University, feted by professional and amateur musicians, sought after by peer and commoner alike, Haydn took most satisfaction, perhaps, in his new-found independence. "How sweet a little liberty tastes!" he writes. "I used often to sigh for freedom—now I have it, in a measure. I appreciate it, too, though my mind is burdened with a multitude of tasks. The knowledge that I am no longer a hired servant repays me for all my trouble." For thirty years Haydn had written for a select group of connoisseurs; now, at fifty-nine, the opportunity to address a wider audience had come to him at last. The change brought with it a new sense of responsibility—to art and to society —a sense of responsibility that found ultimate expression in his great oratorios, *The Creation* and *The Seasons*.

As Mozart's biographer, Otto Jahn, once observed, the difficult task is to portray the Haydn of the fifties, sixties, and seventies. "Thus far we know little, if anything, about him and about the conditions and influences to which he was subject. The Haydn everyone knows is not Mozart's forerunner, but his contemporary and successor." Our knowledge of the musical environment from which Haydn sprang goes further than Jahn's, but for most of us the works of his earlier years still remain uncharted territory. Let us begin, then, on familiar ground—with the music of the post-Mozartian Haydn. We will follow him the more easily through the vicissitudes and complexities of his upward climb if we have first seen the goal at which he aimed. And we will recognize the more readily that his music is something more than an introduction to Mozart and Beethoven, that his role in musical history is something more than that of a pioneer, if we take as our starting point the works of his last period.

During the London years Haydn is preoccupied with instrumental composition; after his return to Vienna "the father of the symphony" tends more and more to write for voices. Up until the time of the composition of *The Seasons* there is no slackening of his pace. The piano variations in F minor; the last three piano-sonatas; a set of three piano-trios dedicated to the Princess Dowager Maria Theresa Esterhazy; a second set dedicated to Princess Marie; a third set for Mrs. Schroeter, his "invariable and truly affectionate" correspondent; a fourth set for Mrs. Bartolozzi, the wife of the London engraver; the single piano-trio in E-flat, afterward rewritten as a piano and violin sonata for Madame Moreau; the six "Apponyi" quartets; and the twelve "London" symphonies: these thirty-five major instrumental works are the fruit of the first five years alone, surely no mean achievement for a man in his sixties. To the next five years belong the eight quartets dedicated to Count Erdödy and to Prince Lobkowitz; four of the last six masses; the revision of *The Seven Last Words;* the Te Deum in C; and the two oratorios. With the composition of *The Seasons* Haydn's creative activity is practically ended. In 1801 he writes the "Schöpfungsmesse," in 1802 the "Harmoniemesse." Then, in 1803, he completes two movements of his last quartet, dedicated to Count Fries. It was never finished. "I am no longer able to work at anything big," he writes to Thomson in the following year. "My age weakens me more and more." Yet for a time his imagination remains as keen as ever: in 1806, on his seventy-fourth birthday, he expresses the conviction that there are no limits to music's possibilities, that what may still be accomplished in music is far greater than what has been accomplished in the past. Often, he says, there come to him ideas through which the art might be advanced much further; his physical limitations, however, no longer permit him to undertake their expression.

"The secret of music's effect lies essentially in this: that in composition everything comes as it must come, yet otherwise than we expect." However one-sided his view of the romantic scene may have been, Eduard Hanslick was a shrewd judge of classical values; in its application to the music of the last quarter of the eighteenth century this brilliant aphorism of his comes very near the mark. The kind of effect he has in mind is not possible in every stage of the development of a style. In the experimental stage its presence is inconceivable; in the conventional stage, which follows, we seldom meet with it. Only when the rules of the game are well established is it feasible for the composer to play on the expectation of his listener. And even then, to play on expectation he must first arouse it. To secure emphasis he must first exercise self-control. He cannot afford to be continually surprising his listener. He must be simple before he is complex, regular before he is irregular, straightforward before he is startling. The composer of the "Surprise" symphony understood the working of these first principles. He could be simple, regular, and straightforward; this is a point that need not be brought home to the modern reader, who is only too apt to exaggerate the extent—or misunderstand the purpose—of this side of Haydn's writing. He could also be original without being eccentric; this the more generous among his contemporaries were always ready to concede. "That sounds queer," Kozeluch once remarked to Mozart, startled by a bold transition in a Haydn quartet, "would you have written it that way?" "Scarcely," Mozart replied, "but do you know why? Because neither you nor I would have hit on the idea."

Eminently suited to the display of the particular sort of originality that consists in playing on the expectation of the listener is the sonata form, as Haydn saw it toward the end of his career. In this type of movement the climax of interest regularly coincides with the beginning of the third part—the return of the principal tonality and the principal idea; artistic success or failure depends largely on the way this climax is hastened or delayed and on the angle from which it is approached. Once the third part has begun the listener's recollection of what has gone before leads him to anticipate the composer's every step; in this part of the design each deviation from the familiar path is a potential source of aesthetic pleasure or disappointment.

The compositions Haydn wrote for London are so full of this kind of originality that it is difficult to single out any one work to illustrate it. Let us choose one of the most familiar—the last of the three symphonies of 1795, the last of all Haydn's symphonies, the so-called "Salomon" symphony in D. Turn to the finale and observe how skillfully Haydn prepares the "return," growing more and more deliberate as he approaches the critical point, wandering further and further from the key at which he intends to arrive, then thinking better of it and making an unlooked-for close that is at once the end of the second part and the beginning of the third; before we have realized it, the "return" has been accomplished. Or turn to the first movement, compare the third part with the first, and observe how artfully Haydn delays restatement of the "second subject"—as is quite usual with him, it is the "first subject" all over again;—only when we have almost given up hope of hearing it does he bring it in at last. It is in the original treatment of just such details as these that the superiority of the London Haydn over the rank and file is most evident. In the compelling audacity of their design, the compositions Haydn wrote for London represent the final development of form in classical music. While he was writing these compositions, plans were already taking shape in his mind for a work that was to make his name last in the world.

"Since time immemorial the Creation has been regarded as the most exalted, most awe-inspiring picture that mankind can contemplate. To accompany this great drama with suitable music can surely have no other result than that of intensifying these sacred emotions in men's hearts and of making them more submissive to the benevolent omnipotence of their Creator." These lines from a letter Haydn wrote in 1801—three years after he had completed *The Creation*—throw a revealing light on the frame of mind in which the aging master approached this most exacting of all the tasks he set himself. For the devout Catholic who habitually began and ended his manuscripts with the words "In nomine Domini" and "Laus Deo," the subject was made to order. The work of composition occupied him for two full years. "I spend much time on it," he said, "because I intend it to last a long time." For once, the composer who "never wrote until he was sure of himself" made systematic sketches. To Griesinger, his first biographer, he confessed that he had half finished his score before its success was apparent to him. "I was never so devout as during the time I was working on *The Creation*," Griesinger quotes Haydn as saying. "Every day I fell on my knees and prayed God that he might give me strength to bring this work to a satisfactory conclusion." Early in 1798, shortly after the composer's sixty-sixth birthday, that satisfactory conclusion was announced. Before the oratorio had been publicly performed, Haydn was at work on *The Seasons*.

"With the decrease of my mental powers, my inclination and the urge to work seem almost to increase," Haydn wrote in June, 1799, to the publishers Breitkopf & Härtel. "Every day I receive many compliments—even on the fire of my last works; no one will believe what trouble and strain I endure to produce them." Goethe's friend Zelter called *The Seasons* "a work of youthful vigor and mature mastery." Schiller's friend Streicher came nearer the truth in 1809 when he called it "a musical debauch." "Without it," he added, "Haydn would assuredly have enjoyed ten more years of activity." Haydn himself said that *The Seasons* had "finished" him.

Haydn often regretted that he was never able to visit Italy. But it is a question whether he would have profited half as much from such a visit as he did from his two visits to England. Without them neither *The Creation* nor *The Seasons* would have been written. The two oratorios owe something to English poetry—one is based on an adaptation from Milton's *Paradise Lost,* the other on Thomson's *Seasons.* They owe more to the English audience and to the anglicized Handel, whose music was virtually new to Haydn when he arrived in London. The Handel Commemoration in 1791 and the "Concerts of Ancient Music" were revelations. To the English composer, Shield, who asked his opinion of "The Nations Tremble" in Handel's *Joshua,* Haydn replied that he had long been acquainted with music, but never knew half its powers before he heard it; when Shield praised the recitatives in Haydn's early oratorio *Il Ritorno di Tobia* (1775), Haydn declared that the recitative "Deeper and Deeper Still" in Handel's *Jephtha* surpassed them in pathos and contrast. Power, pathos, and contrast—these are the secrets of Handel's greatness, and when Haydn returned to Vienna he took them with him. Written for the concerts of the "Society of Noble Amateurs," *The Creation* and *The Seasons* speak to the plain man.

One type of artist is concerned with design, another with expression. Haydn is concerned with both. The classic perfection of the "London" symphonies and the "Apponyi" quartets has its counterpart in the romantic intensity of the works of his last years in Vienna. In the light of later developments Haydn's romanticism may appear somewhat restrained to us; to his contemporaries it was bold and even startling. The rich sonorities of his last quartets and orchestral accompaniments point to Beethoven and to Weber. The simple piety of his *Creation* is no less affecting than the artless realism of his *Seasons.* The ordered lawlessness of his "Representation of Chaos" breaks down old barriers. "It is impossible and contrary to rule that so excellent a piece should be accepted, universally and at once, for what it is and alone can be," Zelter wrote in Breitkopf's journal. "Certain deep-rooted theories, derived from the works of an earlier period, remain eternally at odds with the spirit of progress, leading inevitably to the kind of criticism that is always demanding, but does not know how to accept." Haydn thanked Zelter for praising the "Chaos" by saying: "You could and would have written it just as I did." To which Zelter replied, modestly and with perfect truth: "I could never have written it as you did, great master, nor shall I ever be capable of doing so."

As he approached the end of his career, Haydn became increasingly sensible of the social responsibility of the artist, and of all the testimonials showered on him during his declining years he prized those most that bore witness to his honorable discharge of this obligation. He took particular pride, Griesinger tells us, in the honorary citizenship conferred on him by the municipal authorities of Vienna, seeing in this an illustration of the old saying, "Vox populi, vox Dei." Another tribute of the same kind, simpler, perhaps, but no less sincere, moved him to write what is at once the most revealing and the most touching of all his letters. From the little town of Bergen, capital of the island of Rügen in the Baltic, a society of amateurs wrote to thank him for the pleasure that performing his *Creation* had given its membership.

"Gentlemen: (Haydn replied) It was a truly agreeable surprise to me to receive so flattering a letter from a quarter to which I could never have presumed that the productions of my feeble talent would penetrate. Not only do you know my name, I perceive, but you perform my works, fulfilling in this way the wish nearest my heart: that every nation familiar with my music should adjudge me a not wholly unworthy priest of that sacred art. On this score you appear to quiet me, so far as your country is concerned; what is more, you give me the welcome assurance—and this is the greatest comfort of my declining years—that I am often the source from which you, and many other families receptive to heartfelt emotion, derive pleasure and satisfaction in the quiet of your homes. How soothing this reflection is to me!

"Often, as I struggled with obstacles of all kinds opposed to my works—often, as my physical and mental powers sank, and I had difficulty in keeping to my chosen course—an inner voice whispered to me: 'There are so few happy and contented men here below—on every hand care and sorrow pursue them—perhaps your work may some day be a source from which men laden with anxieties and burdened with affairs may derive a few moments of rest and refreshment.' This, then, was a powerful motive to persevere, this the reason why I can even now look back with profound satisfaction on what I have accomplished in my art through uninterrupted effort and application over a long succession of years."

The fifty most active years of his life—the fifty years between his first compositions and his *Seasons*—coincide with one of the most restless and fruitful half-centuries in all musical history—the half-century between Bach's death in 1750 and Beethoven's first symphony in 1800. Old forms and old methods had gone the way of old ideals; pathos had yielded to sentiment, severity to informality; music had become less comprehensive, more individual, less uniform, more many-sided, less intellectual, more spontaneous. Tastes had changed, and a combination of forces—social, cultural, and artistic—had brought about a complete reversal of musical values. Before the pre-classical movement had reached its height in the music of Bach and Handel, these forces were already working toward its dissolution; by the middle of the century they had undermined the old structure and laid out in bold outline the ground plan of the new.

"We have gradually rid ourselves of the preconceived idea that great music is at home only in Italy. Respect for those illustrious names in *ini* and *elli* is disappearing, and Germans, formerly occupied with the modest business of accompaniment, have raised themselves to the first place in the orchestra of the powers. We no longer listen to the swaggering foreigners, and our scribes, who only yesterday were so bent on propagating fair copies of the empty eccentricities of Italians devoid of ideas, now vie with one another for the honor of making the works of their countrymen known."

So Marpurg wrote in 1749, and it is noteworthy that this somewhat rhetorical declaration of his, far from being a random observation, stands at the very beginning of his *Critical Musician*. That just at this time there should have been a belated reawakening of national feeling among German musicians is highly significant. Having assimilated all that Italy could give, Germany was ready to strike out for herself, and in her leading musical centers—Berlin, Mannheim, and Vienna—native musicians were even now contending for the supremacy.

It was at this moment that Haydn, dismissed at seventeen from the cathedral choir-school in Vienna, faced the problem of shifting for himself. His immediate musical environment, while not precisely dominated by the Italian tradition, was less aggressively Ger-

man than that of Berlin or Mannheim; what is perhaps more important, it was an eminently popular environment, related in a variety
of ways to the everyday life of the community. The popular theater
was in a flourishing condition. Wagenseil, Starzer, and Reutter
were putting the music of the street and the dance-hall to artistic
uses in their serenades and divertimenti; Monn, another Viennese
musician of the older generation, is thought to have been the first
to introduce the minuet in a symphony. Haydn, true to his sur-
roundings, began by composing music of just this kind. One of his
earliest experiments was a serenade, and, according to one account,
it was an improvised performance of this piece that brought him
his first commission and led to the composition of his first "opera,"
Der krumme Teufel. To the same category belong his earliest quartets, written for his first patron, Baron Fürnberg in Weinzierl, and
the numerous divertimenti for various combinations that he wrote
before and during his brief service as musical director to Count
Morzin in Lukavec. "Le Midi" (1761), one of his first symphonies,
already contains a minuet. To recognize the Haydn we know in the
compositions of this early period is no easy matter; at no other time
in his life is the Italian influence more marked. While contemptu-
ously repudiating the "scribbler" Sammartini, whom Mysliweczek
had called the father of his style, Haydn was always ready to acknowledge his debt to Porpora. Berlin and Mannheim are negligi-
ble factors, so far, though by 1760 Haydn was not only a fervent
admirer of Bach's son Carl Philipp Emanuel, but had already gone
so far as to dedicate one of his compositions to Stamitz's patron, the
Elector Karl Theodor. "I wrote industriously, but not quite correctly," Haydn said himself, and when in 1805 a score of his first
mass was discovered and brought to him after fifty-three years, his
comment was: "What pleases me most in this work is a certain
youthful fire."

The next few years brought important changes in Haydn's outward circumstances and in the kind of music he was called upon to
supply. In 1761, on his appointment as second *Kapellmeister* to
Prince Paul Anton Esterhazy at Eisenstadt, he found himself in a
responsible and highly desirable position exceedingly favorable to
the development of his gifts and reputation; in 1762, on Paul
Anton's death and the arrival of his brother and successor, Prince
Nicholas, his responsibilities were materially increased, for the

new employer was not only an ardent music-lover, but an amateur performer as well, and the demand for new compositions was relentless and almost unlimited. Then, in March, 1766, Haydn was made first *Kapellmeister,* and a few months later the opening of the magnificent residence Prince Nicholas had built at Esterház—with its opera house seating four hundred and its marionette theater— again increased his responsibilities, obliging him to devote serious attention to operatic composition, a branch of music in which he had thus far had little experience.

Haydn's first fifteen years at Eisenstadt and Esterház constitute a period that is surely one of the most interesting of his long career: it is the period during which the foundation of his later reputation was laid; during which the works of his first maturity were written; during which he ceased to feel the influence of his lesser contemporaries and, abandoning their conventions, became himself a determining influence in the career of the younger Mozart. Entering the Esterhazy service an almost unknown musician, Haydn began at once to attract attention, not only in Vienna, but in other musical centers. In 1763, Breitkopf's catalogues announce eight "quadros" and six trios for strings, with two concertos and a divertimento for the harpsichord, as available in manuscript; from the same year dates one of the earliest notices of Haydn on record, a manuscript note in an interleaved copy of Walther's *Lexikon* now in the Library of Congress: "Hayden, an incomparable musician and composer, lives in Vienna and distinguishes himself in the writing of fine quartets, trios, and symphonies." The first recorded publication of a work of Haydn's occurred in March of the following year, when the Paris publisher Venier advertised an edition of one of the early quartets in his series "Sinfonie a più Stromenti Composte da Vari Autori" (Opera Decima Quarta) under the title "Les noms inconnus bons à connoitre" (Unknown names worth knowing) in company with compositions by Van Maldere, Beck, Pfeiffer, Schetky, and Fränzl. By 1775 a formidable array of Haydn's sonatas, duos, trios, quartets, and symphonies had been engraved (apparently without the composer's authorization!) in Paris, Amsterdam, and London; the Vienna editions began in 1774 with Kurtzböck's printing of six sonatas. As early as 1766 Haydn is mentioned in magazines published in Leipzig and Hamburg, while in Vienna he was already being called "the darling of our nation." So universal, in fact, was the recognition accorded Haydn by the end of this period that in responding in 1776 to a request for an autobiographical sketch he could write: "In my chamber music I have had the good fortune to please almost everywhere, save in Berlin!"

Successively considered, the compositions of the decade 1765 to 1775 reveal Haydn's steadily increasing mastery of form and content. Not satisfied with the facile polish of his fourth series of quartets (Opus 9, 1769), he strove in those that followed toward greater refinement of workmanship, toward more intense formal concentration, toward the suppression of the episodic and conventional (Opus 17, 1771), resorting in the last series written during this period (Opus 20, 1772) to time-honored contrapuntal devices to enhance the interest and insure the balance of his texture. At the same time Haydn contrived to give his music a more individual note. In their book on Mozart, Wyzewa and Saint-Foix draw attention to certain particularly striking examples of this tendency in the works of the early 1770's—the C-minor piano sonata, the quartets Opus 20 ("à la fois pathétiques et savants"), the "Trauersymphonie," the "Farewell" symphony—and speak of the year 1772 as the "romantic crisis" of Haydn's artistic career. A year or two later, the same writers tell us, still another change took place in Haydn's manner. Now he surrenders to the "galant" style, and henceforward his principal aim is to impress us agreeably or to amuse us with ingenious turns of musical rhetoric.

Then, in 1781, came the publication of the "Russian" quartets (Opus 33), the series that ushered in the style Haydn himself described as "entirely new." Here is the turning-point in his career. Until now Carl Philip Emanuel Bach had been Haydn's principal model; with the appearance of the "Russian" quartets Mozart began to take Bach's place. In the "Paris" symphonies (1786), the "Oxford" symphony (1788), and the two sets of quartets written in 1789 and 1790 for the Viennese wholesale merchant Johann Tost, Haydn attained full maturity, and the transition to the works of the last decade was only a step.

While Haydn had been at work, a new kind of music had grown from tentative beginnings to conscious maturity; his own music had itself passed through every stage in that growth, now following in a path cleared by others, now leading the way. With the possible exception of Handel, no great composer was ever more prolific;

with the possible exception of Beethoven, no great composer ever maintained so fresh an outlook. Keeping pace with contemporary developments and more often anticipating them, Haydn ended even more progressively than he had begun.

HAYDN'S DIVERTIMENTI FOR BARYTON, VIOLA, AND BASS

After Manuscripts in the Library of Congress†

I N 1792, the year of Haydn's return from his first visit to England, the lexicographer Ernst Ludwig Gerber contributed to the *Musical Correspondence of the German Philharmonic Society* for April 25 and May 2 an "Attempt at a Complete Catalogue of Joseph Haydn's Published Works." An introductory paragraph sets forth emphatically the importance of Haydn's contributions to the development of instrumental style, contributions which, Gerber says, have had so marked an effect on the taste of his generation that to all appearance Haydn's manner has become a universal ideal, a standard by which the works of his contemporaries are measured.

Yet [Gerber continues] I need not dwell here on the excellence of Haydn's compositions, the less so since I have already sought to draw my readers' attention to their various merits in my biographical dictionary of musicians. My purpose is rather to observe that it is high time his works were rescued from the obscurity of the countless English, French, German, and Dutch music-publishers' warehouses, large and small, and thus spread before us as a whole; not only as a compliment to this great artist, who now appears to have abandoned Germany forever, but also to advertise to other nations this wealth of masterpieces, for their edification, and as a matter of national pride.

It would seem, to be sure, as though Haydn were himself the man best fitted to compile the complete catalogue I have in mind. Unfortunately, we have nothing to hope for from that quarter; when one of my

†From *The Musical Quarterly*, XVIII (1932), 216–251. Reprinted by permission of G. Schirmer, Inc.

friends approached him in this matter at my request a few years ago he was told that "it would be quite impossible. Furthermore, that many of his works had been destroyed at the time of the fire at Esterház."

One hundred and forty years have elapsed since the publication of Gerber's "attempt," but his remarks have not lost their point. With but few changes they might indeed have been made by a writer of our own day. The project, as Gerber conceived it, has still to be realized in its entirety, though in the list of compositions in the second edition of Gerber's own dictionary, in Pohl's thematic index covering the period 1766 to 1790, and in the thematic indices to the piano sonatas and symphonies in the definitive edition of Haydn's works now being published by Breitkopf & Härtel, we have contributions to the complete, authoritative catalogue which Gerber was the first to propose. In one particular, however, Gerber's expectations have been exceeded. The importunities of friends and admirers may have played some part in reawakening the aging master's interest in the unpublished or forgotten works of his youth. But more probably, as Botstiber suggests, it was the thought of the royalties the publication or republication of these works might now be expected to produce that led Haydn, in 1805, to supervise the drawing up of the document entitled: "A catalogue of all the compositions I recall having completed from my eighteenth to my seventy-third year."[1]

Haydn's catalogue is by no means an entirely complete or absolutely reliable guide to his works. A number of important compositions, including several symphonies, have been overlooked, while inconsistencies in classification and changes in the order of the movements of works in the cyclic forms have given rise to occa-

---

[1] The original manuscript, in the hand of Johann Elssler, Haydn's secretary and majordomo, is preserved in the archives of the Esterhazy family, formerly in Eisenstadt, now in Budapest. Referred to again and again since its contents were first summarized by Bertuch in 1808, the catalogue has never been published, though manuscript copies are to be found in several of the larger libraries. Elssler himself supplied Breitkopf & Härtel with one such copy, and a transcript of this copy, made in 1893 for Friedrich Curtius-Nohl, is in the possession of the Library of Congress. Some of the annotations in this transcript appear to be in the hand of Erich Prieger, to whom it presumably belonged at one time. Facsimiles of three pages of the original, including the title-page, are contained in Alfred Schnerich's *Joseph Haydn und seine Sendung,* 2nd ed. (1926), facing pp. 49, 146, and 147.

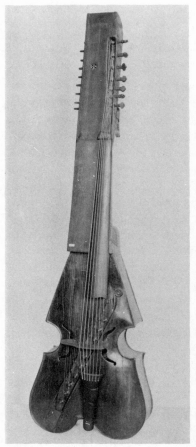

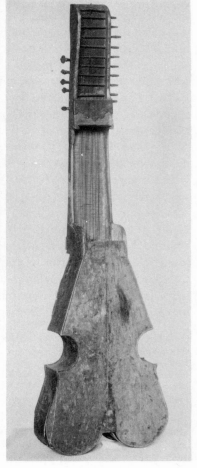

Baryton by J. J. Stadlmann, 1779 (back view).
(FROM THE CROSBY BROWN COLLECTION, METROPOLITAN MUSEUM OF ART, NEW YORK.)

Baryton by J. J. Stadlmann, 1779 (front view).
(FROM THE CROSBY BROWN COLLECTION, METROPOLITAN MUSEUM OF ART, NEW YORK.)

sional duplication. Yet because of the peculiar conditions surrounding the bibliography and chronology of Haydn's works, the value of this manuscript cannot be overestimated. Where the authenticity of a composition attributed to Haydn is questioned, its presence or absence in the catalogue of 1805 may be a determining factor; where it is difficult to establish the original or definitive instrumentation of a work of Haydn's, its place in the catalogue of 1805 may be most significant. And for certain groups of Haydn's minor works this catalogue, including as it does the opening bars of many compositions which, it is to be feared, have been irretrievably lost, affords us information for which we cannot be too grateful. One such group is the long series of divertimenti, duets, sonatas, cassations, and concertos for the baryton with various combinations of other instruments, written during Haydn's first fifteen years at Eisenstadt and Esterház, and intended for the private diversion of Prince Nicholas Esterhazy.

The extraordinary instrument which finds employment in these pieces is a member of the viol family. In size and shape it corresponds roughly to the tenor gamba, its neck being noticeably longer, its body somewhat smaller in scale. Like the *viola bastarda,* or lyra-viola, and its treble counterpart, the *viola d'amore,* the baryton was fitted with sympathetic strings of metal in addition to the usual complement of gut strings. It differed, however, from these instruments in that the peculiar construction of its neck, which was hollow and open at the back, made it possible for the player to reach the sympathetic strings, which passed beneath the fingerboard, with the thumb of his left hand. These strings could accordingly be used to provide a sort of plucked accompaniment to the bowed melody.

Since the baryton was cultivated only in seventeenth- and eighteenth-century Germany and Austria, and there but sparingly, it never became standardized. Instruments with six or seven gut strings were the rule, to judge from the recorded museum specimens; the number of metal strings, usually ten to fifteen, varies considerably, ranging from eight to as many as thirty. Prince Esterhazy's barytons, described by Lucien Greilsamer in his valuable

study "Le baryton du prince Esterhazy,"[2] had seven gut strings and
ten metal strings, but the seventh gut string and the tenth metal
string are seldom, if ever, required for Haydn's music.

The peculiarities of construction and left-hand technic to which
attention has already been drawn are entirely overlooked in several
recent notices of the baryton. For Haydn and his contemporaries,
however, they constituted the instrument's most striking characteristics. "One seems to hear gamba and harp at the same time,"
writes Friedrich August Weber[3] in an essay on the effects of music.
Recalling the baryton-player Karl Franz of Vienna, from 1763 to
1776 a member of the Esterhazy orchestra, Weber continues: "In
1786 I heard him play music written for his instrument by the
indefatigable Joseph Haydn. The delicacy of his bowing, and his
dexterity in drawing out the bass notes by means of the trick I have
mentioned, surpassed the expectations of the most fastidious connoisseurs. His *adagio sostenuto* moved me to tears, something no
other virtuoso has accomplished, before or since." If the baryton
suggested gamba and harp to Weber, for Carl Ludwig Junker,
author of a musical almanac for 1782, it had the effect of mandora
(Mandorzither) and gamba. "Indeed," he adds, "for all its close
resemblance to the *viola da gamba,* the baryton ['the voluptuous
baryton,' he writes in another connection] has in its make-up something of almost every instrument." Another member of Prince
Esterhazy's orchestra to introduce the baryton to a wider audience
was the virtuoso Andreas Lidl, who appeared at a London concert
in 1778, offering "a new favourite overture by Haydn." Dr. Burney was not impressed. "The late Mr. Lidl," he wrote in 1789,

[2] *S. I. M.,* VI (1910), 45–56; see also George Kinsky's note on the baryton in
his catalogue of the Heyer collection, II, 495–504, and Daniel Fryklund's essay
"Viola di bardone," *Svensk tidskrift för musikforskning,* IV (1922), 129–152. These
discussions, based in part on Pohl, contain much information regarding the instrument, the amateur and professional musicians who played it, and the composers
other than Haydn who wrote for it, which need not be repeated here. At least two
barytons are housed in American collections. That at the Metropolitan Museum of
Art, New York, with seven gut strings and twenty metal strings, was built in Vienna
by the younger Stadlmann in 1779; that at the Museum of Fine Arts, Boston, is a
modern copy by Gutsche of Berlin and formerly belonged to the Galpin collection
at Hatfield.

[3] *Musikalische Real-Zeitung* (1788), 182–183.

"played with exquisite taste and expression upon this ungrateful instrument [the *viola da gamba*], with the additional embarrassment of base [sic] strings at the back of the neck, with which he accompanied himself, an admirable expedient in a desert, or even in a house, where there is but one musician; but to be at the trouble of accompanying yourself in a great concert, surrounded by idle performers who could take the trouble off your hands, and leave them more at liberty to execute, express, and embellish the principal melody, seemed at best a work of supererogation."

Haydn makes conspicuous use of these obbligato basses in his baryton pieces and distinguishes them from the melody proper by writing the numbers of the metal strings below the notes indicating their sound.[4] By way of illustration I quote here the Trio for "Pariton con basso solo" from the Minuet in Divertimento 107 for baryton, viola, and bass, apparently the only movement in which Haydn left the problem of accompaniment entirely to the solo instrument. The viola and bass parts are duly marked "tacet."

Divertimento 107
Trio
PARITON CON BASSO SOLO

Baryton

[4]Compare Greilsamer's article, p. 55.

The melody has, of course, to be read an octave lower than written. As a rule Haydn employs but one staff for his baryton parts, writing both melody and bass in the treble clef.

It is abundantly clear, from the movement quoted above and other similar but less extended episodes introducing obbligato basses, that the sympathetic strings of the instrument for which Haydn composed were usually tuned as follows:

In the little duet for two barytons printed by Pohl and reprinted by Greilsamer, the second player uses a *scordatura,* tuning the first metal string to G, the eighth to *c* natural. Contemporary writers, when they allude at all to the tuning of the bowed strings, generally prescribe one of the familiar combinations of fourths with an included third, exceptionally the D-minor tuning. For Haydn's music the following scheme, proposed by Kinsky, seems the most practicable:

Majer's *Neu-eröffneter Theoretisch- und Pracktischer Music-Saal* (2nd ed., 1741) testifies to the perfect plausibility of this tuning. For some reason or other, perhaps because of the unsatisfactory tone-quality of the low D and G strings, Haydn makes little use of the bowed strings in the bass register. I give below (a) the normal, and (b) the extreme range of his music for the baryton (actual sounds an octave lower):

Returning now to Haydn's catalogue, without which our information about this music would be woefully incomplete and lacking in correlation, we find a detailed thematic index listing one hundred and twenty-five divertimenti *a tre* for baryton, viola, and bass; then, under the general heading "Various baryton pieces for the favorite instrument of the late Prince Nicholas Esterhazy," six duets for two barytons, twelve sonatas for baryton and violoncello, seventeen "Cassations Stücke" for combinations of from three to eight instruments including baryton, and three concertos for baryton accompanied by two violins and bass, with the note "163 baryton pieces in all."[5] To these must be added two compositions entered elsewhere in the catalogue: a quartet for harpsichord, two violins, and baryton,[6] and a cantata with baryton accompaniment, "Germany's lament on the death of Frederick the Great." Another necessary addition is the set of twelve little divertimenti for two barytons and bass, overlooked by Haydn, that Pohl saw in autograph at Eisenstadt. Even with these corrections the list is not quite complete, for according to Pohl there were "several" harpsichord quartets.

Thanks to Pohl's conscientious recording, the chronology of Haydn's music for the baryton is fairly well established. None of these compositions can very well have been written before 1762, the year in which Prince Nicholas succeeded to the family titles and established himself at Eisenstadt, while an important document quoted by Pohl, the "Regulativ chori Kissmartoniensis" of 1765, suggests that during the first three years of Prince Nicholas's régime the attention Haydn paid his new employer's favorite instrument was little better than perfunctory. "Capellmeister Hayden is hereby directed to devote himself more diligently to composition than heretofore," so runs the final paragraph of this itemized bill of complaint, "especially to the composition of pieces such as

[5]The complete list printed in Schnerich, pp. 182, 186–188, without the opening themes. Despite the often-quoted story of how Haydn displeased Prince Nicholas by proving that the baryton could be played in the more remote keys, it was limited in practice to D major and related major tonalities. Of the one hundred and twenty-five divertimenti *a tre*, forty-seven are in D, thirty-eight in A, twenty-seven in G, eight in C, and three in F. Only two are in minor: Divertimento 87, in A, and Divertimento 96, in B. As an exception to the general rule, the Trio of the Minuet in Divertimento 96 is in B major.

For the sake of completeness it may be mentioned here that the opening themes of the baryton pieces are also listed in an earlier manuscript catalogue, the so-called "Entwurf-Katalog," compiled by Haydn and his copyist Radnitzky, and preserved today at the Staatsbibliothek in Berlin.

[6]Published as Piano Trio 26 (Edition Peters).

may be played on the gamba, very few of which have come to our notice thus far, and, as evidence of his industry, to send us without fail the first clear copy of each and every new composition."[7] Another document quoted by Pohl in this connection indicates that the Prince's warning did not fail of its intended effect. "I have this moment received from Hayden three pieces which please me very much," Prince Nicholas writes on January 4, 1766, to his superintendent. "You are accordingly to pay him in my name twelve ducats from the treasury and to tell him at the same time that he is to write six more pieces like those he has just sent me, together with two solos, to be delivered as soon as possible."

Influenced, no doubt, by their modest proportions and relative simplicity, Pohl has chosen to regard the duets and the divertimenti for two barytons and bass as the earliest compositions of the entire series. The sonatas and concertos cannot even be dated approximately; as early as 1769, however, the harpsichord quartet circulated in manuscript as a trio, while the cassations, three of which are dated 1775, may all be assigned to the early 70's. "Germany's lament on the death of Frederick the Great," composed in 1786, is apparently the only one of Haydn's compositions for the baryton to belong to a later period.

As to the divertimenti for baryton, viola, and bass, there can be no question but that Haydn's catalogue lists them in the approximate order of their composition. Pohl suggests 1767 as the date when the first forty-eight numbers were completed, and argues that the next twenty-four (No. 49 to 72) must have followed by 1769, and a second set of twenty-four (No. 73 to 96) before the end of the year 1770. The remaining twenty-nine numbers (No. 97 to 125) were presumably finished almost immediately thereafter. The few autographs about which it has been possible to collect positive

[7]Fryklund points out that this reference to "pieces such as may be played on the gamba" need not refer to compositions for the baryton, as Pohl assumes. In one instance, however, Haydn distinguishes bowed and pizzicato passages in a baryton part by marking the one "gamba," the other "pariton," and when Pohl writes (I, 254) "once gamba and baryton alternate" he has, no doubt, some similar instance in mind. It appears, then, that the term "gamba" was sometimes applied to the baryton, so that Pohl's assumption is perhaps justified after all.

information bear out these claims: Divertimento 24 is dated "1766," Divertimento 41 "1767," Divertimenti 79 and 80 "1769," and Divertimento 106 (really 105) "1772."[8] None of the one hundred and twenty-five divertimenti was published in its original form, though many of them circulated in manuscript and, as I shall show later, in printed and manuscript arrangements for other trio combinations. Their existence thus became generally known, as is evident from Burney's statement, in 1789, that Haydn "is said at Vienna to have composed before 1782, a hundred and twenty-four pieces for the *bariton,* for the use of his prince, who is partial to that instrument, and a great performer on it." But just as certain of the baryton divertimenti were later arranged for various combinations of three instruments, so other numbers appear to be themselves arrangements of earlier works for string trio.[9]

A general impression prevails that Haydn's compositions for the baryton have been lost. In 1904 no less an authority than Sir William Henry Hadow informed us that "this vast mass of music has wholly disappeared, except three divertimenti [*i.e.* cassations] and a few inconsiderable fragments."[10] Actually, more than half has been preserved. If we may still rely on Pohl's statements, made

[8]The autograph of Divertimento 24 was advertised by the Berlin dealer Paul Gottschalk in 1930 (*A Collection of Original Manuscripts,* pp. 11–12); that of Divertimento 41 is listed in the catalogue of the Artaria collection (Vienna, 1893) as No. 24. Neither manuscript is mentioned by Pohl (I, 255(. The three he does mention (Divertimenti 79, 80, and 106) belonged at one time to the Viennese composer J. N. Kafka (1819–1886), purveyor of fashionable piano-music and notorious autograph-hunter; they are described in a catalogue of Kafka's collection (Paris, 1881) as No. 27 and 28. The autograph of Divertimento 106, which sold at the Kafka sale for 245 francs, has changed hands several times since 1900; it was last advertised by the Vienna dealer V. A. Heck in 1927 (Catalogue 39, No. 16) at 3,000 Swiss francs! The Heck and Gottschalk catalogues contain facsimiles of Haydn's manuscript.

[9]This is evidently the case with Divertimenti 6, 7, 9, 11, and 17; according to Breitkopf's thematic catalogue for 1772, these numbers are from the six string trios assigned by Pohl (I, 230) to the years 1761 and '62 and published as six sonatas for flute, violin, and bass by Hummel of Amsterdam (Op. 11). The fifth of Hummel's sonatas is an arrangement of movements from a divertimento in G major (Haydn's catalogue, Divertimento 9 "a sei"), published about 1767 as a symphony for five instruments by La Chevardière of Paris (Op. 4, No. 2), listed as a cassation for nine instruments in Breitkopf's thematic catalogue for 1768, and attributed to Michael Haydn by Perger (*Denkmäler der Tonkunst in Österreich,* XIV, 2. Teil).

[10]*The Oxford History of Music,* V, 41.

more than fifty years ago, the duets (with one exception), the sonatas, the concertos, and certain of the cassations have indeed been lost. It is often said that this loss is a result of the fire at Esterház in 1779. But so many of the divertimenti for baryton, viola, and bass have survived, in their original form or in arrangements for other instruments, that it should be a comparatively easy matter to trace the development this type received from first to last at Haydn's hands.

The principal manuscript sources are four:

1. the manuscripts in the archives of the Esterhazy family, formerly at Eisenstadt, now in Budapest;[11]
2. the autographs and copies in the collection formed by the Artaria family of Vienna, acquired in 1897 by Erich Prieger of Bonn and ceded by him in 1901 to the Staatsbibliothek in Berlin;[12]
3. the copies in the archives of the "Gesellschaft der Musikfreunde" in Vienna;[13] and
4. the copies in the collection formed by the Boccherini biog-

[11]Together with the original manuscript of Haydn's catalogue, one autograph from this collection—a divertimento in G major for baryton, viola, and bass (1767) —was exhibited at the "Internationale Ausstellung für Musik- und Theaterwesen," in *Fach-Katalog der Musikhistorischen Abteilung von Deutschland und Österreich-Ungarn* (Vienna, 1832), pp. 262 and 263.

[12]Catalogue (Vienna, 1893), No. 23, 24, 31, 32, and 56. The Haydn manuscripts in this collection were purchased by Domenico Artaria from Elssler in the 1830's; many of them are listed in Elssler's catalogue of Haydn's library ("J. Haydn's Verzeichniss musicalischer Werke theils eigner, theils fremder Composition"), a manuscript now in the British Museum (MS. Add. 32,070).

One hundred and seven trios for various combinations, put into score after the Artaria manuscripts, and including seventy-five divertimenti for baryton, viola, and bass, were disposed of at the sale of the third part of Prieger's private library, Cologne, July 15, 1924 (Catalogue, III, No. 257).

[13]Dr. Victor Luithlen, of the "Gesellschaft der Musikfreunde," informs me that the Society's archives contain only two of the divertimenti in their original form (No. 105 and 109) and twenty-four arrangements, some in contemporary French editions, most of them in old manuscript parts or in scores prepared by Pohl.

Gerber writes that the catalogue issued in 1799 by the Vienna publisher Traeg lists seventy-two divertimenti for baryton, viola, and bass, and, according to Dr. Hermann von Hase, Elssler made copies of all of these for Breitkopf & Härtel. (*Joseph Haydn und Breitkopf & Härtel*, p. 58.) I learn from Dr. Wilhelm Hitzig, Breitkopf & Härtel archivist, that these copies, presumably made for commercial purposes, are no longer in the possession of the firm.

rapher Louis Picquot of Bar-le-Duc, acquired in 1906 by the Library of Congress in Washington.

The manuscripts of the Picquot collection include eighty-two of Haydn's numbered divertimenti for baryton, viola, and bass (thirty-four in their original form, forty-eight in arrangements for other instruments), an unrecorded divertimento in D major for the same combination (not listed in Haydn's catalogue or mentioned by Pohl), and the twelve little divertimenti for two barytons and bass. There are also twenty-four trios for various combinations of string and wind instruments (eleven of them listed neither by Haydn nor by Pohl) and a nine-part divertimento in C major (Haydn's catalogue, Divertimento 17).

Two memoranda prepared by the late Eusebius Mandyczewski, former archivist of the "Gesellschaft der Musikfreunde" and editor-in-chief of the definitive edition of Haydn's works, enable me to state with some assurance that at least one hundred and one of Haydn's one hundred and twenty-five numbered divertimenti for baryton, viola, and bass are still preserved (in their original form or in arrangement) and that as many as eleven of these may be preserved only at the Library of Congress. In 1893, Mahillon published a list of the baryton pieces then known to have survived, locating the manuscripts in the Esterhazy archives, in the archives of the "Gesellschaft der Musikfreunde," and in Mandyczewski's private collection, and citing Mandyczewski as the source of his information. This first list names one duet and ninety divertimenti (by key); curiously enough, the Artaria collection is not mentioned.[14] In 1907, on receiving a thematic catalogue of the Picquot material compiled by the late O. G. Sonneck, then Chief of the Music Division of the Library of Congress, Mandyczewski submitted a list of the manuscripts to be copied for the definitive edition. This second list names sixteen items—among others, the unrecorded divertimento mentioned above; twelve of them are diver-

[14] *Catalogue descriptif & analytique du Musée instrumental du Conservatoire royal de musique de Bruxelles,* I (2nd ed.), 326. Misinterpretation of Mahillon's list is responsible, it appears, for the ambiguous or incorrect statements regarding the holdings of the "Gesellschaft der Musikfreunde" in Kinsky's catalogue of the Heyer collection (II, 500, note 2), in Van der Straeten's *History of the Violoncello* (I, 24), and in Riemann's *Musik-Lexikon* (8th ed., 1916, and following editions).

timenti for baryton, viola, and bass (three in their original form, nine in arrangement). The Library of Congress is accordingly in the enviable position of owning the unique copies of a considerable number of Haydn's unpublished works, one of them a work not recorded by his biographers. It is to be presumed that other sources for some of these compositions have been discovered during the twenty-five years since Mandyczewski's list was compiled; that all of them have been duplicated is at least improbable.

Antoine Vidal wrote in 1878 of a collection of chamber-music in the possession of Louis Labitte of Rheims which contained ninety-three string trios by Haydn, "authentiques, manuscrits et inédits." Among them were the manuscripts of twenty-four baryton divertimenti.[15] Despite certain obvious discrepancies it is, I think, difficult to avoid concluding that the Picquot and Labitte collections were one and the same. Vidal's references to other rarities in the Labitte collection—notably to unpublished works by Boccherini, Gaetano Brunetti, and Cambini, composers in whom Picquot was particularly interested—tend to confirm this identification, for manuscripts bearing the stamp of Picquot's library and corresponding more or less closely to some of Vidal's specifications were acquired by the Library of Congress at the time of the Haydn purchase. If further corroboration is needed, Vidal's comment on the Labitte manuscripts of the baryton divertimenti supplies it. "Ils sont d'autant plus précieux," he writes, "que ce sont des copies authentiques et uniques d'originaux brûlés dans un incendie qui dévora le palais du prince." The most interesting of the Picquot manuscripts, a set of parts in oblong quarto bearing the general title "24 Divertimenti à Pariton, Viola e Basso Del Sig: Giuseppe Haydn, N: i," is indeed an "authentic copy." Though these parts do not have the characteristic Esterhazy binding and are probably not from the Prince's library, they are unquestionably the work of some one of Haydn's own copyists.[16] The handwriting agrees per-

[15] *Les instruments à archet,* III, cxiii, cxxiii, cxxvi, and cxxvii.

[16] Pohl (I, 255, note 46) describes a manuscript with the general title "XXIV Divertimenti per il Pariton col Viola e Basso, Tom. II," dedicated to Prince Nicholas himself. The individual parts, handsomely bound in red leather and gilt edged, are enclosed in a leather case. The manuscript contains Divertimenti 73 to 96; the notation "Tom. II" points, as Pohl says, to the existence of a first volume. Of this

fectly with that in another Library of Congress manuscript (from the Martorell collection, acquired in 1909)—the presentation copy of Haydn's opera *L'Isola disabitata,* sent by the composer himself (probably in 1781) to Charles IV of Spain, then Principe d'Asturias[17]—positively establishing the source of the Picquot manuscript of the divertimenti and pointing to the year 1780 as the approximate date when it was copied.

The period to which Haydn's compositions for baryton belong is surely one of the most interesting of his long career: it is the period during which the foundation of his later reputation was laid; during which the works of his first maturity were written; during which he ceased to feel the influence of his lesser contemporaries and, abandoning their conventions, became himself a determining influence in the career of the younger Mozart. Entering the Esterhazy service in 1761 an almost unknown musician (his first "opera," *Der neue krumme Teufel,* produced in 1751 or '52, had been withdrawn after two performances, his first position as director of Count Morzin's orchestra in Lucavek had been terminated abruptly in 1760, a year or two after his appointment), Haydn began at once to attract attention, not only in Vienna, but in other musical centers. In 1763, Breitkopf's catalogues announce eight "quadros" and six trios for strings, with two concertos and a divertimento for the harpsichord, as available in manuscript; from the same year dates one of the earliest notices of Haydn on record, a manuscript note in Martin Schweyer's interleaved copy of Walther's *Lexikon,* now in the Library of Congress: "Hayden, an incomparable musi-

---

first volume the Picquot manuscript, marked "N: i" and containing Divertimenti 49 to 72, is obviously a copy.

With material from the libraries of J. B. Cartier, James E. Matthew, and F. W. Rust, the printed and manuscript music of the Picquot collection was sold by the firm of Liepmannssohn in Berlin between 1904 and '08 and is described in the Liepmannssohn catalogues 154, 157, 167, and 169. The Haydn manuscripts now in the Library of Congress are not mentioned, though Catalogue 169 includes two collections of divertimenti for baryton, viola, and bass (Nos. 170 and 679)— twenty-four by Burgsteiner, a member of the Esterhazy orchestra from 1766 to 1790, and twenty-four by Neumann. These two collections have the characteristic Esterhazy binding, and Fryklund suggests, on p. 149 of the article already cited, that they may have belonged at one time to the Prince's library.

[17]Pohl, II, 100, 181.

cian and composer, lives in Vienna and distinguishes himself in the writing of fine quartets, trios, and symphonies."[18] The first recorded publication of a work of Haydn's occurred in March of the following year, when the Paris publisher Venier advertised an edition of one of the early quartets in his series "Sinfonie a più Stromenti Composte da Vari Autori" (Opera Decima Quarta) under the title "Les noms inconnus bons à connoitre" (Unknown names worth knowing) in company with compositions by Van Maldere, Beck, Pfeiffer, Schetky, and Fränzl. By 1775 a formidable array of Haydn's sonatas, duos, trios, quartets, and symphonies had been engraved (apparently without the composer's authorization!) in Paris, Amsterdam, and London; the Vienna editions began in 1774 with Kurtzböck's printing of six sonatas. As early as 1766 Haydn is mentioned in magazines published in Leipzig and Hamburg, while in Vienna he was already being called "the darling of our nation." So universal, in fact, was the recognition accorded Haydn by the end of this period that in responding in 1776 to a request for an autobiographical sketch he could write: "In my chamber music I have had the good fortune to please almost everywhere, save in Berlin!"

Successively considered, the compositions of the decade 1765 to '75 reveal Haydn's steadily increasing mastery of form and content. Not satisfied with the facile polish of his fourth series of quartets (Op. 9, 1769), he strove in those that followed toward greater refinement of workmanship, toward more intense formal concentration, toward the suppression of the episodic and conventional (Op. 17, 1771), resorting in the last series written during this period (Op. 20, 1772) to time-honored contrapuntal devices to enhance the interest and insure the balance of his texture. At the same time Haydn contrived to give his music a more individual note. Wyzewa and Saint-Foix draw attention to certain particularly striking examples of this tendency in the works of the early 70's—the C-minor Piano Sonata, the Quartets Op. 20 ("à la fois pathétiques et savants"), the "Trauersymphonie," the "Farewell" Symphony—and speak of the year 1772 as the "romantic crisis" of

<hr>

[18]"Hayden ein unvergleichlicher Musicus und Componist der sich in Wien aufhält und in sonderheit schöne Quartetten Trios u. Sinfonien macht, 1763."

Haydn's artistic career. A year or two later, the same writers tell us, still another change took place in Haydn's manner. Now he surrenders to the "galant" style, and henceforward his principal aim is to impress us agreeably or to amuse us with ingenious turns of musical rhetoric. For a fuller understanding of the development of Haydn's style, and of the Viennese classical style in general, it should be well worth determining to what extent these several trends can be traced in the baryton divertimenti written during the same eventful years, for it is clear that this music played an important part in shaping the ultimate character of Haydn's writing. "Haydn informed me," Carpani reports, "that his compositions for that instrument [the baryton] had cost him much trouble, but that the experience had been of great value to him later in writing for other instruments." And in much the same vein Pohl observes: "The composition of so many of these miniatures would have rendered a less gifted writer incapable of anything better, yet it is precisely here that Haydn seems to have acquired his assurance, his progressive outlook, and, above all, his invaluable capacity for moderation, the quality which we today prize especially in all his works."

The term "divertimento," as Bossler says in his *Elementarbuch der Tonkunst* (1782), is a generic name, applicable to a number of forms, but commonly applied to the cyclic sonata for one or more instruments. Haydn often uses it, particularly during his early period, applying it indiscriminately to solos and ensemble pieces for harpsichord and to chamber music for various combinations of string and wind instruments. It would be virtually impossible to frame a definition broad enough to cover all these compositions, and it is clear that the character and purpose of a piece of music, not its form and instrumentation, decided Haydn's choice of title. His divertimenti—agreeable trifles, hastily written to order—have, generally speaking, only passing interest, apart from the light they throw on the development of his style; for his more serious, more significant work on a small scale he prefers such terms as "sonata," "trio," and "quartet."

In divertimenti for larger combinations Haydn sometimes allows himself as many as nine movements, but those for the baryton are limited, as a rule, to three.[19] Every one of them includes a minuet, now as second movement, now as third; some one of the conventional sonata-movements (generally the Adagio) is almost always sacrificed. When the variation form is used it always appears at the beginning. As regards the type, number, and order of the movements involved, there is, then, no very striking difference between Haydn's divertimenti for baryton and his trios for two violins and bass.[20]

Yet if style is "the outcome of the instinct for adaptation," as Parry has it, we should not expect the similarity between these two groups of compositions to extend beyond an external similarity of form. And in reality they have less in common than appears at first glance. In the divertimenti Haydn writes, not for two instruments of one kind and a third of another, but for three different instruments, each with its peculiar possibilities and limitations. It seems highly probable that the experience he gained in handling this problem in the divertimenti may have helped him to free himself from the conventional texture of the classical trio-sonata with its inevitable imitations and sequences. In the divertimenti, again, Haydn writes, not for soprano and bass instruments, but for instruments confined to the alto, tenor, and bass registers. The effect of this restriction is twofold. On the one hand it obliges him to keep his instrumental voices fairly close together, so that there is not the same need for the harpsichord background as in the trios, where the gap between the violin parts and the bass is often painfully noticeable. On the other hand it encourages him to cross his instrumental voices, so that any one of the three instruments may (and often does) take over the functions proper to either of the others. The divertimenti, finally, are not chamber-music in the accepted sense of the word, but accompanied solos. Prince Nicholas was no democrat where music was concerned and cared little about sharing honors with the professional musicians who assisted him. "In

[19]Divertimenti 2 and 31, with four movements, and Divertimento 97, with seven, are the only exceptions I have noted.

[20]The six trios published by La Chevardière of Paris as Op. 5, by Hummel of Amsterdam as Op. 8, are now available in a modern reprint (Edition Peters, edited by A. Gülzow and W. Weismann). Trio 5 (Pohl, I, 346, No. 18) is not listed in Haydn's catalogue and has been claimed for Michael Haydn by Perger.

future, write solos only in my part," he is reported to have said to the 'cellist Anton Kraft, who courted favor with an occasional composition for his employer's instrument. "It is your duty to play better than I do, and you deserve no credit for it."[21] Haydn doubtless felt an obligation to exploit the baryton at the expense of viola and bass and often does so, though in many movements the three parts are about equally interesting. The instrument has its proper idiom, and there are few divertimenti in which Haydn does not make some use of it. The employment of this idiom gives these pieces what indivduality they have and distinguishes them, even in arrangement, from Haydn's other three-part writing.

Pohl, in speaking of the early quartets, has remarked on the care Haydn lavishes on the trios of his minuets, movements for which the composer appears to have entertained a special affection. In the divertimenti it is at this point that the possibilities of the baryton are regularly displayed. One example of this has already been given. I add here three others: (a) from Divertimento 61, where the baryton supplies a pizzicato bass to the melody played in octaves by bass and viola; (b) from Divertimento 57, where the baryton is contrasted as melody instrument with the viola, as accompanying instrument with the bass; and (c) from a divertimento without number (the apparently unrecorded divertimento previously referred to), where the baryton is used to provide a sort of echo effect.

The disposition of the instruments at (a) is quite usual; such writing has a very odd appearance in arrangement, the baryton bass being commonly assigned to violin or flute. At (c) the fourth sympathetic string has obviously to be tuned to F natural. It will be noted that, even in moderately rapid passages, the metal strings are generally used consecutively and in ascending sequence. Skips and descending passages evidently presented serious technical difficulty. Herein lies perhaps one explanation of the often-repeated statement that certain figures are impracticable on the baryton and that music for it must be specially arranged.[22]

---

[21]Pohl, I, 252–253.
[22]Compare Greilsamer's article, p. 56.

Effects of this kind are also to be found, of course, in the other movements of the divertimento cycle. The Allegros are sometimes based on subjects that lend themselves naturally to performance on the plucked strings (Divertimento 64); the same applies to the fugues that are occasionally made to serve as Finales (Divertimento 67). In the Adagios the baryton often assumes the role of the bass, leaving that instrument free for an inner part, an accompaniment figure, or a fragment of the melody. This is admirably illustrated in Divertimento 56:[23]

[23]Together with movements from other baryton divertimenti, this Adagio has recently been published after an interesting contemporary arrangement for viola d'amore, violin, and violoncello (see the list of modern editions at the end of this article). The two versions should be compared. In arrangement, the composition

Limitations of space prevent my quoting further examples in this connection—of the narrower application of the principle of contrast (Divertimento 106, Moderato, Variation 3); of the use of the baryton's plucked strings in conjunction with the pizzicati of viola and bass (Divertimento 66, Adagio); or of the technical display of the baryton (alternation of plucked and bowed notes, double stops) in variations (Divertimenti 60 and 69).

In the divertimenti, then—and, for that matter, in any similar group of compositions—texture and thematic material are more or less dependent on instrumentation. Yet this music ought not to be considered from the point of view of instrumentation alone; instrumentation has exerted no real influence on its form, and a discussion that leaves form out of account will contribute little to our understanding of Haydn's development. To be sure, his treat-

has gained somewhat in sonority, thanks to the figuration and double-stopping indicated for the viola d'amore; its general disposition, however, is so obviously conditioned by the combination of instruments for which it was conceived that the original is aesthetically more satisfying.

ment of form remains essentially the same (within a given period), regardless of the instrument or combination of instruments for which he writes. The divertimenti, however, comprising as they do a wealth of homogeneous material, chronologically arranged and precisely dated—all of it pertaining to a single decade within Haydn's formative period—constitute a truly ideal field for investigation.

Nowhere is the continuity of Haydn's early work more strikingly attested than in his treatment of the variation form. Wherever he uses it during the period under discussion, its outward appearance is exactly the same.[24] His themes are regularly in duple time (2/4) and rest on a ground bass (often a chaconne formula) which is repeated without essential change as many times as there are variations. His variations are either (1) fresh, more or less individualized counterpoints to the bass, without special reference to the theme itself, or (2) simple, melodic embellishments of the theme, suggesting the type of variation commonly identified with Mozart. The "minore," an inevitable ingredient of Haydn's later variations, is rarely introduced. The last variation is generally a repetition of the theme in its original form, sometimes with an accompaniment more elaborate than that which attended its first statement. In the Quartet Op. 20, No. 4, this is followed by a well-developed, independent coda, but if the divertimenti include examples of this procedure I have failed to notice them.

Yet the divertimenti do afford ample justification for saying that, within the limits prescribed in the preceding paragraph, Haydn's treatment of the variation form gained in breadth and interest during the few years that concern us here. What is more, they anticipate certain progressive features of the quartet variations written at this time. Haydn's growing resourcefulness manifests itself notably in the freedom with which he manages the ground bass. In the earlier divertimenti, as in the earlier quartets, the repetitions of the ground bass are literal. Varied repetition of the ground bass occurs for the first time in Divertimento 60 (ca. 1768)

[24]Compare the variations in Piano Sonata 15 and Symphony 31 (Definitive edition); in Piano Trio 26 (Edition Peters); in the string-quartets Op. 2, No. 6; Op. 3, No. 2: Op. 9, No. 5; Op. 17, No. 3; and Op. 20, No. 4; and in the Quartet Op. 5, No. 4, for flute and strings.

and in the Quartet Op. 9, No. 5 (1769), as a means of heightening the interest of the last variation (the Da capo) in Divertimento 95 (ca. 1770) and in the Quartet Op. 17, No. 3 (1771). The next step is to abandon the convention restricting the ground bass to the bass; in the second variation in Divertimento 106 (ca. 1772) it is assigned to the baryton, in the second variation in the Quartet Op. 20, No. 4 (1772), to the viola. I find no parallel in the quartets to the variations in Divertimento 111, where the ground bass is divided between bass and baryton in the theme and in each of the variations that follow:

Haydn's early variations, conforming as they do to a single, very simple type, lend themselves admirably to comparative analysis. His first essays in sonata form, on the other hand, are relatively heterogeneous. The diversity of the thematic material involved and the elasticity of the form itself discourage regularity; the conventions of the form had not yet become firmly fixed, and its organization varied, not only with the individual school, but with the individual master and even with the individual work. An attempt to reduce the "first movements" of the divertimenti to a formula, or rather to a series of formulas, would make hard reading. Particular interest attaches, however, to Haydn's management of certain specific problems the form presents—the disposition of the "development" and reprise—and a discussion of their solution in the divertimenti, with reference to other works written at this time, will perhaps prove more valuable than general observations.

The "development," in the divertimenti, may begin with a more or less independent episode, but as often as not a literal restatement of the principal subject in the new key (dominant or relative major) follows the double bar. In a number of the early divertimenti this episode or restatement, filling only two or, at the most, four bars, is all that separates exposition and reprise; under these conditions the reprise is conveniently termed "premature." As a rule, however, the "development" attains quite respectable proportions. The general modulatory trend is toward the relative minor, and in about one divertimento in four the section closes with an emphatic cadence in this key, followed by a brief retransition.

Curious and extremely characteristic is the innocent deception Haydn practices on his audience in some of these movements, interrupting the regular course of the "development" by a statement of the principal subject in the original key. This interruption creates the illusion of reprise only to shatter it abruptly by returning at once to the normal order. Wyzewa and Saint-Foix cite Mozart's early use of this "more or less comic device" as evidence of his sensitivity to the influence of Haydn and his Viennese contemporaries. Perhaps its employment was more general than has been alleged; for the purposes of this discussion, however, it is enough that Haydn resorts to it repeatedly in the divertimenti and in other works of the period. An outstanding example of such a "false" reprise (fausse rentrée) occurs in the first movement of the Quartet Op. 17, No. 1 (1771); Haydn's everyday use of the device, illustrated in the first movements of the Quartets Op. 20, Nos. 1 and 4 (1772), is decidedly less effective. In the divertimenti it occurs in every third or fourth number, beginning with Divertimento 7 (1761 or '62), and often follows immediately on the preliminary restatement of the principal subject in the dominant.

The "true" reprise, in the divertimenti, is complete unless anticipated in the "development" by a "false" reprise; under these conditions it may be somewhat abbreviated, beginning now with the second phrase of the principal subject, now with the transition.

We are confronted, then, with two irregular and relatively primitive methods of arrangement in "development" and reprise:

a. transposed restatement, or episode—"premature" reprise (complete);
b. transposed restatement, or episode—"false" reprise—"development" proper—"true" reprise (incomplete).

The actual result is very much the same, whether method (a) or method (b) is applied, and the distinction is largely a matter of proportion and of the presence or absence of proper "development." Method (a) is chiefly employed in the early divertimenti. Method (b), on the other hand, occurs in late as well as early numbers of the series (Divertimenti 117 and 14); its application is well illustrated in the first movement of the Quartet Op. 1, No. 2.[25]

In accepting such sterile mannerisms as the "false" reprise, Haydn defers to the conventions of his time. In other respects, his treatment of sonata form in the divertimenti is distinctly progressive. The modification of the beginning of the reprise in the second movement of Divertimento 88 (ca. 1769), for instance, foreshadows the management of this detail in the best work of Beethoven and Brahms:

Divertimento 88
Allegro   (After an arrangement for violin, viola, and bass)

[25]Sandberger's analysis of this movement (in his *Gesammelte Aufsätze,* I, 257) implies the following proportions: exposition—47 bars; "development" (episode) —8 bars; reprise (complete)—73 bars. As I see it, the "development" (episode, "false" reprise, and "development" proper) comprises 37 bars, the "true" reprise 44.

Jalowetz[26] has quoted a similar passage from the Finale in the Quartet Op. 9, No. 3 (1769). To be sure, the two examples are not strictly parallel. In both cases, however, a desire to give point to the reprise is evident.

It would not be very difficult to pursue this analysis further, taking up one by one the other forms used in the divertimenti, determining the laws that govern their organization, measuring the advance Haydn made in his treatment of them during the period under discussion, and relating them to his other writing in these forms at this time. Yet such further analysis could but confirm what has perhaps been sufficiently demonstrated already—that on the formal side Haydn's early writing is consistent without being un-imaginative, that it steadily becomes more fluent and more individual, and that the same evidences of progress appear simultaneously in each department of his instrumental music. For this reason I shall confine myself, in speaking of the Adagios, Minuets, and Finales, to the quotation of certain singularly characteristic examples.

The Adagios, for all their insistence on the idealized dance-forms of the trio-sonata (notably the Siciliano) tend to corroborate Wyzewa and Saint-Foix's theory that Haydn attained, about 1772, a "romantic" intensity of expression unsurpassed in his later writing. The first movement of Divertimento 96 (ca. 1770) is a case in point:

Divertimento 96
Largo   (After an arrangement for violin, viola, and bass)

[26]"Beethoven's Jugendwerke in ihren melodischen Beziehungen zu Mozart, Haydn und Ph. E. Bach," *Sammelbände der Internationalen Musik-Gesellschaft,* XII (1910–11), 417–474.

It is no mere coincidence that Haydn reverts, in the opening bars of this Largo, to the language, if not to the form, of the classical chaconne; throughout this period the "romantic" impulse which gave birth to the magnificent fugues in the Quartets Op. 20 leads him to resort, again and again, to the idiom of an earlier day. Since for Haydn emotional intensity is closely associated with the use of the minor mode, the baryton divertimenti, written for an instrument limited in practice to the commonest major keys, include fewer "romantic" movements than might otherwise have been the case. But in major, too, Haydn manages now and then, as in Divertimento 117 (after 1772), to achieve a distinctly individual type of expression:

[27]For evidence of the extent of Haydn's technical and temperamental development during his first years at Eisenstadt and Esterház, this example need only be
compared with the Adagio in Divertimento 1 (before 1765), recently published
after a contemporary arrangement for violoncello obbligato, violin, and bass.

Haydn indulges his fondness for the grotesque and bizarre in the
Quartet Op. 20, No. 4 (1772), with a "Minuetto—Allegretto alla
zingarese," in Piano Sonata 26 (1774) with a "Menuetto al ro-
vescio," carrying this tendency toward caricature to an extreme in
Divertimento 52 (ca. 1768) with a deliberately eccentric "Menuetto alla zoppa" (Limping Minuet) and "Trio al contrario":

Elsewhere, particularly in the Trios, he turns to contrapuntal refinements as a relief from the conventional minuet-style. It may as well be admitted here, however, that the strictly contrapuntal movements in the divertimenti do not reveal Haydn in a very favorable light. The "Canone in diapente" which serves as Minuet and Trio in Divertimento 94 (ca. 1770) seems to me distinctly inferior to other examples of this kind in the symphonies (No. 23 and 44) and piano sonatas (No. 25) of the period, and since this minuet is already available in modern edition, I prefer to quote a specimen of free contrapuntal writing—the Trio of the Minuet in Divertimento 84 (ca. 1769):

Divertimento 84
Trio
Allegretto   (After an arrangement for violin, viola, and bass)

Uninteresting enough in itself, Haydn's use of the fugue in the divertimenti acquires a certain reflected interest because of the prominent place he assigns to this form in the Quartets Op. 20. The most ambitious (and least felicitous) of these essays is the Finale in Divertimento 101; its heading, "Fuga a 3 sogetti in contrapuncto doppio," suggests a real connection with the double, triple, and quadruple quartet-fugues, but arouses expectations that remain unfulfilled. This movement and other similar movements in the divertimenti are in no wise compatible with the corresponding movements in the quartets, and if the fugue in Divertimento 101 is taken as fairly representative of the sort of counterpoint Haydn could write on the spur of the moment in 1772, it follows that the fugues in the Quartets Op. 20, which date from the same year, cannot have been written without long, continuous, and determined application.

In 1780 the firm of Artaria in Vienna brought out the first of a long series of publications devoted to Haydn's works—the original edition of his "Sei Sonate per il Clavicembalo, o Forte Piano," Op. 30. A curious feature of this edition is the following "Avertimento," drafted by Haydn himself and designed to forestall malicious criticism injurious to the sale of the work:

> Among these sonatas are two movements which begin with the same theme, namely the Allegretto scherzando of Sonata I and the Allegro con brio of Sonata V. The composer explains in advance that he has done this purposely, modifying the continuation of the movement in each case.[28]

The baryton divertimenti afford further evidence of the pleasure Haydn took in such "second versions." In the first movement of Divertimento 4 an episode from Divertimento 3 is worked over and extended; the second subject of the Allegro in Divertimento 82 is a revision of the parallel passage in Divertimento 80. An idea developed in the second of the twelve little divertimenti for two barytons and bass recurs in the Trio of the Minuet in Divertimento 35 and again in Piano Sonata 36, one of the six sonatas already referred to in this connection. The Allegro in Divertimento 64 (ca. 1768) affords what is perhaps the sole example of a connection between the baryton divertimenti and the symphonies. This movement, obviously the beginning of the "Alleluja" Divertimento mentioned by Pohl,[29] is a sort of gloss on the Allegro in the "Alleluja" Symphony 30 (1765); the thematic material of the two movements is exactly the same, its development quite different,

---

[28]Haydn's original draft read somewhat differently; see Artaria and Botstiber, *Joseph Haydn und das Verlagshaus Artaria* (Vienna, 1909), pp. 8 10.

[29]I, 254.

except for two intentionally parallel passages. But the Trios of the Minuets in Divertimenti 89 and 91 provide the most arresting example of this practice. Pohl, without mentioning its derivation from an earlier number of the series, quotes the "second-version"[30] as "an example of the charming movements these unassuming divertimenti contain." The exquisite refinement of the little movement is the more apparent when it is compared with the "primitive version":

Such deliberate parallels as these point, not to the poverty of Haydn's invention, but to his ability to recognize, in a single theme, a wealth of possibilities. Indeed, his store of ideas must have been almost unlimited if he could afford to throw away charming thoughts and ingenious turns of phrase on "occasional compositions" for the idle entertainment of his patron. Though the greater part of Haydn's music for the baryton never became widely known he turned surprisingly little of it to practical account, to judge from the few traces it has left in his work in other fields. Päsler has pointed out that the opening Andantino of Divertimento 37 (in G) is also utilized as the opening Allegro of Piano Sonata 3 (in C).[31] Yet in this instance it is, as Päsler says, impossible to determine which of the two versions is the original. The identity of the theme of the Variations in Divertimento 38 (in A) and the "Il Maestro e lo Scolare" Variations (in F) for piano four-hands has been noted

[30]II, 306–307.
[31]Definitive edition, Serie 14, Bd. I, p. xx.

by Weigl.[32] Here the version for the baryton (ca. 1767) is clearly
the original, unless Pohl's date for the piano four-hand version
(1778) is open to question. Divertimento 111 reappears in
Haydn's catalogue as Cassation 14 for baryton and four other
instruments ("a cinque"); Divertimento 114 is also to be found
under this rubric as Cassation 6. "[In 1781], on the Prince's return
from Paris, where he had been delayed somewhat longer than
usual . . . he was greeted with a chorus in G major (2/4), 'Al tuo
arrivo felice' adapted by Haydn from a movement of one of his
baryton trios [Divertimento 116, Allegretto], obviously a favorite
with the Prince. In the same way the Prince's recovery from illness
was celebrated on another occasion with a baryton piece in D major
(3/4) [Divertimento 115, Adagio], accommodated to the text 'Dei
clementi.' "[33]

In admitting to Carpani that the composition of his music for the
baryton had proved a valuable experience, Haydn has given us his
own estimate. These pieces, after all, were laboratory experiments,
intended for private performance only. Haydn retained a fatherly
interest in them, listing them in the catalogue of 1805 and keeping
a careful record of the copies in his possession, but seems to have
considered them unsuited for publication. If a number of them
were published during his lifetime, this generally took place without his knowledge or consent; the arrangements in which they
appeared were, for the most part, the work of others,[34] and we
have no way of knowing that they had his approval.

> Haydn was not responsible for all the editions in which his works
> were published [Dies tells us in his *Biographische Nachrichten* (Vienna,
> 1810)]. Many of his compositions, the first ones not excepted, have
> suffered all sorts of transformations at the hands of speculators. Even
> today there is trouble between Haydn and a nameless individual who
> obtained possession of certain of Haydn's early works and has never

[32]*Handbuch der Violoncell-Literatur,* 3rd ed. (1929), p. 70. A parallel case is
Haydn's set of "favorite variations" for piano two-hands (1774) on the Minuet in
the Quartet Op. 9, No. 2 (1769).

[33]Pohl, II, 191.

[34]Päsler (Definitive edition, Serie 14, Bd. I, p. xx) speaks of the arrangement
of Simrock's "Six Trios à l'usage des comançans" as "schwerlich von Haydn selbst
verfasst."

returned them to their rightful owner. These works, written for the baryton, were favorites of the late Prince Nicholas Esterhazy.

We know, however, of one authorized edition of selections from the baryton pieces—Artaria's "Six Divertissements à 8 Parties Concertantes," Op. 31 (Vienna, 1781), five of which are arranged from the cassations for baryton with other instruments, the baryton part assigned to a flute. And we have reason to believe that single movements from one of the divertimenti for baryton, viola, and bass also appeared in an authorized edition. The divertimento in question is No. 97, the seven-movement divertimento written, according to Pohl, in honor of the Prince's birthday; the edition is Forster's "Six Trios for Two Violins and a Violoncello or German Flute," Op. 38 (London, 1785?).[35]

Haydn's style underwent a remarkable change (or series of changes) during the decade 1765 to '75, and, as I have tried to show, this change is no less remarkable when measured in the baryton divertimenti than when measured in the string-quartets or in any of the other forms he cultivated. The exact nature and extent of this change cannot be understood fully unless his entire production is taken into account; since the divertimenti fill in for us what would otherwise be breaks in the chain of development it is almost imperative that they be given careful consideration. If they are the conscientious handiwork of an honest craftsman rather than the spontaneous creations of an inspired artist, the craftsman keeps pace with the artist—and sometimes anticipates him. Even were we no longer able to accept the divertimenti at their face-value, they would still hold for us the peculiar interest that attaches to every study and every sketch by the master whose influence on his con-

[35]The immediate source of Forster's Op. 38 appears to have been a manuscript bearing the title "Sei Divertimenti a tre, Violino 1mo o Flauto Traver., Violino 2do, e Violoncello" (British Museum MS. Egerton 2379, ff. 125–148), written by Haydn's copyist Radnitzky and signed by the composer himself. These divertimenti were sent to Forster for publication on May 31, 1784; for their copyright, with that of nine symphonies and six sonatas, Haydn received £70, a very fair price, considering that some of this music had already been published on the continent. To judge from the description of the "Sei Divertimenti" in the catalogue of manuscript music in the British Museum (III, 198), they are the same as those recently reprinted by Zimmermann of Leipzig as Op. 100. The fourth number of Zimmermann's series is a transposed arrangement of Divertimento 97.

temporaries and successors was so marked, whose style, as Gerber says, became "a universal ideal."

When Haydn's compositions for the baryton are published in the definitive edition, with appropriate critical and bibliographic comment, this article will have fulfilled its purpose. Until then it should serve, despite its obvious limitations, to make this music a little more accessible to musicians in general than it has been in the past. A number of the problems it presents remain unsolved. That these unsolved problems are not more numerous is due, in large part, to friends and correspondents in Europe and in this country who have generously placed their time and their experience at my disposal —to Professor Otto Erich Deutsch and Dr. Victor Luithlen, of Vienna; to Dr. Wilhelm Hitzig, archivist to the firm of Breitkopf & Härtel in Leipzig; to Dr. Georg Kinsky, of Cologne; to Professor Johannes Wolf, Director of the Musikabteilung at the Preussische Staatsbibliothek, Berlin; to Miss Barbara Duncan, Librarian of the Sibley Library at the Eastman School of Music; to Professor Otto Kinkeldey, Librarian of Cornell University; and to Professor Dayton C. Miller, of the Case School of Applied Science.

COLLATION OF THE LIBRARY
OF CONGRESS MANUSCRIPTS OF
THE DIVERTIMENTI WITH
HAYDN'S CATALOGUE

(With notes on certain numbers not included in the MSS. and references to contemporary and modern editions)

MANUSCRIPTS

A   "24 Divertimenti à Pariton, Viola e Basso Del Giuseppe Haydn. N:i." Parts; contemporary MS. (ca. 1780). "Nos. 77 à 100 du Catalogue thématique." Numbered 1 to 24. (M 351. A2H48.)

B   "J. Haydn—Trios Inédits—Bariton, Viola et Basso." Parts (in portfolio); 19th century MS. (ca. 1850), perhaps copied for Picquot. Contains 11 divertimenti for baryton, viola, and bass and the 12 little divertimenti for 2 barytons and bass. Numbered 1 to 12. (M 351. A2H521–532.)

C   "Collection des Trios de J. Haydn; la plupart Inédits." Parts (bound in 3 vols.); contemporary Italian and French MS. A composite collection, consisting of 17 distinct MSS. Contains 66 trios for strings and 3 for 3 flutes, 47 of them arrangements from the baryton divertimenti. Numbered 1 to 69. (M 351. A2H43.)

D   "J. Haydn—Trios Inédits—Violino, Viola et Basso." Parts (in portfolio); contemporary German and Spanish MS. The German MSS. are marked "Ex rebus Francisci Hofmanni" and "I R I A de Wielandt." Contains 10 trios, 6 of them arrangements from the baryton divertimenti. "Nos. 101 à 110 du Catalogue thématique." Numbered 1 to 10. (M 351. A2H501–510.)

CONTEMPORARY EDITIONS

As a result of the present confused state of Haydn bibliography it has not been possible to compile an ideally complete list of the contemporary editions in which arrangements of the baryton divertimenti appeared. Besides those named below, other arrangements, about which I have no reliable information, were issued by the Paris publishers Bailleux, La Chevardière, and Sieber. Sieber's trios ("considérés comme apocryphes," according to Vidal) include an arrangement of Divertimento 123 (the MS. arrangement in the Library of Congress has been marked "Gravé chez Sieber"); this series probably duplicates the collection later published by Zumsteeg of Stuttgart. In the same way, the trios issued by Bailleux and La Chevardière, and certain Berlin and Vienna editions not mentioned below, probably duplicate one or other of the publications named.

Le Menu   Trois divertissemens dont les deux premiers pour un violon ou flûte, un second violon et basse, le troisième pour un premier violon ou flûte, un alto et basse. Paris, Le Menu [1771?] Library of Congress. British Museum: Bruxelles, Van den Berghen [1770?] Le Menu's Divertisemens 2 and 3 are Haydn's Divertimenti 35 and 21.

Op. 11   Six sonates à flûte, violon & violoncello. Amsterdam, Hummel [1771?] Not seen; title after Zur Westen; thematic index, Breitkopf 1772. Breitkopf lists Hummel's

164   ESSAYS ON MUSIC IN THE WESTERN WORLD

Op. 11 as "VI. Trii a 2 Flauti e Basso." Hummel's Sonates 1, 2, 3, 4, and 6 are Haydn's Divertimenti 9, 7, 6,
and 11 (all transposed), and 17 (original key).

Simrock A   Six trios pour flûte, violon & violoncello. Liv: I. Bonn,
Simrock [1804?] Sibley Library. Contains Divertimenti
109, 118, 100, 82, 103, and 110 (all transposed).

Simrock B   Six trios pour deux violons & violoncelle à l'usage des
comançans. Bonn, Simrock [1807?] Not seen; title after
Päsler. Contains Divertimenti 39, 37, 38, 36, 35, and
34.

MODERN EDITIONS

Zumsteeg   Sechs Divertimenti für Violine, Viola und Violoncell.
Hefte I–II. Stuttgart, Zumsteeg [1864–69]. Contains
Divertimenti 123, 103, 101, 114, 124, and 108. Zumsteeg's Divertimenti are in G, A, C, D, G, and A; the
same keys, in the same order, are given by Whistling for
Hummel's Op. 21, published in Berlin about 1785, and
it seems probable that Hummel's publication (or the
publication by Sieber referred to above) was Zumsteeg's
source.

May   Op. 21. 12 leichte Streich-Trios. Rev. und zum Vortrage
bearb. von J. May. Für 2 Violinen und 'Cello. Bd. II.
Heilbronn a. N., Schmidt [1898]. Also arranged for 2
violins and viola. Contents same as Simrock B.

Tillmetz   Sechs Trios für Flöte, Violine und 'Cello. Für Flöte und
Klavier bearb. von Rudolf Tillmetz. Hefte 1–2. Leipzig,
Zimmermann [1903]. Contents same as Simrock A.

Prieger   Siciliano für Violine, Viola, Violoncell. Music supple-
ment to the program of a concert given by the Rosé
Quartet, Bonn, Beethovenhalle, February 6, 1909. With
note by Erich Prieger. Haydn's Divertimento 51 i.

Heuberger   Zwei Divertimenti für Violine, Viola und Violoncello.
Hrsg. von Rich. Heuberger. Wien, Robitschek [1914].
Heuberger's Divertimento 1 is Haydn's 38 i, 94 ii, and
38 iii; Heuberger's Divertimento 2 is Haydn's 113 i and
ii, 95 ii, and 81 iii. According to Altmann, this publication was first issued by the Universal-Edition of Vienna
in 1902.

Neue Zeitschrift	Divertimento Nr. 106. Music supplement to the *Neue Zeitschrift für Musik,* LXXXIII, No. 4 (January 27, 1916). After the autograph, then in possession of Josef Liebeskind of Leipzig. Haydn's catalogue: Divertimento 105.
Corroyez	Sept trios pour divers instruments. Sonates à trois des maîtres du XVIII siècle. (Répertoire de musique de chambre pour instruments à vent ou à cordes ad lib. 2me collection.) Paris, Buffet Crampon, *1925.* Corroyez's Trio 2 is Haydn's Divertimento 36, in E-flat.
Ruyssen	Deux divertissements pour baryton. Transcrits pour violoncelle par C. A. P. Ruyssen. Paris, Schneider, *1925.* Arranged for 2 'cellos, for 'cello and piano, and for 2 'cellos and piano. Contents same as Heuberger.
Dittrich	Sechs Trios für Flöte, Violine und 'Cello. Neuausg. von Richard Dittrich. Leipzig, Zimmermann, *1926.* Dittrich's Trio 4 is Haydn's Divertimento 97 i, vi, and vii, in G.
Fitz	Drei leichte Streichtrios für Violine, konzertierende Viola und 'Cello. Hrsg. von Oskar Fitz. Erstdruck. Kassel, Bärenreiter-Verlag [1926]. Fitz's Trio 3 is Haydn's Divertimento 1.
Lemacher	Zwölf ganz leichte Streichtrios. Hrsg. von Heinrich Lemacher. Heft 1. M.-Gladbach, Volksvereins-Verlag [1927]. Contents same as Simrock B.
Meyer	Divertimento für Viola d'amour, Violine und Violoncello. Hrsg. von Clemens Meyer. Hannover, Nagel, 1930. Haydn's Divertimento 56 i, 34 ii, 78 iii, in E-flat; Trio of Menuetto not identified.

Abbreviations:
B—bass; Fl—flute; V—violin; Va—viola; Vc—'cello.
The letters A, B, C, and D refer to the Library of Congress MSS.
†—not included in the Library of Congress MSS.
*—Mandyczewski's list (1907).

1. A major: Andante—Allegro—Menuetto. C 34 (V, Va, B, in D). Fitz 3, after an arrangement for V, Vc obbligato, and B in the archives of the Gesellschaft der Musikfreunde, copied by Anthony Schaarschmidt in 1765: Andante—Menuetto Allegro.

2. A major: Allegretto (con variazioni)—Arioso (Adagio)—Menuetto—Finale (Presto). C 1 (2 V, B). C 64 (Vc, Va, B, beginning in C, ending in G): Arioso (Adagio)—Menuetto (not the same as that in C 1)—Allegretto (con variazioni).

3. A major: Allegro—Menuetto—Presto. C 63 (Vc, Va, B, in G).

4. A major: Moderato—Menuetto—Allegro molto. C 61(V, Vc, B, in G).

*6. A major: Moderato più tosto adagio (con variazioni)—Menuetto —Finale. C 65 (Vc, Va, B, in G). Breitkopf 1769, Trio 1 (Fl, V, B, in D). Op. 11, No. 3 (in D).

*7. A major: Moderato—Menuetto—Presto. C 66 (Vc, Va, B). Breitkopf 1769, Trio 2 (Fl, Va, B, in D). Op. 11, No. 2 (in C).

9. A major: Andante cantabile—Menuetto—Finale (Allegro). C 11 (2 V, B). C 62 (Vc, Va, B). Breitkopf 1772, Trio 2 (V, Va, B). Op. 11, No. 1 (in D). Autograph (V, Va, B) in the Artaria collection (Pohl, 1, 230).

†10. A major: Moderato. Breitkopf 1772, Trio 4 (V, Va, B).

11. D major: Adagio—Menuetto—Finale (Presto). C 28 (V, Va, B). Breitkopf 1772, Trio 5 (V, Va, B). Op. 11, No. 4 (in F).

*14. D major: Adagio cantabile—Allegro di molto—Menuetto. C 31 (V, Va, B).

*15. A major: Adagio cantabile assai—Allegro di molto—Menuetto. C 30 (V, Va, B).

*16. A major: Moderato—Menuetto (Poco allegretto)—Final (Presto). C 27 (V, Va, B). Breitkopf 1772, Trio 3 (Vc, Va, B).

17. D major: Adagio più tosto cantabile (con variazioni)—Adagio—Menuetto. C 32 (V, Va, B). Breitkopf 1772, Trio 1 (V, Va, B), also Trio 1 (Vc, Va, B). Op. 11, No. 6.

†18. A major: Adagio. Breitkopf 1772, Trio 5 (Vc, Va, B).

*19. A major: Moderato—Menuetto—Finale (Presto). C 29 (V, Va, B).

21. A major: Moderato—Menuetto—Presto. C 26 (V, Va, B). Le Menu 3.

†24. D major: Moderato—Menuetto (Allegretto). Breitkopf 1772, Trio 4 (Vc, Va, B). See note on autographs, this article, p. 222, note 8.

†25. A major: Adagio. Breitkopf 1772, Trio 2 (Vc, Va, B).

31. D major: Adagio cantabile—Menuetto—Allegro molto—Adagio. C 35 (V, Va, B).

†34. D major: Moderato—Menuetto—Allegro. Simrock B 6. The Menuetto (but not the Trio) is 2nd movement of Meyer.

†35. A major: Pastorella (Adagio)—Allegro molto—Menuetto. Le Menu 2. Simrock B 5.

36. D major: Adagio—Allegro di molto—Menuetto. C 5 (2 V, B). Simrock B 4. Corroyez 2 (in E-flat).

†37. G major: Andantino—Adagio—Menuetto. Simrock B 2.

†38. A major: Poco andante—Menuetto—Presto. Simrock B 3. The Poco andante and Presto are 1st and 3rd movements of Heuberger 1.

39. D major: Adagio—Allegro—Menuetto. C 9 (2 V, B), without Menuetto. Simrock B 1. Autograph in the Artaria collection (Catalogue, 1893, No. 23).

†40. D major: Moderato. Autograph in the Artaria collection (Catalogue, 1893, No. 24).

†41. D major: Moderato. See note on autographs, this article, p. 228, note 8.

49. G major: Adagio—Allegro—Menuetto. A 1.

50. D major: Andante (con variazioni)—Allegro di molto—Menuetto Moderato). A 2.

51. A major: Siciliano (Adagio)—Allegro—Menuetto. A 3. Siciliano published by Prieger.

52. D major: Adagio—Allegro—Menuetto alla zoppa (Trio al contrario). A 4. The Adagio is preceded by 8 introductory measures of recitative (D minor: Adagio).

53. G major: Moderato—Menuetto—Finale (Allegro). A 5.

54. D major: Moderato—Menuetto (Un poco allegretto)—Finale (Presto). A 6.

55. G major: Moderato—Menuetto—Finale (Allegro di molto). A 7.

56. D major: Adagio—Allegro moderato—Menuetto. A 8. The Adagio is 1st movement of Meyer.

57. A major: Adagio—Menuetto (Un poco allegretto)—Finale (Presto). A 9.

58. D major: Moderato—Menuetto—Finale (Allegro di molto). A 10.

59. G major: Adagio—Allegro—Menuetto (Poco allegretto). A 11.

60. A major: Adagio (con varizioni)—Allegro—Menuetto. A 12.

61. D major: Allegro—Andantino—Menuetto (Allegretto). A 13.

62. G major: Allegro—Menuetto—Finale (Presto). A 14.

63. D major: Adagio—Allegro—Menuetto. A 15.

64. D major: Allegro—Menuetto (Un poco vivace)—Finale (Presto). A 16.

65. G major: Allegro (Haydn's catalogue: Adagio!)—Menuetto—Finale (Allegro assai). A 17.

66. A major: Adagio—Allegro di molto—Menuetto (Allegretto). A 18.

67. G major: Allegretto—Menuetto—Finale (Allegro di molto). A 19.

68. A major: Adagio—Allegro di molto—Menuetto. A 20.

69. D major: Adagio (con variazioni)—Menuetto (Allegretto)—Finale (Presto). A 21.

70. G major: Scherzando, e presto—Andante—Menuetto. A 22.

71. A major: Allegro moderato—Menuetto (Un poco allegretto)—Finale (Allegro di molto). A 23.

72. D major: Adagio—Allegro assai—Menuetto (Allegretto). A 24.

73. G major: Andante (con variazioni)—Menuetto (Allegretto)—Finale (Presto). B 5. C 37 (V, Va, B).

74. D major: Adagio—Allegro—Menuetto (Allegro). C 38 (V, Va, B).

75. A major: Allegro moderato—Menuetto (Allegretto)—Finale. C 39 (V, Va, B).

76. C major: Moderato—Menuetto—Finale (Scherzo, Presto). C 40 (V, Va, B). Breitkopf 1772, Trio 3 (V, Va, B).

77. G major: Adagio—Allegro con spirito—Menuetto (Allegretto). C 41 (V, Va, B).

78. D major: Andante (con variazioni)—Menuetto (Allegretto)—Finale (Presto). C 42 (V, Va, B). The Finale is 3rd movement of Meyer.

79. D major: Moderato—Menuetto (Allegretto)—Finale (Presto). C 43 (V, Va, B). See note on autographs, this article, p. 135, note 8.

80. G major: Moderato—Menuetto (Allegretto)—Finale (Presto). C 44 (V, Va, B). See note on autographs, p. 135, note 8.

81. D major: Un poco adagio (con variazioni)—Menuetto—Finale (Vivace). C 45 (V, Va, B). The Finale is 4th movement of Heuberger 2.

82. C major: Adagio—Allegro—Menuetto (Allegretto). C 46 (V, Va, B). C 67 (3 Fl): Adagio—Menuetto (Allegretto)—Allegro. Simrock A 4 (in D).

83. F major: Adagio—Allegro—Menuetto. C 47 (V, Va, B).

84. G major: Allegro moderato—Menuetto (Allegretto)—Finale (Presto). C 48 (V, Va. B).

85. D major: Adagio—Allegro—Menuetto (Allegretto). C 49 (V, Va, B).

86. A major: Adagio—Allegro—Menuetto (Allegretto). C 50 (V, Va, B).

87. A minor (Haydn's catalogue: A major!): Adagio—Allegro di molto—Menuetto. C 51 (V, Va, B).

88. A major: Adagio—Allegro—Menuetto. C 52 (V, Va, B).

89. G major: Moderato—Menuetto (Allegretto)—Finale (Presto). C 53 (2 V, B).

90. C major: Moderato—Menuetto (Allegretto)—Finale (Presto). C 54 (2 V, B).

91. D major: Moderato—Menuetto (Allegro)—Finale (Presto). C 55 (2 V, B). Trio of the Menuetto published by Pohl, II, 306–307.

92. G major: Allegro—Menuetto (Allegretto)—Finale (Presto). C 56 (V, Va, B).

93. C major: Allegro di molto—Menuetto—Finale (Presto). C 57 (V, Va, B).

94. A major: Allegretto—Menuetto (Allegretto, Canone in diapente) —Finale (Presto). C 58 (V, Va, B). The Menuetto is 2nd movement of Heuberger 1.

95. D major: Allegro di molto (con variazioni)—Menuetto (Allegretto)—Finale (Presto). C 59 (V, Va, B). The Menuetto is 3rd movement of Heuberger 2.

96. B minor: Largo—Allegro—Menuetto. C 60 (V, Va, B).

97. D major: Adagio—Allegro di molto—Menuetto—Polonese— Adagio—Menuetto (Allegretto)—Finale (Fuga, Presto). B 11. The Adagio, Menuetto II, and Finale are 1st, 2nd, and 3rd movements of Dittrich 4 (in G). "Fatto per la felicissima nascita di S. A. S. Prencipe Estorhazi" (Pohl, I, 254, note 45). See Divertimento 117.

*98. D major: Adagio—Allegro moderato—Menuetto. D 2 (V, Va, B).

†100. F major: Moderato—Menuetto—Presto. Simrock A 3 (in B).

101. C major: Allegro—Menuetto—Finale (Fuga a 3 sogetti in centrapuncto doppio). B 2. Zumsteeg 3.

*102. G major: Moderato—Menuetto—Finale (Presto). D 1 (V, Va, B).

†103. A major: Moderato—Menuetto—Scherzando (Presto). Simrock A 5 (in C). Zumsteeg 2.

†105. G major: Poco adagio (con variazioni)—Menuetto (Allegretto). *Neue Zeitschrift.* See note on autographs, p. 135, note 8.

106. D major: Moderato (con variazioni)—Menuetto—Finale (Presto assai). B 8. D 3 (V, Va, B).

*107. D major: Andantino—Menuetto—Finale (Allegro). B 6.

†108. A major: Moderato—Menuetto—Finale (Allegro assai). Zumsteeg 6.

109. C major: Adagio—Allegro—Menuetto. Simrock A 1 (in D).

†110. C major: Moderato—Menuetto—Finale (Presto). Simrock A 6 (in D).

*111. G major: Adagio (con variazioni)—Menuetto (Allegretto)—Finale (Presto). B 7. Also listed in Haydn's catalogue as Cassation 14 "à cinque."

112. D major: Allegro—Menuetto (Allegretto)—Finale (Presto). C 36 (V, Va, B).

113. D major: Adagio—Allegro di molto—Menuetto (Allegretto). B 4. The Adagio and Allegro di molto are 1st and 2nd movements of Heuberger 2.

114. D major: Moderato—Menuetto—Finale (Fuga, Presto). B 9. Zumsteeg 4. Also listed in Haydn's catalogue as Cassation 6.

*116. G major: Allegretto (con variazioni)—Menuetto—Finale (Allegro di molto). C 68 (3 Fl). D 5 (V, Va, B).

117. F major: Adagio—Allegro—Menuetto. B 1, with the note: "Fatto per la felicissima nascita di S A S: Principe Esterhàzi." (See Divertimento 97.) D 8 (V, Va, B).

†118. D major: Allegro—Menuetto (Allegretto)—Presto. Simrock A 2 (in G).

120. D major: Adagio—Menuetto (Allegretto)—Finale (Presto). B 3. C 33 (V, Va, B).

121. D major: Moderato—Menuetto (Allegretto)—Finale (Presto assai). D 7 (V, Va, B).

122. A major: Adagio—Allegro—Menuetto. D 6 (V, Va, B).

123. G major: Adagio cantabile—Allegro—Menuetto (Allegretto). D 10 (V, Va, B), with the note: "Gravé chez Sieber." Zumsteeg 1.

†124. G major: Moderato—Menuetto (Allegretto)—Finale (Presto). Zumsteeg 5.

125. G major: Adagio—Menuetto—Finale (Presto). D 9 (V, Va, B).

*"Divertimento a tre per il Pariton, Viola, Violoncello del Giuseppe Haydn. No. 10." B 10.

NOTES ON A HAYDN
AUTOGRAPH†

Writing in the Report of the Librarian of Congress for 1933, the Chief of the Music Division announces the purchase, by the Library, of a hitherto unknown Haydn autograph, the original manuscript of a piano sonata in E-flat major.

No piano work of Haydn's is more often played or more generally admired; few have received less attention from his biographers. The little we know about it goes no further than the plain facts of its publication, and these can be summed up in very few words. The sonata appeared in two "original" editions—one published by Artaria & Co. of Vienna in December 1798, another published by Longman, Clementi & Co. of London sometime between October 1799 and January 1800. Artaria's edition is dedicated to a Viennese pianist, Fräulein von Kurzböck; the title-page of Longman's edition describes the work as composed "expressly" for Mrs. Bartolozzi, a London amateur. The evidence admits two interpretations. On the one hand is the dedication to Fräulein von Kurzböck,

†From *The Musical Quarterly*, XX (1934), 192–205. By permission of G. Schirmer, Inc.

suggesting composition in Vienna; on the other hand is the dedication to Mrs. Bartolozzi, suggesting composition in London. How is this apparent contradiction to be explained? To whom did Haydn really dedicate the sonata? Does it belong among works written before, or after his departure from London in August 1795? When, where, and under what circumstances was it actually composed?

The Library's manuscript not only answers these questions, but clears up for all time certain puzzling entries in Haydn's list of his compositions for England, pointing the way to a logical and satisfying solution of the problem in chronology presented by his last works for the piano. Time and place of composition are precisely indicated in the autograph, which is inscribed: "Londra $\overline{794}$." The pianist for whose use the sonata was intended is also specified, but her name is neither Kurzböck nor Bartolozzi. The manuscript is headed: "Sonata composta per la celebre signora Teresa de Janson."

The name "Jansen" (so spelled) is not altogether new to Haydn literature. It occurs among names of London pianists in the diary of the first English visit. It occurs again among names of London publishers and patrons in the list of compositions that formed part of one of the two diaries of the second visit. Thinly disguised, it occurs a third time among entries for June 4, 1807, in Dies's *Nachrichten.*[1]

---

[1]The anecdote in connection with which it is here introduced was evidently a favorite of Haydn's; Dies heard the story from him more than once. It concerns a German violinist, an amateur with the technic of a professional and a singular weakness for losing himself in the higher altitudes near the bridge, a weakness of which Haydn was resolved to cure him.

"This amateur," says Dies, "often visited a Miss J**, a pianist of considerable ability with whom he was in the habit of playing. Without saying a word to anyone, Haydn composed a sonata for piano and violin, called it 'Jacob's Dream,' and sent it through trusted hands, sealed and unsigned, to Miss J**, who did not wait long before trying over the sonata—to all appearances an easy one—with her friend. What Haydn had foreseen then came to pass; the amateur broke down on the high notes, where the passage-work was overloaded. Miss J**, guessing that the unknown author had had Jacob's ladder in mind, no sooner noticed how her partner was climbing up and down—now awkwardly and unsteadily, now reeling and skipping—than she was so diverted by the business that she could no longer conceal her amusement. The amateur meanwhile cursed the composer and confidently asserted that he knew nothing about writing for the violin.

"Five or six months later, when the authorship of the sonata came to light, Miss J** rewarded Haydn with a present."

Elssler's catalogue of Haydn's library (British Museum, MS. Add. 32,070) lists

Except for these few brief appearances, Therese Jansen is a stranger to the musical scene. We know only that Haydn met her in London during his first visit, that he renewed her acquaintance in London during his second visit, and that he remembered her and spoke of her in Vienna ten to fifteen years later. Though he considered her a brilliant performer, she seems never to have appeared in public. She is not mentioned in Haydn's correspondence; she is not mentioned in Doane's *Musical Directory* (1794), which purports to list the names and addresses of a number of London amateurs; she is not mentioned in any biographical dictionary of musicians. So far as musical biography is concerned, she is an unknown quantity and would no doubt remain so, had she not become the daughter-in-law of a very distinguished artist and the mother of an equally distinguished actress. Miss Jansen and Mrs. Bartolozzi are the same person, and Mrs. Bartolozzi, the mother of Madame Vestris, was the wife, not of Francesco Bartolozzi, as Haydn biography has always supposed, but of his son Gaetano.

Haydn's biographers give us only a bare outline. To fill it in, we must turn to the biographers of Bartolozzi and Vestris. Tuer and Pearce[2] supply the essential details. But the best informed and most helpful of all the writers who have mentioned Therese Jansen is the author of an anonymous pamphlet published in London in 1839: *Memoirs of the Life, Public and Private Adventures of Madame Vestris.*[3] This writer describes himself as "a near relative"; what he has to say I shall quote in his own words, filling in the gaps in his narrative with information derived from other sources.

among the "Geschriebene Musicalien": Jacob's Dream, ein Allegro fürs Pianoforte.

[2]A. W. Tuer, *Bartolozzi and His Works,* 2 vols. (London, 1882); C. E. Pearce, *Madame Vestris and Her Times* (London, 1923).

[3]Pearce (*op. cit.,* pp. 38–39) calls this a "considerably bowdlerized" edition of a pamphlet published without printer's name in 1830. Other anonymous "memoirs" were published in London without date by John Duncombe and William Chubb, and in New York "at 107 Fulton Street" in 1838. As sources for the biography of Therese Jansen these earlier pamphlets have little to recommend them: they do not mention her by name, they misstake her relationship to Francesco Bartolozzi, and they give the place and date of her marriage, and of her daughter's birth, incorrectly, if at all. Mr. G. Wallace Woodworth, of the Division of Music, Harvard University, has kindly compared for me the Harvard copies of the London "memoirs," and I am indebted to him for information regarding the differences between them.

Mademoiselle Therese Jansen was the daughter of M. Jansen, the first dancing master of his age in Germany, his native land. He was brought to this country by Earl Spencer and Lord Mulgrave, under whose patronage Miss Jansen likewise immediately began teaching that beautiful and graceful art. Several of the very highest families benefitted by her instructions, and she was eminently successful; so much so, indeed, that she and her brother, Mr. L. Jansen (who taught dancing only because he was bred to it by parental authority—music being his decided forte), realized rather more than two thousand pounds per annum. They resided at No. 14, Great Marlborough-Street, and they were both musical pupils of the immortal Clementi.

Tuer supplies the probable place and approximate date of Therese's birth: the elder Jansen came to England from Aix-la-Chapelle, and since Therese was 73 at the time of her death in Calais in 1843, she must have been born about 1770. As to her studies with Clementi, Tuer's claim that she had the reputation of being the best of his school is supported by Bertini,[4] who names her as one of Clementi's three most distinguished pupils, with Cramer and Field. Clementi's Opus 33, a set of three piano-trios published about 1795, was dedicated to her; Dussek honored her in 1793 with the dedication of his Opus 13, a set of three sonatas for piano and violin, and again in 1800 with the dedication of his Opus 43, a "grand" sonata for the piano alone. Therese Jansen-Bartolozzi was evidently a person of considerable prominence in the musical world of Haydn's day, a pianist who enjoyed the friendship and respect of the leading composers for her instrument.

Her brother Louis began his career as a composer in 1793 with the publication of three piano-sonatas (Op. 1) and eighteen "favorite" minutes; his Opus 6, a "grand" piano-sonata published about 1802, was dedicated to his sister. In later life his talents seem to have been chiefly applied to the production of military and patriotic piano-pieces.[5] An obituary notice in the *Revue et gazette musicale de Paris* for November 19, 1840, supplies a few further details.

> Louis Charles Jansen, born at Aix-la-Chapelle in 1774, brother of Mrs. Bartolozzi—widow [sic] of the celebrated engraver of that name, and uncle of Madame Vestris—for years an ornament to the musical

[4] *Dizionario storico-critico* (Palermo, 1814–15), II, 73; see also Max Unger, *Muzio Clementis Leben* (Langensalza, 1914), p. 111.

[5] The Library of Congress has copies of "Buonaparte's Defeat," "The Siege of Bajados," "The Grand Battle of Waterloo," and "The Surrender of Paris."

profession, has just died in a poorhouse in Northumberland Street, Marylebone. This man, whose compositions endeared him to artist and amateur alike, who had the honor of dining with George IV when he was still Prince of Wales, was supported during his last days by public charity.

Before introducing the mother of his heroine, the author of the *Memoirs* has this to say about her father.

> Sir F. Bartolozzi's only offspring, G. Bartolozzi, was born at Rome, and had come to England with his father. His mother was never in this country. At first he followed the occupation of his father; but, not being able to endure confinement, he at length became a picture-dealer and general trader in everything that might present itself in his various journeys to and from Italy. Indeed he was so very successful that in a few years he accumulated an independent fortune and purchased an estate at Venice, with a country residence about fifty miles distant from that celebrated city. . . . Signor Bartolozzi was a very fine violin and tenor player and could boast of having introduced into this country the very first double-bass player in the world—Signor Dragonetti, the very prop of the Italian Opera House.

To make this sketch complete I need only add that Gaetano Bartolozzi was born in 1757 and that he was away on one of his periodic visits to the Continent during the early part of Haydn's second stay in England.[6] Traveling in company with his fellow Venetians Bianchi and Dragonetti, he had only just returned to London when he met the young woman who was to become his wife.

The scene of this meeting, which took place early in 1795, was a musical party at Colonel Hamilton's,[7] and if we follow the author

[6]G. B. Cimador, letter of October 14, 1794 (Heyer sale, 1927, No. 414).

[7]In Leicester Street, Leicester Square. The author of the *Memoirs* speaks of Colonel Hamilton's "pugilistic notoriety." J. T. Smith, in *Nollekens and His Times* (London, 1828), recalls having seen him spar with Mendoza in his drawing-room. On September 29, 1790, when Humphreys and Mendoza fought at Doncaster, Colonel Hamilton acted as umpire. This "gentleman pugilist" was also an amateur musician. Smith tells of a visit he paid, with Nollekens, to Gainsborough. "The artist was listening to a violin, and held up his finger to Mr. Nollekens as a request of silence. Colonel Hamilton was playing to him in so exquisite a style that Gainsborough exclaimed: 'Now, my dear Colonel, if you will but go on, I will give you that picture of the boy at the stile which you have so often wished to purchase of me.' . . . As Gainsborough's versatile fancy was at this period devoted to music, his attention was so riveted to the tones of the violin that for nearly half an hour he was motionless, after which the Colonel requested that a hackney-coach might be sent for, wherein he carried off the picture."

of the *Memoirs* the proposed match proved immediately acceptable to all concerned. Bartolozzi had originally planned to return at once to Italy; now he changed his mind and took a small house at Northend, near Walham Green. The couple was married at St. James's Church, Piccadilly; the date of the ceremony was May 16, 1795;[8] the witnesses were Charlotte Jansen, Francesco Bartolozzi, a certain Maria Adelaide de las Heras, and[9] Haydn himself. Through the kindness of the late Professor J. William Hebel, of Cornell University, I am able to reproduce in facsimile the signatures to the entry in the parish register.

> After spending the honeymoon at the Star and Garter, at Richmond, the bride and bridegroom went to their residence at Northend, where they resided for some time. Here Mrs. Bartolozzi suffered a double miscarriage. In less than twelve months they removed to the upper part of the house of Mr. Wetherell, upholsterer, No. 72 Dean-street, Soho, where our hero [Madame Vestris] was born in the year 1797.

During the month following this event, which occurred on May 2,[10] Bartolozzi took steps to wind up his affairs in London with a view to leaving for the Continent with his wife and daughter. An advertisement of Christie's, first published in *The Times* for June 10, gives us the approximate date of their departure.

CAPITAL PRINTS, DRAWINGS, AND COPPER PLATES
By Mr. Christie
AT HIS GREAT ROOM, PALL-MALL, ON FRIDAY, THE 23 INST. AT
12

> The genuine and entire STOCK of capital and valuable Prints, Drawings, and Copper-plates, some of which have never been published, and a few pleasing Cabinet Pictures, the property of G. BARTOLOZZI, retiring from business: Comprising an extensive assemblage of prints, of the finest impressions, drawings by Cipriani and Bartolozzi, and among the plates, a capital engraving in strokes, after the celebrated picture of the Madona del Sacco, of A. del Sarto, at Florence, by Bartolozzi, lately finished, and which may be truly deemed the finest plate ever executed by that artist. To be

---

[8] *The Sun*, May 23, 1795.

[9] Pohl, III, 55. Unless Bartolozzi refers to his marriage in the letter in which he informs Artaria that Corri & Dussek have published the "Apponyi" quartets (Pohl, III, 309), it is difficult to understand how Botstiber, knowing neither the date of the ceremony nor the name of the bride, learned of Haydn's connection with it.

[10] G. P. Laurie, *Sir Peter Laurie: A Family Memoir* (Brentwood, 1901), p. 152.

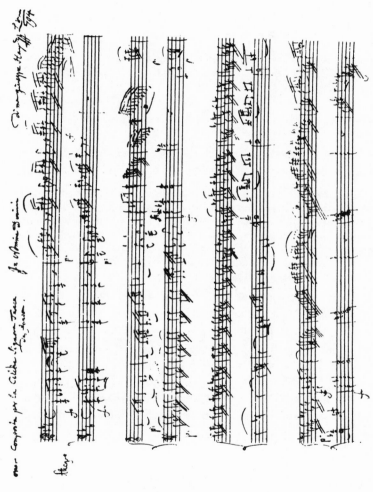

Facsimile of the first page in Haydn's autograph of the Piano Sonata in E flat. (COURTESY OF THE LIBRARY OF CONGRESS.)

Signatures in the parish-register entry of the marriage of Gaetano Bartolozzi and Therese Jansen, showing Haydn's signature among the names of the witnesses. (See p. 173.)

> viewed two days preceding the Sale. Catalogues may be had in Pall-Mall; and at the Rainbow.

According to the author of the *Memoirs,* the Bartolozzis, after leaving London, went first to Paris.

> From the capital of France, Mr. Bartolozzi proceeded to Vienna to prepare for the reception of his wife, whom he left under the care of a friend of the Jansen family, the Marquis del Campo, ambassador to the Court of England from the King of Naples. In due time Mrs. Bartolozzi joined her husband at Vienna; and the family, soon after, going to Venice, remained there until the ravages of the French army . . . had deprived Bartolozzi of his estates and forced him to return to England.[11]

A "card" printed in *The Times* for January 8, 1800, gives us the approximate date of this return.

> Mr. Bartolozzi, jun., respectfully informs the Ladies and Gentlemen who have formerly honored him with their patronage and recommendation, that being now returned from Italy, he means to resume giving Lessons in Drawing.

From this "card" and from Christie's advertisement it is clear that Bartolozzi and his family spent not more than two years and

[11]Marquis Bernardo del Campo, mentioned in the diary of Haydn's first London visit, was the Spanish (not Neapolitan) ambassador to London. By October 5, 1796, when his government declared war on England, he had left London for Paris, where he had charge of Spanish interests until the appointment of Azara in 1798. The French occupation of Venice, which left Bartolozzi's countrymen "without a zechino," as the author of the *Memoirs* has it, began on May 17, 1797. When General d'Hilliers withdrew his troops on January 18, 1798, the Bartolozzis were probably still *en route.*

a half on the Continent. At some time during these two years and a half they were in Vienna. Allowing six months to a year for Mrs. Bartolozzi's stay in Paris, we may place her arrival in Vienna late in 1798 or early in 1799. Whatever the date, she was very probably there when her husband's old friend Dragonetti, passing through Vienna on his way to Italy in the spring of 1799, visited Haydn and saw the score of the *Creation*.[12] And it cannot have been long after this that Bartolozzi ordered from Haydn his copy of the score: the list of subscribers printed with the first edition in February 1800 includes the name "Bartolozzi, Junior," without address.

Unquestionably there is a connection between Mrs. Bartolozzi's visit to Vienna, the publication there of the sonata Haydn wrote for her, and the subsequent publication of the sonata in London. Assuming, as I think we may, that Mrs. Bartolozzi at first controlled all publication rights in the work,[13] we can easily guess what happened. The simplest explanation is that Mrs. Bartolozzi (or her husband acting for her) ceded her Continental rights to Artaria or to Haydn himself, directing her London agents to forestall unauthorized English reprints by bringing out an independent edition at once. But it is also possible that the Vienna edition was itself unauthorized[14] and that Mrs. Bartolozzi, learning of its existence, took steps to protect her English rights.

In any case, publication in London occurred during Mrs. Bartolozzi's absence, for on October 29, 1799, Longman announced: "In a few days will be published, a new sonata for the Piano Forte, by Dr. Haydn."[15] The interesting thing is that the Vienna edition appears to have followed an inaccurate copy of the autograph, while the London edition was obviously engraved by someone who had Haydn's original before him. The manuscript still shows the

[12]Pohl, in *Grove's Dictionary*, 3rd ed. (1927–28), II, 92.

[13]Had Haydn been in a position to release the sonata in 1794, he would presumably not have waited until 1798 to do so. Griesinger's letters to Härtel (Pohl, III, 138–140) throw some light on the real state of affairs. His letter of May 25, 1799, reports that Haydn will try to persuade certain patrons of his to consent to his submitting commissioned works for publication; his letter of June 12, 1799, contains this significant sentence: "Bay [Clementi's agent] is also clamoring for piano sonatas, but he [Haydn] has not yet been able to supply him."

[14]In September 1791 Artaria published, without Haydn's permission, the sonata in E-flat written for Marianne von Genzinger.

[15]*The Times*; publication is advertised on January 7 and February 28, 1800.

red-crayon marks that Longman's engraver made in "laying out" the plates, and the blank page that follows the slow movement in the autograph is actually reproduced in Longman's edition, the foot of the preceding plate being marked "Page 13 blank"!

Having brought the Bartolozzis back to London, the author of the *Memoirs* goes on to speak of the domestic arrangements they made on their arrival. His statement that they took apartments in Oxford Street over premises occupied by Peter Laurie is confirmed by Laurie's godson and biographer, who recalls that the Bartolozzis were already living at the Oxford Street address, where they appeared to have been in residence for some time, when his godfather settled there on May 1, 1801.[16]

It is evident, however, that the family did not go directly to Oxford Street on returning to London. Bartolozzi's "card" fills in a gap in the anonymous narrative. For a time—perhaps only for a few months—the family lived at "No. 82 Wells-street, Oxford-street," the address mentioned in *The Times*. When we come to discuss the chronology of Haydn's last works for the piano, this seemingly irrelevant detail will prove significant.

At this point we can afford to part company with the author of the *Memoirs*. What he and other pamphleteers have written about Mrs. Bartolozzi's later life reflects little credit on her and less on them. Her portrait seems not to have been preserved. If her daughters Lucia Elizabeth and Josephine resembled her at all, she must have been very attractive at the time of her marriage. When Haydn knew her she was in her twenties; the one extant account of her personal appearance describes an elderly woman.

> In a clever caricature sketch of "Calais Market," by Miss M. A. Cook, sister of George Cook, the well-known engraver, Madame Gaetano Bartolozzi is represented dressed in the costume of the period. She was evidently inclined to corpulence, and wears an enormous bonnet decorated with a prodigious quantity of flowers—a complete flower-garden. She is described as a very vain woman, with highly coloured—her enemies said enamelled—cheeks, who prided herself on the smallness of her feet and ankles. This foible is taken advantage of in the caricature referred to, where she appears with her dress slightly raised, showing an ankle and foot of elephantine proportions.[17]

[16]Laurie, *op. cit.*, pp. 49, 54.
[17]Tuer, *op. cit.*, I, 24.

Had Haydn dedicated only one work to Mrs. Bartolozzi, there would have been reason enough to devote these few pages to establishing her identity; for one thing, her close association with Clementi, hitherto unnoticed by students of Haydn's music, throws a new light on the traces of Clementi's influence that Abert, Shedlock, and other critics have detected in his mature piano-style. But the sonata in E-flat is only one of a number of works that Haydn dedicated to her. From the list of his compositions for England we know that several sonatas were written for "Miss Janson." According to one transcript of the list there were two such works; according to another, three. And in the spring of 1797, nearly two years after his return to Vienna, a set of three piano-trios, dedicated to Mrs. Bartolozzi, was published in London by Longman & Broderip. Altogether, Haydn wrote five—possibly six—major works for her, nearly one-third of his last contribution to piano literature. With the sole exception of Princess Marie Esterhazy, wife of Nicholas II, to whom three sonatas and three trios were dedicated, no other woman was so honored.

Haydn's last works for the piano have received relatively little attention from his biographers. Pohl's comment on them is the least satisfactory part of his article for *Grove's Dictionary*. Botstiber, Artaria, and von Hase contribute much that is new without attempting a solution of the problem as a whole. The Library of Congress autograph removes one of the principal difficulties. And the detailed information we have regarding Mrs. Bartolozzi's movements during the nineties enables us to dispose of another: the riddle of the so-called "English" sonata in C. The original edition of this work—"Composed expressly for and Dedicated to Mrs. Bartolozzi, Printed for and to be had of the Proprietor, 82 Wells Street and of the Publisher, J. & H. Caulfield, 36 Piccadilly" —has been variously dated "1791" (Riemann and Päsler) and "1793" (Botstiber).[18] Since it is dedicated to Mrs. Bartolozzi it cannot have been published before May 1795; since it is numbered "Opus 79" it was probably published after Opus 78 (the sonata in E-flat), that is, after October 1799. The address of the "proprietor"

---

[18]Franklin Taylor writes in his edition of Haydn's piano sonatas (Augener): "First published in London early in the nineteenth century (the exact date is uncertain)."

—"82 Wells Street"—proves conclusively that the correct year is
1800, and there is no longer any reason to assume, as editors and
critics have assumed in the past, that the sonata in C was composed
during Haydn's first visit to England.[19]

With this difficulty out of the way it becomes possible to raise the
question: Did Haydn write any piano music at all during the first
London period? Negative evidence indicates that he did not. From
December 15, 1790, when he first left Vienna, to January 19,
1794, when he left Vienna for the second time, no new work of
his for the piano made its appearance. For the moment, the sonatas,
trios, and smaller pieces of 1789 and 1790 claimed the entire
attention of his publishers and public. The "new" trio that figures
on the program of Salomon's eighth concert was in reality an old
one, written in Vienna,[20] yet Haydn refers to it as his most recent
(letzte) piano sonata in writing to Frau von Genzinger on December 20, 1791. Up to this time, then, he had written nothing new
for the piano. The absence of any reference to a new piano work
in later letters from London makes it at least unlikely that the last
six months of his stay were more fruitful. And, as I shall show
presently, Haydn's list of his compositions for England suggests, if
it does not prove, that he first returned to the instrument in 1793,
on completing the "Apponyi" quartets.

Once we exclude the possibility of Haydn's having begun the
composition of his last piano works in London, the problem of
arranging them in approximate chronological order becomes
relatively simple. A table printed at the end of these notes
[pages 186–87] presents a solution that makes possible an intelligent, critical approach to the music itself. If it differs here and
there from the partial solutions previously brought forward, it
has at least the positive advantage of agreeing with the most important single document bearing on the question—Haydn's

[19]According to Pohl, who seems to be quoting from the correspondence with
Breitkopf & Härtel, Haydn's comment on the sonata was: "Not to be printed." Mrs.
Bartolozzi had evidently learned to protect her rights. (*Grove's Dictionary,* 3rd ed.,
II, 575.)

[20]Peters No. 11; Breitkopf & Härtel No. 24. At this concert, which took place
on April 20, 1792, the piano part was played by Hummel, then a boy of thirteen.
The title-page of Longman's edition adds "As performed by Master Hummel at M.
Salomon's Concert."

own account of what he wrote for England.

As already intimated, this account formed part of one of the two diaries of the second English visit. It covers the period from January 1791 to August 1795 and, besides enumerating the works themselves, specifies the exact number of leaves required for each manuscript.[21] From this circumstance one might argue that what we have is no mere list, written down from memory, but an actual record in which works were entered at the time—and in the order —of their composition. This argument is given at least a semblance of plausibility when we compare the order in which the works are set down with the known order as established by dated autographs and other conclusive evidence. The document itself has disappeared. But before its disappearance it was copied independently by two of Haydn's first biographers—Griesinger, who prints a German translation, and Dies, who gives the original English wording.[22] In both texts the arrangement of the list is the same, and in both texts the piano works are grouped together, as below, between the entry for the "Apponyi" quartets, composed in 1793, and the entry for "Dr. Harrington's Compliment" ("What Art Expresses"), which belongs to the second London period.

Griesinger		Dies
[9] Drey Sonaten für Broderiep	18 [Blätter]	3 Sonates for Broderip
[10] Drey Sonaten für Preston	18 "	3 Sonates for P——
[11] Zwey Sonaten für Miss Janson	10[23] "	3 Sonates for Ms. Janson
[12] Eine Sonate in F minor	3 "	1 Sonate in F minore
[13] Eine in g	5 "	1 Sonate in g
[14] Der Traum	3 "	The Dream

[21]Where it is possible to verify these "exact" figures, there are always discrepancies between them and the actual specifications of the autographs. The original manuscript of the opera *Orfeo* (1791) fills, not 110 folios, as indicated in Haydn's list, but *132*, or without the overture, *121*. Some other examples are: the Symphonie concertante (1792)—*40*, not 30 folios; the six "Apponyi" quartets (1793)—*99*, not 48 folios; the two divertimenti for two flutes and violoncello (1794)—*9*, not 10 folios; the last three "London" symphonies (1795)—*118*, not 72 folios.

[22]Griesinger's text, printed in the *Allgemeine musikalische Zeitung* for August 2, 1809, and reprinted in his *Biographische Notizen* (1810), is followed by Gerber (1812), Pohl (1867), and Botstiber (1927); Dies's text, printed in his *Biographische Nachrichten* (1810), is followed by Carpani (1812) and Stendhal (1814).

[23]The Library of Congress autograph alone has ten leaves.

Unless Dies is right in mentioning three sonatas for "Miss Janson" instead of two, Haydn's list fails to account for the sonata in D, written in England, according to his own statement,[24] for "a lady who retained the original manuscript." And unless Dies is right in repeating, as his forty-third and last item, the entry "3 Sonates for Broderip," which Griesinger, who has forty-two items, gives only once, Haydn's list fails to account for the trios dedicated to Mrs. Schroeter, for the first entry must refer to the earlier set published by Longman & Broderip, dedicated to Marie-Anna von Hohenfeld, the Princess Dowager. Where the two texts disagree, a better case can always be made out for Dies than for Griesinger, yet Pohl and Botstiber reprint the Griesinger text without even mentioning the existence of another.

Haydn's reference to a "Sonate in g" presents real difficulty unless we include among the works of the London years a composition which Pohl assigns, with some hesitation, to an earlier period —the sonata in G for piano and violin, first published in 1794.[25]

A more serious difficulty is the chronological arrangement of the three solo sonatas. Karl Päsler, who edited them for Breitkopf & Härtel's complete edition, inferred the order C, D, E-flat. The incomplete and in part untrustworthy evidence he had left him no alternative. Our position is different; while our information goes further and is more reliable, it does not commit us to any one solution.

We have reason to believe that all three sonatas were written for one person; we infer that they constitute an "opus." We know that the sonata in E-flat was composed in 1794; we infer that the sonatas in C and D belong to the same year. We cannot determine the actual order of the three sonatas; we can only suppose it to have been an order consistent with the uniformly progressive character of Haydn's later writing.

External evidence admits half-a-dozen chronological arrangements, internal evidence only one. The first of the three sonatas for "Miss Janson" is in E-flat, the second in D; the sonata in C is at once

[24]Hermann von Hase, *Joseph Haydn und Breitkopf & Härtel* (Leipzig, 1909), p. 51.

[25]The remaining items are identified in my chronological table.

the last of the series and the last of all Haydn's works for the piano alone.[26]

What followed was piano chamber-music. Before leaving London Haydn had finished his three trios for Mrs. Schroeter, the last item on his list; Longman published them within a few months after his departure. Next in order is the single trio in E-flat minor, which the autograph dates "1795"; though Haydn does not count it among his English works, Griesinger speaks of it as having been written in London.[27] The four remaining trios do not figure in Haydn's list and were evidently written after his return to Vienna. The set dedicated to Mrs. Bartolozzi, published by Longman in May 1797,[28] may have been finished as early as June 1796; about this time Haydn signed a new contract with his English agent and from thenceforward sent no more piano music to London.[29] The single trio in E-flat major is precisely dated in Haydn's correspondence; on April 16, 1796, he asks Härtel to have more patience with him[30] and seven months later, on November 9, sends the promised sonata "at last."[31]

How each of these details contributes to a solution of the whole problem is indicated in my chronological table, which combines with other information the various conclusions and conjectures to which this discussion has led.

---

[26]The second movement of the sonata in C is a revision of an earlier work—an Adagio in F, probably composed in Vienna, where it was separately published in June 1794. The last movement breaks with the limitations of the old five-octave keyboard, making repeated use of the so-called "additional keys" which Beethoven introduces for the first time in the "Waldstein" sonata of 1805.

[27]Pohl, III, 214. Botstiber, in reprinting Haydn's dedication to Madame Moreau, omits the significant date "1er 9bre 1803," from which it follows that priority belongs to Traeg's edition, published in August of that year, and to the dedication to Fräulein von Kurzböck.

[28]*The Monthly Magazine and British Register,* III (1797), 388.

[29]Griesinger, letter of June 12, 1799 (Pohl, III, 139–140).

[30]Hase, *op. cit.,* p. 6.

[31]Julien Tiersot prints the full text of this second letter in *Rivista musicale italiana,* XVII (1910), 372–373, and in his *Lettres de musiciens* (Turin, 1924), pp. 72–73; von Hase, without Haydn's original before him, dates it "Ende des Jahres 1795."

HAYDN'S LAST WORKS

No.	Work	Dedication	Place and Date of Composition
1	Variations in F minor	Barbara Ployer Baroness von Braun	Vienna, 1793 *Autographs:* Vienna, National- bibliothek; New York Public Library
2	Sonata in G, with violin	None	Vienna? 1793?
3	3 Trios in A, G minor, and B-flat, with violin and violoncello	Marie-Anna von Hohen-feld, Princess Esterhazy	Vienna? 1793?
4	3 Trios in C, D minor, and E-flat, with violin and violoncello	Marie von Liechtenstein, Princess Esterhazy	Vienna? 1793?
5	Sonata in E-flat	Therese Jansen-Bartolozzi Magdalene von Kurzböck	London, 1794 *Autograph:* Washington, Li- brary of Congress
6	Sonata in D	Therese Jansen-Bartolozzi?	London, 1794?
7	Sonata in C	Therese Jansen-Bartolozzi	London? 1794? Adagio: Vienna? 1793?
8	"Jacob's Dream," sonata with violin		London, 1794?
9	3 Trios in D, G, and F-sharp minor, with violin and violoncello	Mrs. Schroeter	London? 1795?
10	Trio in E-flat minor, with violin and violoncello	Magdalene von Kurzböck Madame Moreau	London, 1795 *Autograph:* Liepmannssohn, V e r s t e i g e r u n g s k a t a l o g 62 (1932) No. 32
11	3 Trios in C, E, and E-flat, with violin and violoncello	Therese Jansen-Bartolozzi	Vienna? 1796?
12	Trio in E-flat, with violin and violoncello	None	Vienna, 1796 *Autograph:* Lengfeld,, Katalog 42 (1932), No. 394 (Fragment)

[32]Dates of publication are based on Artaria-Botstiber and other sources, and on contemporary advertisements. References in columns 7 and 8 are to the Peters and Breitkopf & Härtel editions. of the smaller piano pieces, piano and violin sonatas, piano sonatas, and piano trios, and (in

FOR THE PIANO[32]

London Edition	Continental Edition	Peters	Breitkopf	Haydn's List
Clementi, April 1802	Artaria (Op. 83), Jan. 1799	1	1	1 Sonate in F minore
	Artaria (Op. 70), June 1794	1	6	1 Sonate in g
Longman & Broderip (Op. 70), Nov. 1794	Artaria (Op. 71), July 1795	13, 17, 9	7, 14, 13	3 Sonates for Broderip
Preston (Op. 71), between Nov. 1794 and Oct. 1795	Artaria (Op. 72), end of 1795	21, 22, 23	18, 19, 20	3 Sonates for Preston
Longman, Clementi (Op. 78), between Oct. 1799 and Jan. 1800	Artaria (Op. 82), Dec. 1798	1	1 (52)	Sonate for Miss Janson
	Breitkopf & Härtel (Op. 93), Dec. 1804	32	37 (51)	Sonate for Miss Janson
Caulfield (Op. 79), 1800	None Adagio: Artaria, June 1794		22 (50)	Sonate for Miss Janson
None	None			The Dream
Longman & Broderip (Op. 73), Jan. 1796	Artaria (Op. 75), beginning of 1796	6, 1, 2	6, 1, 2	3 Sonates for Broderip
	Traeg (Op. 101), Aug. 1803	18	15	
Longman & Broderip (Op. 75), May 1797	Artaria (Op. 78), Oct. 1797	3, 4, 5,	3, 4, 5	
	Artaria (Op. 79), Oct. 1797	8	12	

parentheses) to the Breitkopf & Härtel *Gesamtausgabe*. In Augener's edition of the complete piano works (Riemann) the sonatas in E-flat, D, and C are numbered 38, 23, and 35.

EARLY MUSIC PUBLISHING
IN THE UNITED STATES†

B Y one of those strange coincidences which delight the historian and at the same time provide the essayist with convenient points of departure, the year 1787, which saw the writing of the Constitution of the United States, saw also the solid beginnings of music publishing in this country as a separate and independent enterprise. The scene of these beginnings was Philadelphia, the publisher and composer a certain William Brown, the engraver John Aitken; the publication itself bore a dedication to no less a person than Francis Hopkinson, signer of the Declaration of Independence and our first native composer. *Three Rondos for the Piano Forte or Harpsichord. Composed and Humbly Dedicated to the Honourable Francis Hopkinson, Esq. by William Brown. Philadelphia. Printed and Sold by the Author. Price Two Dollars. J. Aitken Sculp*—so runs the full title of this musical landmark, which the composer-publisher himself, in inviting subscribers, had called "the first attempt of the kind in America."

Of the several persons connected with this "first attempt," it is Aitken who interests us most. In 1788 we meet with him again as the engraver of Hopkinson's *Seven Songs;* in 1789 as the engraver of Reinagle's *Chorus Sung before Gen. Washington.* What interests us still more is his anonymous, yet evident, share in the publication of the one piece of music which has come down to us from the

†From *Papers of the Bibliographical Society of America*, XXXXI (1937), 176–179; read at a meeting of the society, Philadelphia, December 30, 1937. Reprinted by permission of the Council of the Bibliographical Society of America.

188

various local celebrations of the ratification—Reinagle's *Federal March as Performed in the Grand Procession in Philadelphia the 4th of July 1788.* Jeweler, goldsmith, engraver, composer, and proprietor of a "musical repository," John Aitken was associated with music in Philadelphia for nearly twenty years, and as late as 1802 published and deposited for copyright a musical advertisement of his own composition, *The Goldsmith's Rant. A New Song: Sung by the Sons of the Immortal Tubalcain,* in connection with which he called special attention to his readiness to supply "silver cyphers for carriages."

Without attempting to trace, step by step, the steady growth, from these tentative beginnings, of the flourishing industry which was already firmly established by the turn of the century; without attempting to follow, in detail, the development of this industry on the technical side, its substitution of lithography for engraving, its introduction of the illustrated title-page, one may characterize the catalogues and the practices of our first music publishers in one phrase—they were essentially English. And quite naturally so. The musical likes and dislikes of our forefathers were those of their contemporaries in London; our early concert programs were reproductions—on a small scale, to be sure—of those arranged by Salomon and Pleyel. In a similar way the catalogues of our first music publishers echo those of their British colleagues; indeed the publishers themselves were, for the most part, Englishmen, and more than one of them had simply transferred his operations from the Old World to the New. Reinagle, Carr, and Hewitt thrive in the main, as do Longman and Preston, on Arnold, Shield, Dibden, and Hook; the Continental composers who figure in their advertisements—the "English" Bach, Haydn, Mozart, and Pleyel—are those sanctioned by acceptance in London. As to physical appearance, the actual publications differ at first from the English product only in imprint and in their uniformly inferior execution. In format and style the one is scarcely to be distinguished from the other. So far as practice is concerned, one could wish that the tradition had been quite different. For to the perpetual embarrassment of bibliographer, historian, and collector, our early music publishers had learned from English example that sheet music, to sell continuously, ought never to be dated and that engravers' plates are, by the same token, best left unnumbered.

The result, of course, is a more or less hopeless bibliographic tangle, and no one at all familiar with the very real difficulties involved will be greatly surprised to learn that, when the first recorded copy of the original sheet-music edition of the *Star-Spangled Banner* came to light here in Philadelphia some twenty years ago, it was described in an illustrated magazine article as a mere curiosity and that it required the combined talents of Mr. Dielman of the Maryland Historical Society, Mr. Muller of the New York Public Library, and Mrs. Redway, a specialist in musical Americana, to establish its definite priority. Yet with ordinary luck and a little experience with musical problems the average bibliographer can establish the publication date of a comparable Continental edition in a few minutes. Until about the year 1820, when the practice of copyrighting sheet music became general here, we are wholly dependent, for dates of publication, on publishers' addresses (at best uncertain guides), contemporary advertisements (when they can be found), and occasional publishers' plate numbers. After 1820 the situation, if somewhat improved, is still far from ideal. Many publications, among them the musically important early editions of the German classics, were, in their very nature, ineligible for copyright. And, to cite but one example of the sort of complication that may arise, even in this period, publisher A may register a copyright claim, then transfer his plates to publisher B, who, after reissuing the publication with his own imprint, may transfer them in turn to publisher C, who adds a serial plate number of his own—a by no means hypothetical case. I have in mind a particular issue of the *Star-Spangled Banner,* bearing a copyright claim for 1843, actually struck off sometime between 1849 and 1852, according to Mr. Muller's calculations, but not finally placed on sale until 1856. Here copyright claim yields one result, imprint a second, publisher's number a third.

My point, to put it as simply as possible, is that in this field—one that is only just beginning to arouse the interest of the general bibliographer and collector of Americana—there is much spadework yet to be done. If for the period prior to 1800 we can still make good use of O. G. Sonneck's classic study, *The Bibliography of Early Secular American Music,* the period 1800–1850 remains, for the most part, uncharted territory. Before the problem can be dealt with as a whole, special studies of single localities, even single publishers, must be undertaken. And if I have succeeded, this morning, in prompting even one such study, I shall feel well satisfied and shall know that I have not wasted your time.

VERDIANA IN THE
LIBRARY OF CONGRESS†

F OR years, the Music Division of the Library of Congress in
Washington has been widely known as a center for the study of
operatic history—widely known, though perhaps not as widely
known as it deserves to be. When Oscar Sonneck, the first Chief
of the Division, began the systematic development of its resources
in 1902, there were not more than 60 operas in full orchestral score
on its shelves. When he left the Library in 1917 there were something like 2,500 to 3,000, and in addition the Library had succeeded in acquiring the important Schatz collection of opera librettos, consisting of 12,000 distinct items. With justifiable pride,
Sonneck could call these resources unrivaled. As one of Sonneck's
successors, I too take enormous satisfaction in them, even though
little was done, or could be done, to add to them during my brief
tenure. Thus when Maestro Medici proposed that I take an active
part in the deliberations here in Venice, it seemed to me that I
could offer nothing more useful or more appropriate than an account of the resources in Washington for the study of Verdi's
works and their history.

Since the publication of the catalogue of dramatic music in 1908,
Washington's collection of Verdi operas in full orchestral score has
nearly doubled in size. It consists today of 24 items, printed and
manuscript, representing 18 of the 26 works. Wanting are scores

†From *Atti del primo congresso internazionale di studi verdiani* (Parma, 1969), pp.
452–457, in Italian translation; read at a meeting of the congress, Venice, August
2, 1966. Reprinted by permission of the Instituto di Studi Veridani, Parma.

of the two earliest operas, of *I Lombardi, I Due Foscari, Alzira,* and *Stiffelio,* and of *Les Vêpres siciliennes* and *Don Carlos.* It goes without saying that a collection as large and as comprehensive as this one could not have been assembled without the co-operation of Verdi's publisher—the printed score of *Falstaff* in the so-called memorial edition was presented to the Library of Congress by the house of Ricordi, while the manuscript score of *Nabucco* is a transcript of the one in the Ricordi archives, made in 1911. Among the remaining manuscript scores, three were copied for the firm of Francesco Lucca, and one of these—that of *I Masnadieri*—can claim a special interest, for its title-page records performances of the work by a traveling company that appeared in Bergamo, Bologna, Cesena, Ferrara, Alghero, Cremona, Urbino, Verona, Stresa, Rimini, and Intra-Pallanza, the dates of these performances ranging from the carnival of 1847/48 to August 1867.

Following the publication of the catalogue of 1908, Sonneck began work on a new and improved edition, brought up to date, and by 1915 the task had been practically completed. This new edition was never published, although in 1921 Sonneck decided to include the extraordinarily interesting preface he had written for it in his *Miscellaneous Studies in the History of Music.* Knowing that Sonneck's manuscript, in the form of a card catalogue, was still at the Library in Washington, knowing also from my own experience with it that its entries are as a rule far more detailed and informative than those of the old published catalogue, I asked to have the Verdi entries copied for use in preparing this report. The result was disappointing, although not altogether unexpected. Fifty years ago, musicology had scarcely begun to concern itself seriously with Verdi's works and the development of his individual style, and Sonneck, who was ready to take infinite pains in describing opera scores of the seventeenth and eighteenth centuries, does not even record that Washington's manuscript scores of *Macbeth* and *Simon Boccanegra* represent these works in their original versions, content-ing himself with minimal entries.

Probably not more than 3,000 to 3,500 of the 12,000 opera librettos of the Schatz collection are entered in Sonneck's well-known *Catalogue of Opera Librettos Printed before 1800.* For the re-mainder—the librettos of the nineteenth century—there is no pub-lished list and no unpublished card-index; the only access to this enormous body of material is through Schatz's own *Hand-Katalog*, written on over-sized folios similar to those used for commercial ledgers—one such folio is reproduced in facsimile in Sonneck's first volume. Here again I asked to have the Verdi entries copied.

With 92 items, the list is a long one. And to name only a few of the outstanding pieces is to suggest that it is also select. It extends from 1840 to 1893, from the original edition of *Un Giorno di regno* to the original edition of *Falstaff*. Other operas represented by the original editions of their librettos are *I Due Foscari*, *Il Corsaro*, *Stiffelio*, *Les Vêpres siciliennes*, *Macbeth* (in the revised version), *Aïda*, and *Otello*. Noteworthy also is an early edition of *La Forza del destino* (St. Petersburg, 1876), with text in Italian and Russian. Where the intransigence of political or ecclesiastical censorship has imposed changes in title, time, place, and dramatis personae, Schatz has sought to acquire copies of the text in each of its forms, and he has generally succeeded. Thus *Nabucco* appears also as *Nino*, *Ernani* as *Il Proscritto, ossia Il Corsaro di Venezia*, *Giovanna d'Arco* as *Orietta di Lesbo*, *Stiffelio* as *Guglielmo Wellingrode* and *Aroldo*, *Les Vêpres siciliennes* as *Giovanna de Guzman* and *Batilde di Turenna*. Had I asked for copies of the entries under Rossini, Bellini, or Donizetti, I should, of course, have obtained a similar result. The same is true of composers like Cherubini, whose earlier works are listed in the published catalogue with a frustrating cross-reference to the projected but non-existent catalogue of nineteenth-century librettos. For later works by these men, one is again thrown back on Schatz's manuscript, which has in some cases been supplemented by individual bibliographies, also manuscript. Among the composers so treated are two contemporaries of Cherubini's—Giovanni Simon Mayr and Ferdinando Paër.

From the first, the main collections of primary sources for the study of Verdi's works and their history have been in the possession of the house of Ricordi, the Museo della Scala, and the Villa Verdi at Sant'Agata, and today one needs to add to these the rapidly growing collections of the Istituto di Studi Verdiani at Parma. To suggest that, as a potential center for Verdi research, the Library of Congress in Washington ranks with any one of these institutions would be a manifest absurdity. All I aim to suggest is that, even where Verdi is concerned, Washington's resources ought not to be ignored or under-estimated and that it would be an excellent thing if complete copies of the manuscript catalogues of Sonneck and Schatz were made accessible somewhere in Italy where they could be consulted without loss of time by anyone interested.

It remains for me to thank Dr. Harold Spivacke, the present Chief of the Music Division of the Library of Congress, and Mr. Wayne Shirley, his able assistant, for their prompt and helpful replies to my inquiries. Summary lists of the materials in Washington, sufficiently detailed for purposes of identification, are appended to this report, and I am turning over to the Institute in Parma the whole of the relevant correspondence, together with all photostats and microfilms that I have received.

APPENDIX A

Full Scores of Operas by Verdi
Owned by the Library of Congress

I. ENGRAVED SCORES

Unless otherwise specified, all scores listed below were issued by the firm of Ricordi, Milano, and are with Italian text only.

	Date of Issue or Copyright	Publisher's Number
Aïda		97825
Aïda	1913	113954
Un Ballo in maschera	1914	113939
Falstaff	1893	96180
Falstaff[1]	1912	113953
La Forza del destino		98646
Othello[2]	1894	——
Otello	1913	113955
Rigoletto		98189
Rigoletto	1914	113960
La Traviata[3]		21366–21376
La Traviata	1914	113958
Il Trovatore[4]		——
Il Trovatore	1913	113957

[1]Gift of G. Ricordi.
[2]Issued in Paris by G. Ricordi; French version.
[3]Printed from the original plates at a date well before 1915.
[4]Printed from old plates at a date well before 1915.

2. MANUSCRIPT SCORES

Unless otherwise specified, all scores listed below are with Italian text only.

Attila	For F. Lucca, Milano.
La Battaglia di Legnano	For Choudens, Paris, with title "Patria."
Il Corsaro	For F. Lucca; Italian text with added French; on the title-page a reference to a performance in Trieste in 1848.
Ernani	German text, with added Italian.
Giovanna d'Arco	For Giovanni Ricordi.
Luisa Miller	Italian text with added French; performances listed on the title-page extend from 1850 to 1852.
Macbeth	For Tito di Giovanni Ricordi; original version.
I Masnadieri	For F. Lucca; performances listed on the title-page extend from 1847 to 1867.
Nabucco	A transcript of the copy in the Ricordi archives, made in 1911.
Simon Boccanegra	Original version.

APPENDIX B

The Verdi Librettos of the Schatz Collection

The several columns of this second tabulation supply, for each libretto, the following information: the Schatz number, a short title, the place of publication, the date of publication or performance wherever one or both of these is specified, the place of performance wherever this is specified, and an indication of the language or languages in which the text is printed (E = English; F = French; G = German; I = Italian; R = Russian). First editions are distinguished by an asterisk (*). Dates of publication without parentheses are imprint-dates, those within parentheses are performance-dates mentioned on the title-page; I have not attempted to supply dates for those librettos for which no imprint- or performance-date is specified. In no case, however, is the date of publication later than 1908, the year in which the collection was offered to and purchased by the Library of Congress.

10619*	AIDA	Cairo	1871	Cairo	IF
10620	AIDA	Milan	(1874)	Berlin	G
10621	AIDA	Milan			IG
10622	AIDA	Paris	1876	Paris	IF
10623	ALZIRA	Milan	1846		I
10624	ATTILA	Florence	1846	Florence	I
10625	GLI UNNI E I ROMANI	Palermo	1854	Palermo	I
10626	ATTILA	Stuttgart	1854	Stuttgart	G
10627	LA BATTAGLIA DI LEGNANO	Milan			I
10628*	IL CORSARO	Milan	(1848)	Trieste	I
10629	DON CARLOS,[1] in 5 atti	Paris	(1867)	Paris	F
10630	DON CARLO, in 5 atti				I
10631	DON CARLOS, in 5 atti	Darmstadt	1868	Darmstadt	IG

[1]"Deuxième édition."

10632	DON CARLOS, in 5 atti	Berlin	1868		IG
10633	DON CARLOS, in 4 atti	Berlin			IG
10634	DON CARLOS, in 4 atti	Boston			IE
10635*	I DUE FOSCARI	Milan	1844	Rome	I
10636	DIE BEIDEN FOSCARI	Weimar	(1856)	Weimar	G
10637	ERNANI	Milan	1844	Milan	I
10638	IL PROSCRITTO[2]	Naples	1847	Naples	I
10639	HERNANI	Hamburg	(1847)	Hamburg	G
10640	HERNANI	Stuttgart	(1847)	Stuttgart	G
10641	ERNANI	Boston			IE
10642	HERNANI	Dresden	1849	Dresden	G
10643	HERNANI	Berlin	1861	Berlin	IG
10644	ERNANI	Wiesbaden			IG
10645*	FALSTAFF	Milan	1893	Milan	I
10646	FALSTAFF	Milan	1893	Vienna	IG
10647	FALSTAFF	Milan			G
10648	LA FORZA DEL DESTINO	St. Petersburg	1876		IR
10649	LA FORZA DEL DESTINO[3]	Milan			I
10650	GIOVANNA D'ARCO	Milan	1847	Venice	I
10651	ORIETTA DI LESBO	Milan	(1845)	Rome	I
10652	I LOMBARDI	Milan	1844	Milan	I
10653	DIE LOMBARDEN	Berlin	1845	Berlin	IG
10654	DIE LOMBARDEN	Hamburg	(1849)	Hamburg	G
10655	DIE LOMBARDEN	Stuttgart	(1849)	Stuttgart	G
10656	I LOMBARDI	Boston			IE
10657	JERUSALEM	La Haye	1853		F
10658	GERUSALEMME	Milan	(1850)	Milan	I
10659	LUISA MILLER	Milan	1851	Milan	I
10660	LUISA MILLER	Boston			IE
10661	MACBETH	Milan	1847		I
10662*	MACBETH	Paris	1865	Paris	F
10663	I MASNADIERI	Milan			I
10664	NABUCODONOSOR	Venice	1843	Venice	I
10665	NEBUCADNEZAR	Berlin	1844	Berlin	IG
10666	NABUCODONOSOR	Stuttgart	(1844)	Stuttgart	G
10667	NEBUKADNEZAR	Stuttgart			G
10668	NINO	London	1846	London	IE
10669	OBERTO	Genoa	(1841)	Genoa	I
10670*	OTELLO	Milan	1887	Milan	I
10671	OTHELLO	Milan			G
10672	RIGOLETTO	Milan	(1851)	Trieste	I
10673	VISCARDELLO	Milan	(1852)	Bologna	I
10674	RIGOLETTO	Hamburg		Hamburg	G

[2]"Ossia Il Corsaro di Venezia."
[3]"Nuova edizione."

10675	RIGOLETTO	Berlin	1860	Berlin	IG
10676	RIGOLETTO	Paris	1857	Paris	IF
10677	RIGOLETTO	Paris	1865		I
10678	SIMON BOCCANEGRA	Naples	1858	Naples	I
10679	SIMON BOCCANEGRA	Vienna	1882	Vienna	G
10680*	STIFFELIO	Milan	1850	Trieste	I
10681	GUGLIELMO WELLINGRODE[4]	Milan	1851	Florence	I
10682	AROLDO[5]	Milan	(1857)	Rimini	I
10683	LA TRAVIATA	Milan	1856	Milan	I
10684	VIOLETTA	Milan	1854	Florence	I
10685	LA TRAVIATA	London	1858	London	IE
10686	VIOLETTA	Vienna	1858		G
10687	LA TRAVIATA	Berlin	1860	Berlin	IG
10688	VIOLETTA	Berlin	(1860)	Berlin	IG
10689	VIOLETTA[6]	Paris	1870	Paris	F
10690	LA TRAVIATA	Königsberg			G
10691	THE ESTRAY	Boston			IE
10692	IL TROVATORE	Milan	1853	Trieste	I
10693	LE TROUVERE	Paris	1872		F
10694	DER TROUBADOUR	Vienna			G
10695	DER TROUBADOUR	Berlin	1860	Berlin	IG
10696	UN BALLO IN MASCHERA	Milan	(1868)	Venice	I
10697	EIN MASKENBALL	Berlin	(1861)	Berlin	IG
10698	AMELIA	Vienna	1862		G
10699	AMELIA	Stuttgart	(1862)	Stuttgart	G
10700	AMELIA	Berlin	1867		G
10701	DER MASKENBALL	Hamburg	(1862)	Hamburg	G
10702	DER VERHÄNGNISVOLLE MASKENBALL	Königsberg		Königsberg	G
10703*	UN GIORNO DI REGNO	Milan	1840	Milan	I
10704	IL FINTO STANISLAO	Milan	(1845)	Venice	I
10705*	LES VEPRES SICILIENNES	Paris	1855	Paris	F
10706	GIOVANNA DE GUZMAN	Milan			I
10707	I VESPRI SICILIANI	Milan			I
10708	BATILDE DI TURENNA	Milan	1857	Naples	I
10709	DIE SICILIANISCHE VESPER	Vienna			G
10710	DIE SICILIANISCHE VESPER	Berlin	1870		G

[4] "Con cambiamenti."
[5] "Nuova poesia . . . e musica nella massima parte quella di Stiffelio."
[6] "Nouvelle édition."